How to Create and Manage a
Hedge Fund

Founded in 1807, John Wiley & Sons is the oldest independent publishing company in the United States. With offices in North America, Europe, Australia, and Asia, Wiley is globally committed to developing and marketing print and electronic products and services for our customers' professional and personal knowledge and understanding.

The Wiley Finance Series contains books written specifically for finance and investment professionals as well as sophisticated individual investors and their financial advisors. Book topics range from portfolio management to e-commerce, risk management, financial engineering, valuation and financial instrument analysis, as well as much more.

For a list of available titles, please visit our Web site at www.WileyFinance.com.

How to Create and Manage a
Hedge Fund

A Professional's Guide

STUART A. McCRARY

John Wiley & Sons, Inc.

Published by John Wiley & Sons, Inc., Hoboken, New Jersey
Published simultaneously in Canada

For general information on our other products and services, or technical support,
please contact our Customer Care Department within the United States at 800-
762-2974, outside the United states at 317-572-3993 or fax 317-372-4002.

Wiley also publishes its books in a variety of electronic formats. Some content that
appears in print may not be available in electronic books.

Library of Congress Cataloging-in-Publication Data:
McCrary, Stuart A.
    How to create and manage a hedge fund : a professional's guide / Stuart A.
McCrary.
        p.   cm.   (Wiley finance series)
    Includes bibliographical references.
    ISBN 0-471-22488-X
    1. Hedge funds.   I. Title.   II. Series.
HG4530.M38 2002
332.64'5—dc21
                                                                    2002001892

Printed in the United States of America.

10 9 8 7 6 5 4 3

To my loving wife, Nancy

acknowledgments

I want to thank everyone who assisted me in writing this text. I received invaluable comments from Dr. Christopher Culp, Peter F. Karpen, Philip Ryan, Ricardo Cossa, and John Szobocsan, who spent many hours reviewing drafts and offering suggestions. I also thank Kevin Foley, Steven A. Edelstein, Michael Griffin, Tom Barron, David Knorowski, Lummezen Mondal, and Philip Erban, who each made important suggestions to me about the text.

I must also thank my wife, Nancy, and children, Kate, Lauren, and Douglas, who endured my absence while writing and revising this text.

SMcC

contents

This book is intended for anyone interested in creating and managing a hedge fund. Individuals trading on exchange floors, within broker-dealers, on bank currency desks, or in mutual funds, commodity pools, and other hedge funds may have a track record as a basis for a hedge fund start-up. Organizations such as mutual funds, insurance companies, and family offices may have the investment experience and infrastructure to run a hedge fund but need additional information about how to operate in a levered, unregulated environment.

Beginning with general descriptive information in Chapters 1 through 8, the book advances to rather technical and specialized chapters on performance mathematics, legal, accounting, market, and other topics. Each chapter was written so that the reader needs little prerequisite knowledge. Nevertheless, those readers with limited knowledge of the hedge fund industry will find the book easier to understand if the chapters are read in order.

The book should be valuable to anyone who wants in-depth knowledge of hedge funds. Salespeople at broker-dealers can learn much about the inside operation of a hedge fund and thereby provide better coverage and effectively cross-sell other products. Lawyers, accountants, and tax specialists can learn about their clients' businesses to help customize professional services to their clients' needs. These readers will be most interested in the less technical chapters (Chapters 1–7 and Chapter 16) and the one or two chapters addressing technical material in the reader's field.

Employment in the hedge fund industry is growing rapidly along with the size of assets under management. Students, those working in related fields, and those seeking a career change into the hedge fund industry can learn enough about the business from this book to work for a fund. These readers should study the chapters that relate to their own specializations (Chapters 8 through 15) after reading the background material.

disclaimer

Starting a hedge fund without proper legal, accounting, and tax advice is foolhardy. Professional advisors should be consulted early in the process of creating a hedge fund. The discussion of these and other topics is intended to facilitate those professional relationships and is not sufficiently detailed, up-to-date, or reliable to preclude relying on this advice.

Some of the material in this book is very technical and involves issues where professional judgment is imperative. Material may be outdated. Nearly every hedge fund formation involves unique aspects that may contradict statements in this book.

The information in this book is believed to be reliable, but it is up to the reader to confirm everything with the fund's lawyers, regulators, accountants, and tax professionals.

Nothing in this book is intended as legal, accounting, or tax advice and should not be construed as such.

CHAPTER 1

Introduction to Hedge Funds

Alfred Jones created the first hedge fund in 1949. This fund resembled the most common type of fund today. The fund was created as a limited partnership. The fund invested in long and short positions in common stocks and used a modest amount of leverage.

For nearly decades the general public knew almost nothing about this secretive group of investors. The press and the public generally became aware of hedge funds in the late 1980s and early 1990s due to the actions of several large funds such as those run by George Soros and Michael Steinhardt. These funds were classified as "global macro" funds.[1] Despite the reference to hedging in the name "hedge fund," this type of fund did not resemble most people's impression of a hedge. Instead, these funds made speculative bets on currencies, stock markets, and interest rates around the world.

Macro funds frequently made market-moving news. It was widely reported in the press that George Soros and his Quantum Funds were responsible for breaking a policy of maintaining a high exchange value for the British pound (although George Soros and many economic historians place the blame elsewhere). Macro funds were also blamed (in many cases wrongly so) for forcing emerging market economies into the hands of the International Monetary Fund (IMF).

These funds offered high risk and high rewards to investors. Many types of strategies are bound by a variety of factors that limit the total size of a fund. Macro funds have much less problem scaling up their strategies to ever-larger size positions. Several funds grew to incredible size and their clout in the market grew along with their asset size and trading volume.

Along with the growth of the global macro hedge fund, a trend emerged from the trading desks of major broker-dealers. Senior traders who had expertise and a solid track record in a variety of markets discovered they could set up hedge funds and increase their take-home pay.

Wall Street has been called a young man's game and quite a few highly successful traders have retired at a young age. Broker-dealers have horizontal organizations and few senior traders advance to general management. Some partnerships even have an expectation that their partners will retire at 50 to 55 years of age to make room for young hopefuls.

The hedge fund provides traders a new place to practice their craft with a very different business model. Traders in a broker-dealer are employees who deploy the firm's capital. Through a hedge fund, senior traders discovered they could sever the employment relationship with the broker-dealer and substitute capital from third-party investors. Instead of a salary, the hedge fund management company collected a management fund (at one time as much as 2 percent of money under management, now more typically 1 percent) that resembled a salary. Instead of a bonus, the hedge fund collected incentive fees (typically 20 percent of net return). These Wall Street transplants found they could charge these fees, provide an attractive return to investors, and earn as much or more than their counterparts at the broker-dealers.[2]

Hedge funds do not contain the incentive to retire early. In fact, the principals' years of experience make a fund more appealing to potential investors. Frequently the fund is marketed almost exclusively on the earning potential of the principal traders.

More recently, most of the growth in hedge funds has occurred in types of funds that resemble neither the home-run-hitting fund nor the trader emeritus fund. Funds are created around the marketing strength of a financial institution, not the trading expertise of individuals. They are created to fill the identified needs of investors. Issues such as correlation, lower risk, style purity, and an ability to track a subbenchmark are much more likely to be the genesis for a new fund. These funds are more likely to be created by mutual fund managers, banks, insurance companies, broker-dealers, or investment counselors than by individual entrepreneurs.

WHY INVEST IN HEDGE FUNDS?

Investors decide to allocate funds to hedge funds for several reasons: (1) to increase the return on the portfolio; (2) to diversify the returns of assets within the portfolio; and (3) to reduce risk. An investor may consider one or more of these factors when evaluating hedge funds for a portfolio.

In connection with the first reason, it can be noted that hedge funds have performed well compared to many traditional investments. Historical performance is prominent in most hedge fund marketing literature. Clearly, after the fact, many hedge funds have performed well in both absolute return and relative to aggregate stock and bond returns. Some funds have done well, regardless of the aggregate return for the industry, and that is enough to make them appealing to many investors.

During the 1980s and early 1990s, the funds capturing the attention of investors and the media had extremely high returns (and extremely high risk) and were very large. These funds were mostly global macro funds. Although these types of funds still exist, hedge funds are generally less committed to capturing high returns and this style has fewer assets under management, even while the size of the hedge fund industry has grown substantially.

Fortunately for the industry, aggregate returns have been attractive. Several academic studies[3] and countless industry studies have demonstrated that *ex post* return for hedge funds has been attractive, especially when adjusted for risk.

The second major reason to invest in hedge funds, diversification, involves a statistic called *correlation*. This idea is developed much more thoroughly in Chapter 13; for now, suffice it to say that correlation measures the extent to which returns of one asset are associated with returns of another asset. Investors have long realized the value of diversification. The adage "don't put all your eggs in one basket" applies because stocks often don't move together and a port-folio can be less risky than its component stocks.

Two assets in the same industry provide less risk reduction from diversification than a combination of unrelated companies. A well-diversified portfolio combines the returns of many assets often with some effort devoted to identifying returns that are not correlated.

There are limits to the risk reduction from diversification. As the number of stocks in a portfolio increases, the risk of the portfolio approaches the risk of aggregate averages such as the Standard & Poor's 500 Index (S&P), which still has substantial risk. There can be fairly high correlation between stocks, bonds, and even real estate. This correlation means that the resulting portfolio will have risks that cannot be eliminated by diversification.

Hedge funds generally have low correlation to traditional stock and bond indices. Table 1.1 shows correlations between the S&P 500 Index[4] and hedge funds[5] by strategy. The fund styles with the lowest correlations provide the largest impact in reducing risk for the portfolio.

The third major reason individuals and institutions invest in hedge funds is to reduce the risk of the overall portfolio. Clearly, diversification serves that function. However, even without the benefit of diversification, many hedge funds have lower risk than traditional assets.

TABLE 1.1 Hedge Fund Styles' Correlation to S&P 500 Returns

Hedge Fund Style	Correlation
CSFB/Tremont Hedge Fund Index	.51
Convertible arbitrage	.11
Dedicated short bias	−.78
Emerging markets	.48
Equity market neutral	.46
Event driven	.54
Fixed Inc arbitrage	.09
Global macro	.29
Long/short	.61
Managed futures	−.10

TABLE 1.2 Historical Volatility of Hedge Fund Returns

Hedge Fund Style	Volatility (%)
CSFB/Tremont Hedge Fund Index	9.54
Convertible arbitrage	4.93
Dedicated short bias	18.89
Emerging markets	19.75
Equity market neutral	3.34
Event driven	6.36
Fixed income arbitrage	4.19
Global macro	13.73
Long/short	12.26
Managed futures	11.32
S&P 500	15.09

Table 1.2 shows a measure of risk called *historical volatility*.[6] Nearly every category of hedge fund has a lower volatility of return than the S&P 500. Even without the benefit of diversification, hedge funds can lower the return volatility of a portfolio without lowering the expected return of the portfolio.

GROWTH OF ASSETS UNDER MANAGEMENT

Although hedge funds have existed since 1949, much of the growth in the hedge fund industry has occurred since 1990. Market observers estimate that some 200 hedge funds existed by 1968,[7] but, surprisingly, only 68 funds could be identified by 1984. The number of hedge funds has grown from an estimated 1,373 in 1988 to an estimated 5,830 in 1998, a growth of 325 percent for the period or 15.6 percent per year (see Figure 1.1). Other sources estimate that the number of funds grew in the 1990s by nearly 26 percent per year.[8]

Although precise information about the number of hedge funds is not available, it seems certain that the number of outstanding funds is rising at a slower rate at the latter part of this time interval. In the early periods, the number of funds was estimated to have grown by 20 percent annually. In contrast, the growth since 1996 has been below 10 percent per year.

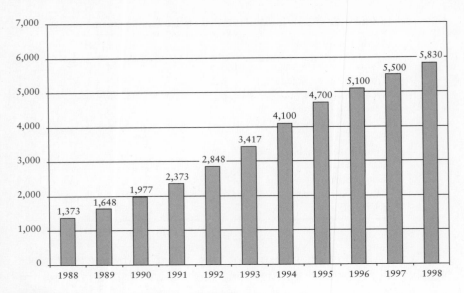

FIGURE 1.1   Estimated Number of Hedge Funds
(*Source:* Van Hedge Fund Advisors International.)

Growth in assets under management has risen faster than the growth in the number of funds (see Figure 1.2). Based on the data shown in Figure 1.2, it can be determined that the assets under management grew by 640 percent in the same period. In 1988, hedge funds managed an estimated $42 billion. By the end of 1998, assets had risen to $311 billion, representing an annualized growth rate of 22.2 percent.

Although the assets under management grew up to twice as fast as the number of funds, the average size of hedge funds actually declined over the same period. This counterintuitive condition resulted from the demise of most of the extremely large macro hedge funds that dominated the hedge fund markets in the 1980s. In other words, while most hedge funds grew in size during the period, they grew in part by capturing new assets and in part by receiving investments formerly concentrated in very large hedge funds. The average hedge fund now manages between $50 million and $100 million.

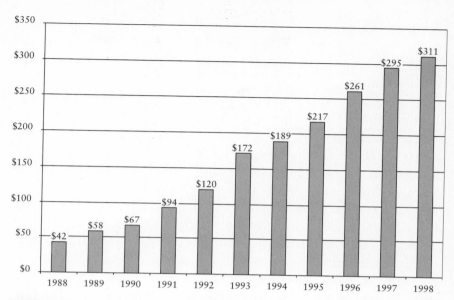

FIGURE 1.2 Estimated Hedge Fund Assets Under Management ($ billions) (*Source:* Van Hedge Fund Advisors International.)

DEFINITION OF A HEDGE FUND

Many descriptions are used to define hedge funds. The President's Working Group on Financial Markets defined hedge funds as "a pooled investment vehicle that is privately organized, administered by a professional management firm. . . , and not widely available to the public."[9] Attempts to define hedge funds only work if they are somewhat ambiguous because the range of business types and investment strategies that can be classified as a hedge fund is quite large. Further, there is no consistent difference between hedge funds and other types of investments.

In general, hedge funds are a limited liability investment pool run by a separate manager. The investment manager is hired by the fund, but generally the manager sponsors the fund and is responsible for marketing it. Consequently, there is not an arm's-length relationship between the fund and its manager.

Hedge funds are typically structured as a limited partnership or a limited liability corporation in the United States but may be a traditional corporation if the fund is organized in a tax-free or low-tax offshore country.

Hedge funds typically employ leverage, including both long and short positions. They may invest in a narrow class of assets and often have considerable freedom to change the nature of those investments.

Hedge funds usually charge a combination of a management fee (a fixed percentage of assets in the fund) and an incentive fee. The investments are valued periodically for the purpose of calculating those fees. Many hedge funds do not value the assets daily and those that do value the assets frequently may disclose the information to few people. In addition, investors frequently are severely restricted from withdrawing funds.

Many hedge funds differ from the foregoing description. Many other investment products share some of the previously cited characteristics. The following sections distinguish hedge funds from other common investment products.

Comparison of a Commodity Trading Advisor to a Hedge Fund Manager

The Commodity Futures Trading Commission (CFTC) and the National Futures Association (NFA) regulate investment pools that rely on physical commodities, futures, and futures options. The NFA (the self-regulatory body that implements the regulations of the CFTC) identifies a business unit called a commodity pool, which resembles a hedge fund in many ways. Similar to a hedge fund manager, a commodity pool operator (CPO) manages the pool. Alternatively, a commodity trading advisor (CTA) manages individual accounts with similar investment style and fee structure. Managers can act as both a CPO (for commingled money) and a CTA (for individual accounts).

The largest commodity pool operators define the expectations for a commodity pool. Monroe Trout, Paul Tudor Jones, Bruce Covner, and John Henry run the largest examples of commodity accounts. There are thousands of CPO and CTA organizations and while they can differ markedly, they typically employ leverage by using futures, collect management and incentive fees, and most often trade based on historical price patterns.

Margin requirements and the risk level of the positions limit the degree of leverage in managed futures accounts. Margin requirements are higher than some levered cash market trading, where completely margin-free trading is sometimes possible (government bonds and over-the-counter derivatives, for example). Therefore, the actual leverage employed is sometimes considerably below the leverage theoretically possible in a hedge fund. In practice, commodity accounts, such as global macro hedge funds (which have the similar combination of multiple long and short positions), usually carry excess cash.

Many hedge fund managers register as a CPO and many funds register as a commodity pool. The NFA requires this registration even when futures are not the primary investment assets in the fund. These hedge fund managers could be called CPOs. They are generally not called commodity pool operators, however, to distinguish them from CPOs, who only invest in exchange-traded futures and options.

CPOs, who invest only in futures and options carried on the books of a broker (also called a *futures commission merchant* or FCM) have dramatically simpler accounting than a hedge fund. The futures statement preserves the cost basis of positions and marks them to market. It is typical to run the books of a commodity pool by extracting all the financial results from the futures statement. The CPO must, of course, proof and reconcile the statements but is spared a separate accounting of these transactions.

In contrast, a hedge fund generally has cash positions that are financed with short-term borrowings, thus creating an incredibly large number of journal entries for the accountants to track. In addition, the hedge fund may have over-the-counter derivative securities that it must mark to market internally. As a result, most hedge funds maintain their own accounting records or contract out for accounting services.

Tax reporting is also notably simpler for a commodity pool because futures and futures options are granted a special tax status. All gains and losses on these assets receive 60 percent long-term and 40 percent short-term capital gains tax treatment. In other words, all realized gains are treated as if 60 percent of the gain corresponded with a one-year holding period to be taxed at the lower capital gains rate. Similarly, 40 percent of the gain is reported as short term and taxed at each investor's ordinary tax rate regardless of the actual holding period. As a result, the CPO can report only the annual net change in the value of the commodity account.

This simplification applies only to gains and losses, not to revenues and expenses, which must still be allocated to pool investors. However, the CPO does not need to preserve the holding period or cost basis of individual purchases and sales. The combination of these differences makes accounting in a hedge fund dramatically more complicated than a commodity pool.

The fee structure in a commodity pool is similar to the fees in a hedge fund. At the time of this writing, a management fee of 2 percent of assets (annually) and an incentive fee of 20 percent of profits is typical for commodity pools, whereas hedge funds are more likely to charge 1 percent of assets and have a 20 percent incentive fee. Commodity pools (and hedge funds) may profit from the commissions charged on pool transactions by executing futures through an affiliated FCM, by charging the pool commissions higher than actually paid to the FCM, or by using the commissions as a sales incentive for third parties that market the fund. A hedge fund, however, may also charge for cash market execution and for financing long and short levered positions.

A commodity pool has the same issue of transparency as a hedge fund. A transparent fund discloses positions to its investors. A commodity pool is not required to disclose positions to pool investors. Certain investors demand transparency, and hedge funds and commodity pool operators each can run separate accounts for those investors. However, separate accounts are much easier to administer with futures-only accounts because the individual accounts run by a hedge fund must establish credit relationships with all the broker-dealers they trade with. They may need to create derivative trades directly for the benefit of the separate account if the positions exist in the hedge fund. As a result, separate accounts must be fairly large for a hedge fund manager. In contrast, a separate futures account needs only enough money to create proportionally smaller positions with reasonably small tracking error.

Comparison of Mutual Funds to Hedge Funds

On the surface, mutual funds appear to be similar to hedge funds. Both are investment pools. Generally, hedge funds calculate a net asset value similar to mutual fund procedures, although the presence of leverage in a hedge fund affects the calculation. The largest amount of money in both types of funds is invested in publicly listed common stock. Even the returns are similar for many types of funds, when adjusted for differences in leverage.

The differences between hedge funds and typical mutual funds are actually fairly large. Mutual funds are free to invest in most of the assets that hedge funds buy and sell. However, the range of assets within a particular mutual fund is much smaller than that of a hedge fund, and the types of assets carried in a mutual fund do not vary much over time.

Mutual funds typically calculate and publish the net asset value (NAV) of their shares daily. Hedge funds frequently calculate their NAV only on days when entry and exit is possible (monthly or quarterly) and do not make the NAVs available to the general public.[10]

Mutual funds publish complete details of their positions, including issues and quantities, albeit only quarterly and with a delay. Hedge funds tend not to provide these details to the public at large and some will not provide them to any investor.[11]

Most mutual funds allow entry or exit any business day of the year. In contrast, hedge funds allow transactions only monthly or quarterly. In addition, hedge funds sometimes impose lockup provisions, prohibiting exit for a period of time.

A small number of mutual funds use leverage to increase return. Leverage is not typical of mutual funds and almost never exceeds 2:1. Although atypical, there are mutual funds that carry short positions.

In contrast, although there are unlevered hedge funds, they are the exception. Leverage in hedge funds often runs from 2:1 to 10:1

(depending on the type of assets held) and can run higher than 100:1. It is worth warning that leverage is not a good proxy for risk. For a given strategy, it is generally true that more leverage will increase risk. It is also generally true that the highest leverage is applied to the least risky assets (matched positions in U.S. Treasury securities). Although there are some hedge funds wildly more volatile than the typical mutual fund, the average hedge fund is less volatile than an unlevered investment in the S&P 500 Index.[12] The typical hedge fund has very little in common with the stereotypical high-stakes gambler often portrayed by the news media.

Mutual funds are allowed to use derivative securities, including futures and options. They tend to use these instruments as substitutes for traditional investments, rather than as a source of leverage. Also, for the most common derivative trade (covered call writing), the derivative strategy actually reduces portfolio risk.

The management fees in mutual funds resemble the hedge fund management fees. Since hedge fund management fees have declined from 2 percent to 1 percent over time, there is not much difference in the size of the management fee for the typical mutual fund and hedge fund,[13] and they are calculated similarly.

Although mutual funds can collect performance-based incentive fees, most do not, and the incentive fees are almost always smaller than the smallest hedge fund incentive fees. Mutual funds are barred from charging incentive fees on most funds. Securities law only allows incentive fees when all the investors are wealthy enough that they could have invested in a private hedge fund structure anyway.

As if to prove there are exceptions to every rule, several mutual funds are operating quite similarly to hedge funds. These new vehicles use leverage, carry long and short positions, and may charge an incentive fee.

Comparison of Private Equity Funds to Hedge Funds

Private equity funds can be divided imprecisely into venture capital funds and leveraged buyout funds. Both are organized as limited partnerships or limited liability corporations, as are hedge funds. As a result, they are not taxed at the fund level. Instead, as with hedge funds, all economic results are passed through to investors and taxed only on the investors' returns. These funds have a fee structure that is fairly similar to hedge fund fees, although much of the incentive fee may be postponed until investments are sold. The line separating hedge funds from venture funds and leveraged buyout funds is further blurred by hedge funds that invest a portion of their assets in new ventures and deal arbitrage.

Private equity fund investors may have little or no ability to withdraw capital from the fund until the manager liquidates. In contrast, hedge funds generally allow investors to increase their investment or withdraw funds monthly, quarterly, or annually. Some hedge funds, especially those that have material real estate and private equity investments, may resemble venture funds for a portion of the hedge fund assets. These hedge funds use a technique called *sidepocket allocations* (see Glossary) that are not routinely marked to market, postpone incentive funds until the assets are sold, and completely prohibit the investor from withdrawing those funds associated with the side pocket allocation.

FEE STRUCTURES

Unregistered investment companies are practically unregulated as to how they assess fees on investors. The funds must disclose the fees in advance, must be allocated fairly across different classes of investors, and should be calculated on a reasonable basis for each period. Fees in hedge funds are much higher and considerably more complicated than fees charged by registered investment companies.

Management Fee

Hedge funds assess a flat fee based on the assets under management. The fee is usually between 1 percent and 2 percent per year. However, the fees are generally assessed monthly (or at least as frequently as investors are allowed to enter and exit the fund). For example, for a fund assessing 2 percent per year, 0.1667 percent of the assets (2%/12) may be charged each month. The fee applies to the NAV of the fund. This fee is generally due whether the fund makes or loses money.

Despite the sound of the phrase "net asset value," the fee is actually applied to the investors' equity in the fund. In other words, the netting reduces the asset value by the liabilities of the fund. The fund manager may assess a fee to the fund in aggregate or assess each investor individually, depending on how the partnership records are maintained. Usually the limited and general partners are assessed the same fees.

Incentive Fee

Hedge funds charge a performance fee, typically 20 percent of the return. For example, if the fund experiences a 10 percent return in a month, an incentive fee of 20 percent of that amount (not divided by 12 because these are nominal, not annualized returns) is charged to the fund and indirectly to the investors. Typically, incentive fees are not refunded if the fund experiences a loss in subsequent months.

All or nearly all hedge fund managers charge management fees and incentive fees. The rest of the fees described are not universally assessed.

Surrender Fee

A surrender fee is assessed as a percentage of redemption amount for exiting investors. Sometimes this fee is paid back into the fund to compensate the remaining investors for the transaction costs caused by the need to liquidate assets for the redemption. When the fee is paid to the management company, it serves as a source of additional revenue for the manager and acts as a deterrent to investors considering leaving the fund.

Hurdle Rate

A variation on the incentive fee sets a rate below which no incentive fees are collected. For example, if a fund has a 6 percent hurdle rate (annual), then incentive fees are collected only on the return that exceeds 6 percent in a year (or 0.50 percent in a given month).

High-Water Mark

Although incentive fees are generally not refunded following a loss, the investors are usually protected so that the manager earns no fee for making back a loss. In a typical structure, returns are determined by the NAV of a unit of participation in a fund. Each time the NAV reaches a new high level, the incentive fee is assessed. When a decline in NAV occurs (a loss is experienced), no incentive fee is assessed until the NAV exceeds the highest NAV used for incentive fee calculations.[14] Some funds maintain high-water marks for each individual investor and may trace multiple high-water marks on individuals if they add to their investments after a loss.

Lookback

Although not a typical structure, some management companies rebate an incentive fee if a subsequent loss erases a gain shortly after an incentive fee is charged. One type of lookback refunds the incentive fee when losses occur within 3 months of the high-water mark.

Miscellaneous Fees

The management company is free to charge a variety of fees if they are adequately disclosed to the investors. The fund may be assessed a ticket charge for purchases and sales handled by the management company. For leveraged positions, a financing fee is sometimes charged for handling levered long and short financing transactions. Sometimes the manager charges the fund a commission that is higher than the commission actually charged by the futures commission merchant.[15]

BEST PRACTICES FOR HEDGE FUND MANAGERS

Throughout this book, we conclude several sections with a discussion of best practices. Governmental regulators and industry groups have compiled recommendations for hedge fund managers to encourage fair treatment of investors, protect the fund from credit and other risks, and encourage a healthy, self-sustaining business. These best practices recommendations are not universally accepted. However, these sections summarize the conventional wisdom. See the Bibliography for reference to specific documents on best practices.

NOTES

1. See Chapter 3 and the Glossary for a description of this and other types of hedge funds.
2. The impression from coverage in the financial press is that traders at hedge funds probably make more than traders at broker-dealers. However, large movie deals for blockbuster actors do not trickle down to starving actors waiting on tables. Similarly, there are many traders who started funds that never really paid off.
3. See Thomas Schneeweis, Richard Spurgin, and Vassilios N. Karavas, "Alternative Investments in the Institutional Portfolio," AIMA commissioned paper, updated summer 2000; available at http://www.aima.org/aimasite/research/AIIP%2020000.pdf.
4. Standard & Poor's 500 performance data from Bloomberg; hedge fund data from CS First Boston/Tremont, August 31, 1996, through August 31, 2001.
5. Hedge fund sector data from CS First Boston/Tremont. See Chapter 3 for a description of styles.
6. Volatility measures the standard deviation of returns. See Chapter 13. The data used for the volatility estimates are the same data from CS First Boston/Tremont used for correlations in Table 1.1.
7. *A Case for Hedge Funds,* Tremont Partners, Inc., and Tass Investment Research Ltd., page 5.

8. Ibid.
9. *Hedge Funds, Leverage and the Lessons of Long Term Capital Management,* President's Working Group on Financial Markets, April 1999, page 3; available at http://www.ustreas.gov/press/releases/docs/hedge fund.pdf.
10. Although NAVs and returns are published by several hedge fund data sources, each organization limits the distribution of those data to qualified investors.
11. When a hedge fund provides this detail to investors, that disclosure is much more timely.
12. A large number of mutual funds are less volatile than the S&P 500, too, simply because they carry cash balances.
13. Of course, some hedge funds are considerably higher than 1 percent and some mutual funds (especially index funds) are notably lower than 1 percent.
14. If the high in NAV occurs midperiod, that level would not represent the high-water mark. Instead, the level at month-end or quarter-end that had been used for incentive fee calculations would be the high-water mark.
15. These above-market futures commissions can be used to compensate intermediaries that raise investment funds for the hedge fund.

CHAPTER 2

Building a Valuable Business

Newspapers and trade publications carry many stories about hedge funds. At least once a year, we read about a large hedge fund that has closed, often under turbulent conditions. This chapter explores reasons why hedge fund businesses have had short lives and discusses ways in which the businesses created can be made valuable to their potential buyers.

It is important, first, to distinguish the hedge fund from the management company. A hedge fund is an investment partnership that contains money, investments, and, usually, debt. The hedge fund may employ no individuals. The hedge fund hires a management company to provide investment services. The management company generally hires the investment professionals, accountants, computer specialists, and marketing staff. In most cases, the principals of the management company create the hedge fund business entity.

When a hedge fund is closed, often the management company is dissolved. The management company sometimes remains and operates like a private trust company for the benefit of the hedge fund's principal owners. In most cases, the management company will not survive after the hedge fund has closed. Here are some examples:

- For decades, Michael Steinhardt ran a very successful macro hedge fund, Steinhardt Partners. A macro fund makes unhedged investments in a collection of equities, currencies, and debt securities.[1] Michael Steinhardt and the fund enjoyed good name recognition and a reputation for high-risk/high-reward trading, averaging nearly twice the return of the Standard & Poor's (S&P) 500 Index.

In the first quarter of 1994, the fund, which was invested in a variety of European fixed-income assets, lost nearly 30 percent. Despite having endured significant volatility in the past, the fund was closed and the management company ceased running hedge fund assets.

- In 1995, a pair of fixed-income arbitrage funds run by Fenchurch Capital Management experienced significant losses. Within months, the funds shrank by more than 90 percent (a combination of 35 percent investment loss and rapid withdrawal of funds). Prior to 1995, the funds enjoyed one of the best performance records for low-risk hedge funds. The management company was not able to survive the event because (1) all investors were invested in a single strategy and (2) marketing efforts had created unrealistic expectations about risk.

- In 1998, losses forced the Federal Reserve to arrange a bailout of Long Term Capital Management (LTCM). Prior to the crisis that led to the bailout, LTCM experienced very high returns. The fund was run by an extremely well-regarded team of seasoned investment professionals and decorated academic advisors. After the crisis ran its course, hundreds of millions of dollars were withdrawn and the fund was closed.

- Until March of 2000, Julian Robertson ran a family of value stock hedge funds, including the Tiger Fund. The fund created long and short positions with leverage using a traditional investment philosophy favoring value stocks. Performance in the Tiger Fund was always volatile, but the fund did not survive the huge appreciation of technology stocks in 1999.

- Jeffrey Vinik ran the large Magellan Fund at Fidelity Investments. Although guilty of a couple visible missteps (in particular, a poorly timed and controversial movement out of stocks and into bonds),

Vinik achieved a fair return for investors while in control of the fund, an impressive achievement considering problems associated with running a very large fund. After a short period running a hedge fund and generating very high returns, Vinik announced he was returning public funds and would focus just on partner wealth.

These management companies were not sold to other investment managers. Although the managers earned high fees while open, the owners received nothing for the future revenues that might have been derived from managing money into the future.

Why does a hedge fund's management company not have equity value? Perhaps the most direct explanation is that previous profits have been removed from the firm. Frequently, in a medical or law practice, nearly all the annual revenues are paid out each year. This keeps the value of the business low so that new young partners can buy into the business for less money.

In professional partnerships, interests are frequently bought and sold at book value. Most other businesses value the future stream of revenues so that existing owners benefit from rising earnings directly and also in raising the market value of their interest in future revenues.

However, if the hedge fund is organized around a star, the business may be worth little without that star. Without the leadership (and possibly even with the star), performance may be expected to return to normal levels. Possible buyers of the management company expect that much of the money raised on the reputation of the star will exit the fund if the investment team is replaced. It is often said that a money manager's assets walk out the door each night.

Few funds survive longer than 7 years. Funds close for a variety of reasons. A key employee may retire. An investment style may go out of favor. Short-term losses may scare investors out of funds. A high-water mark provision may motivate a fund manager to close a fund following losses.

When a fund is marketed primarily by touting recent excellent performance, the money raised because of that performance may be difficult to retain when performance suffers. Any strategy has periods of better and worse performance because real exogenous events affect the returns. Strategies differ in their sensitivity to these factors. A variety of random factors add to the variability of returns even for excellent managers.

Sometimes a management company markets based on an excellent record of risk control. Fund managers who have created a pattern of return that produces reasonably high returns and particularly low volatility of return have a valuable product worth bragging about. The problem with this approach is that it tends to attract a risk-intolerant group of investors. Despite best intentions, future performance may be more volatile and investors may be unforgiving about unforeseen problems.

When the funds under management are not "sticky,"[2] the revenues derived from managing those assets cannot be expected to persist into the future. For this reason, if the manager must replace exiting investors due to rapid turnover, the management company as a business is worth little. In other words, a buyer would need to market to bring in new money whether the buyer purchases the fund or starts de novo, so there is little reason to pay a premium for an existing business.

One type of hedge fund called a *fund of funds* is an exception to this pattern. A fund of funds is a hedge fund that invests in a portfolio of hedge funds. When major financial institutions have bought existing hedge funds, they are generally fund of funds managers. Through careful selection of their investments and with the benefit of diversification, these funds are more stable and less exposed to returns that could end a separate fund.

CREATING A MANAGEMENT COMPANY WITH EQUITY VALUE

It is possible to create a management company that has value. For each of the examples of hedge funds and their managers that closed, there are examples of managers who have endured market disasters.

For example, Michael Vranos ran a fund called Ellington Capital Management. In the fall of 1998, the fund was under siege from lenders.[3] Lenders forced the bankruptcy of the Granite Fund when mortgage derivatives lost value in the market. In contrast, the Ellington fund escaped the raiders by aggressively liquidating positions before creditors took control.

More recently, Bulldog Capital Management managed to preserve its business despite consecutive monthly losses of 44 percent and 77 percent in its Foxhound Fund, a 9-year-old small cap fund.[4] Although Foxhound Fund was liquidated, many investors moved to other Bulldog funds and the management company survived to run the other investment products.

It is possible to see substantially different business strategies in the mutual fund industry. For example, the Janus group of funds enjoyed huge success in the 1990s. The funds placed heavy weight on the high-tech stocks that were driving the market indices rapidly higher. With this concentration, fund performance was excellent and assets under management grew rapidly. In contrast, Fidelity Management Company has regularly added new and different funds with different styles, risk levels, asset mix, marketing channels, and fee structures. While the Fidelity business benefited much less from the high returns in tech stocks in the 1990s, their business suffered much less when the same stocks tumbled in 2000–2001.

While a diverse business model also diversifies business revenues, a countervailing trend in hedge funds proves there are several wrong ways to translate the supermarket of mutual funds into the hedge fund world. It is fundamental to any business that you must satisfy consumer needs or wants. From the accounts in the popular press, it is tempting to think this means providing very high returns using risky strategies and lots of leverage. In fact, this type of fund represents a small part of the business and little of the growth in hedge fund assets.

The hedge fund business thrives on providing a pattern of return not available from conventional assets. This might mean low correlation to overall stock and bond returns, a pattern of modest return with very low risk of loss, or a variety of other features. However, it is very important that the returns are predictable.

Predictable returns do not imply that investors know what the return will be each month. Rather, the returns follow a predictable pattern of cause and effect. If you create a short equity fund, it is more important to make money when markets decline than to avoid losses when markets advance. If you create a convertible arbitrage fund, it will have good and bad months together with other convertible arbitrage funds if you invest the way you claim to invest.

This predictability of returns favors style purity. Sophisticated hedge fund investors are interested in blending in some hedge fund returns to manage the pattern of return for the overall portfolio. These investors seek out pure examples of a hedge fund strategy to make certain they get the performance they seek.

This concept relates to a second major point: It is usually best to keep the fund's strategy as pure as possible and to market the fund honestly. If the fund manager does not believe the stated investment product will produce the best returns in the future, it is much better to start a new fund with new objectives than to transform an existing, relatively pure fund. Of course, hedge fund investors would be free to disagree with the manager and keep the money in the old fund/old strategy.

Honesty also means that investors should have reasonable expectations about the fund. Investors with unrealistic return expectations will not remain long-term investors. Investors who fail to recognize the chance for major losses will not be around after a period of poor performance and might invite lawsuits seeking restitution of losses. Therefore, it is important to market attainable results. Clients should understand in advance the types of external events that could lead to good and bad results for their investment. And the management company should prepare investors for the worst periods the client is likely to experience in advance of the losing period.

It is vital to maintain good customer relationships. Customers may sound happy when the returns are good, but they are not likely to voice their reservations about remaining in the fund. Having an active dialog with clients throughout makes them much more likely to remain through periods of poor performance.

The client contact at a star fund tends to be poor. Generally, the star focuses all the attention on producing great returns, which probably is the best use of the star's time, but who then has little time to build a relationship with the investors. Instead, a monthly newsletter written by the manager replaces direct contact. Typically, the primary purpose of the letter is to reinforce the status of the manager as a star.

It is better to build a personal relationship between the investor and members of the management company. In addition to preparing the investor for the inevitable bad times, the client contact provides an opportunity to educate the investor. Because hedge funds may only be offered to individuals and institutions that satisfy several legal tests designed to limit access to unsophisticated investors, managers generally do not view this role of education as important. But the manager is the best expert on all aspects of that fund and one of the most knowledgeable about its strategy. Certainly, the investor knows less about these matters than those in the fund. Yet, educating the investors is one of the most effective ways to make the money stickier.

Some managers (hedge fund, mutual fund, commodity traders, etc.) like to blend multiple strategies with a single fund. This approach is appealing because diversification can reduce the extreme swings in return without lowering overall return. Only the most naïve investor picks the funds with the highest return without regard to risk. This diversification appears to make the fund more appealing by improving the inevitable trade-off between risk and reward.

Of course, many investors can diversify the hedge fund returns by investing in more than one fund, each with a pure style. A manager can combine the returns of two or more funds (not necessarily run by the same manager) and produce all the benefits of diversification without compromising style purity. However, potential investors who get performance data from a third party (a summary of the major performance benchmarks is included in Chapter 9) would see the data only at the fund level.

This blending of funds is exactly the idea behind a fund of funds. Funds that invest in other funds are generally organized as hedge funds but invest exclusively in a collection of hedge funds. Several different methods are used to engineer a pattern of return that the manager believes is superior to individual fund returns.

Because certain types of hedge funds respond to outside shocks differently, it is possible to combine funds to accomplish certain purposes beyond diversification. An investment in several hedge funds may be superior to an investment in any individual fund. For example, convertible arbitrage funds do well in periods of rising volatility. Investment in a convertible arbitrage fund can be used to engineer a particular pattern of return or mitigate a pattern already present in a portfolio.

Some strategies excel when borrowing spreads widen. Others do well when markets decline. These idiosyncrasies may apply to a broad category of funds or to specific funds or particular managers.

If investors have sufficiently large hedge fund assets, they can create a synthetic fund of funds. For example, a family office or foundation may invest in several separate hedge funds using the same methods as the fund of fund operator, perhaps customizing the portfolio to its specific needs.

MISTAKES FREQUENTLY MADE BY
FUND MANAGERS

John Bowen has written an insightful book on the entrepreneurial issues in setting up an investment advisory or financial planning business.[5] Although the investment product is notably different than a hedge fund, much of his advice is relevant for a hedge fund manager. Bowen has created a list of 13 common mistakes made by investors that lead to poor valuation of the management company. It is instructive to review the list, which has been adapted here to apply to the specific problems of creating a hedge fund management company.

1. *The fund tries to be all things to different types of investors.* Hedge fund managers generally do not have this problem. In fact, managers coming from Wall Street trading houses generally create very specialized funds reflecting their specific experience. Unlike an investment advisor who primarily runs separate accounts for individual clients, hedge fund investments are usually commingled into a fund. Fund managers are motivated to produce a return having the largest appeal.

This is not always the case. Many fund managers also run segregated accounts for large investors that may differ from the commingled hedge funds. These separate accounts generally resemble the hedge fund positions. When used to create additional transparency,[6] customize leverage, or accommodate tax considerations or other incremental variations to the overall strategy, these separate accounts can be valuable, especially to a small manager. However, carried to excess, these separate accounts hoping to achieve different objectives can divert a small fund manager's attention sufficiently to interfere with sound management.

2. *The manager has no written goals for improvement.* Here, improvement means a variety of things in addition to performance. Tracking investment performance is a major part of the self-assessment required of a fund manager. It may be less important that a fund underperformed a particular benchmark (the S&P 500 Index, for example) because hedge fund returns often are not expected to track published indices. Indeed, much of the value in making hedge fund investments is that they do not track such indices.

However, if the fund is following a quantifiable model, the management company should measure the tracking error between theoretical performance and actual returns. The management company should also track the theoretical performance and continue to review the reasonableness of the investment philosophy.

In addition, the management company should delineate specific marketing goals, set deadlines to install and upgrade systems, and monitor individual employee performance. All too often, investment managers also serve as business managers but devote too little attention to running the money management business.

3. *Client-monitoring systems are poor.* Security regulations require thorough record keeping of individual flows into the fund. Although this analysis may be completed accurately and on a timely basis, it often is not shared with marketing or client-contact staff.

Fund managers should realize that client sensitivity to short-term performance hinges on previous experiences with the fund, investment objectives of the investor, knowledge and sophistication of the investor, cost basis, holding period, tax situation, and a variety of additional factors. Funds could improve their retention of assets by improving contact with the client.

4. *Marketing is done without a plan.* A marketing plan for a hedge fund must account for a variety of factors. In the United States, private placement provisions prohibit explicit advertising. To complicate matters, even within the United States, the manager must adopt different ways to reach high net individuals, endowments, and pension plans. Marketing to offshore investors must account for different regulations in foreign countries, language and cultural differences, time differences, and inconvenient travel requirements.

The target market for a hedge fund depends on the type of returns investors should expect. High-risk, high-return funds appeal to investors who are using hedge funds to increase the return. Low risk, lower return, and lower correlation to stocks and bonds appeal to portfolio investors, especially pensions and endowments. It is unusual that a fund would appeal to both groups of investors.

The target market for a hedge fund will change over time. Many investors will not invest in a new fund with a short track record and a small amount of money under management.[7] Often, the only investors who will consider a new fund are friends, relatives, and work associates. A new fund can also turn to fund of fund managers who have already raised investment funds. These managers often play a role similar to that of a venture capitalist by directing funds to new hedge funds, and they typically extract favorable treatment, including lower fees, participation in hedge fund fees, and long-term access to capacity.[8]

An offshore fund does not need to comply with U.S. security law, even if a U.S. manager runs the fund. Managers must comply with the laws of each country in which they conduct business. Although securities laws are more lax in other locations, fund managers must rely on legal counsel to ensure they comply with marketing regulations.

5. *Different returns are provided to different investors.* Hedge funds tend to provide a more consistent experience for individual investors than investment counselors managing individual accounts.

Because hedge funds commingle the assets, investors generally experience uniform returns. (Individual difference will remain as investors enter and exit the fund at different times.) For certain clients, some funds negotiate special fee arrangements that create incrementally different net returns. These differences are fairly minor compared to the range of returns different investors earn in a bank trust department or with an investment counselor.

Investors inherently experience different returns because of varied holding periods, specific tax rates, and interaction with other assets in client portfolios. These differences mean that clients will react differently to returns, creating a complicated client-management task for a hedge fund.

6. *Management fails to act beyond the short-term tactical decisions.* Any business must avoid the trap of focusing on short-term to the exclusion of long-term issues. Short-term priorities for a hedge fund always involve attention to investment performance. Certainly, no fund should sacrifice performance. From time to time, other issues demand short-term attention, including news and economic events that affect the fund or its reputation, staffing issues, and liquidity crises. It is important that the management company has sufficient staff so that there is time to focus on long-term plans, priorities, new business opportunities, pricing, and marketing issues.

7. *Too much time is spent delivering performance and not enough managing expectations.* This foible of investment counselors is generally not a problem for hedge fund managers. Hedge fund fees are high, so it is counterproductive to dwell on limits to returns or advertising worst-case possible returns.

8. *Too much free advice is given as a marketing tool.* This fault identified by Bowen pertaining to investment advisors is generally not a fault of hedge fund managers.

9. *The fund centers too much around a few key individuals.* It is flattering to be revered by the press because of past outstanding performance. Very few stars tend to emerge from the investment community and fewer remain stars for long. One way to extract value

from that star status is to create a business that does not rely on being a demigod while also extracting as much value from the cult status directly.

For example, a highly visible manager of a global macro fund should (and usually does) invest in a variety of traditional or inventive investment products. Faced with an easy time to raise money and limits on the ability to scale the business up in size, the manager can help preserve the returns on existing funds by not exceeding the practical capacity limitations and developing a portfolio of products to allocate administrative and marketing costs over different funds.

10. *Maximizing fee income is emphasized over net profit.* There are several ways a hedge fund can limit net income that differ somewhat from Bowen's examples. Although salaries of trading staff are generally the largest expense, much of that is variable cost. That is, bonuses are large when incentive fees are high (following periods of outstanding performance) and low when fees are low (following periods of poor performance or withdrawal of funds under management). It is tempting to worry little about these expenses. However, large, expensive staff salaries can dilute the profit from hedge fund fees.

Because bonuses for key investment professionals are often paid at the discretion of the management company, a classic zero-sum game develops. If the fund managers can pay the smallest compensation and retain the individuals, the net income rises for the benefit of the owners of the management company. Too often, disgruntled employees leave to become competitors, costing the past employer much more than the bonuses of key personnel.

Managers should ask how much money could be effectively employed with the investment strategies in place. Managers often convince themselves that they can effectively run larger and larger pools of money. Most investors believe that growing beyond an optimal size will lower return. If this happens, net revenue is limited by reduced incentive fees and could lead to withdrawals from the fund.

11. *Technology is poorly utilized.* This deficiency does not appear to be a systematic problem for hedge fund managers.

12. *Costs are poorly controlled.* Because hedge fund fees are higher than most other forms of asset management, revenues are high when returns are good. A fund is wise to reinvest some of that revenue into expenses that will ensure the continued success of the fund. Unfortunately, it is difficult to distinguish effective expenditures from poor ones in advance.

Hedge funds can run into trouble when returns are poor or the fund experiences unexpected withdrawals. Frequently, these reversals of fortune are completely beyond the control of the management company. When they occur, the management company may be thrown into a cost-cutting spiral very damaging to the manager.

13. *Effective alliances and partnerships are not developed.* For a variety of investment strategies, there can be better and worse forms of ownership. A large sales organization in a broker-dealer might be the perfect complement for an investment product. Ownership by a highly regarded parent can lend credibility to a new strategy. For these reasons, it might be better to affiliate with a partner.

In contrast, a fund linked to a tainted parent might gain marketing advantages from severing and becoming independent. Or a parent motivated by broad objectives may not be motivated to maximize performance for investors or even maximize net income from that business. Similarly, a prestigious financial institution may refuse to lend its name to a hedge fund because of the risk of damage to its reputation if fund performance is poor.

Like any business, founders of a hedge fund may place too much value on remaining independent. Others might find a quick cash-out enough motivation to sell out despite the best interest of the owners of the management company and the fund participants.

THE BUSINESS OF THE BUSINESS

The typical hedge fund has been set up by an investment specialist who has often spent most of his or her early efforts producing the investment return. If successful in creating an attractive return, these fund managers must soon create the essential parts of a complete management company: internal controls, marketing, payroll, and an office environment. These business functions may seem like a luxury to the nascent fund operator, but may end up making the difference between success and failure.

Ideally, the founders should have sufficient resources to focus on the management company from the outset. For financial institutions starting a hedge fund, such resources are readily available.

With care, the organizers can build a management company that can create a particular hedge fund product and survive even if the fund strategy goes out of favor. The management company should be capable of managing several hedge funds with different strategies. This diversity may be valuable to the marketing staff and greatly increases the chance of long-term survival of the management company.

NOTES

1. This strategy and several others are defined in detail in Chapter 3.
2. Sticky funds are assets being managed that are not likely to be removed from the fund.
3. *Wall Street Journal,* February 12, 1999.
4. Pete Gallo, "Foxhound Fund Liquidates; Investors Migrate to Other Bulldog Funds," *The Alternative Edge,* March 19, 2001, page 11; available at http://www.hedgeworld.com/news/alt_edge.
5. John J. Bowen, Jr., *Creating Equity,* Securities Data Publishing Books, New York, 1997, pp. 10–15.
6. Transparency refers to whether investors receive details about actual positions held for their benefit.
7. Institutional investors frequently set thresholds for the percentage of a fund they will own. They often want to make substantial investments in fewer funds, so they refuse to consider smaller funds. For example, an investor who wants to make up no more than 10 percent of a fund and wants to invest $10 million cannot consider funds smaller than $100 million.
8. An early investor may get the right of first refusal. Any time the fund is willing to accept additional investments, the early investor may get the opportunity to provide the funds. This right can be extremely valuable if the hedge fund is successful and in high demand.

CHAPTER 3

Types of Hedge Funds

Hedge fund managers follow a variety of strategies to create attractive returns for investors. It is useful to categorize individual funds into broad styles to allow investors to understand roughly the risks inherent with a particular fund so they can quickly focus on those funds most appropriate to introduce into their portfolios.

This chapter describes the most popular hedge fund strategies. There can be tremendous differences between two hedge funds even within the same category. Also, hedge funds may employ more than one strategy at a time. Despite these differences, it is possible to point to fundamental investment risk factors (stock returns, interest rates, credit spreads, and volatility are the most useful) that explain much of the differences between returns for different hedge fund strategies.

FUND STRATEGIES

Several organizations, including TASS, Evaluation Associates, MAR-Zurich, (Managed Account Review), CSFB/Tremont, Hennessey, and Van Hedge, collect hedge fund performance data. These organizations separate hedge funds into categories. In most cases, the data providers categorize a fund similarly. Funds are sometimes assigned to different categories due to differences in the definition of their categories and human judgment.

Divisions in the plant or animal kingdom suffer from some ambiguity, but these organisms are definitely either flora or fauna. Hedge funds do not need to stay true to a single investment philosophy. Funds that combine multiple strategies can either be classified as mixed or one of the multiple strategies. In addition, the nature of their business can change over time.

With that caveat in mind, here are descriptions of the major fund styles.

Long/Short Equity

This type of manager is generally not market neutral. Instead, the fund can be long or short and will change from long to short from time to time. The fund can have substantial exposure to specific sectors and even individual companies.

The long/short equity hedge funds represent a large amount of hedge fund assets, up to a third of all money invested in hedge funds. Funds that are primarily long or short may be categorized as long/short equity by one data service and differently by other providers.

Some long/short equity hedge funds commit most of their efforts toward buying and selling the right stocks (or stock sectors). Other funds focus more on market direction, fairly freely swinging from market long to market short. More typically, a manager will overlay a market exposure on an ongoing stock selection program.

It is difficult to get consistent performance results on the long/short strategy. In one data set, the strategy is moderate risk and provides moderate returns. Results from another source show the strategy to be one of the highest performing hedge fund sections with very high risk. Perhaps the lack of consistency in performance of the sectors is caused by the lack of consistency in categorizing individual managers. In any case, it is important to review the performance of the individual funds in this category to decide if the performance is appropriate for the investor.

Equity Arbitrage

The equity arbitrage fund buys or sells a basket of stocks and hedges with a future. In its purest form, the fund buys the appropriate amount of every stock in the basket/index. In practice, a subset of stocks may serve as a proxy with relatively small tracking error. Also, with the proliferation of equity derivatives, including a variety of futures, these funds can trade combinations of futures, perhaps using positions in individual issues to fine-tune the relationship.

This strategy produces moderate returns with moderate risks. Investors in equity arbitrage funds might also invest in convertible bond arbitrage or fixed-income arbitrage funds. Equity arbitrage funds have had slightly higher volatility of returns than these other arbitrage strategies but with sufficient returns to justify the increased risk. Still, the sector has substantially less risk than broad market averages. This sector has fairly high correlations to stock indices and other equity hedge fund strategies (45–50 percent).

Equity Pairs Trading

Equity pairs trading involves buying and selling two very similar companies or similar securities issued by a single company. The companies generally are involved in very similar product markets, although they can differ in terms of financial leverage, product qualities, pricing, and other ways. Sometimes, pairs trading is used to create exposure to a comparatively small subsidiary (long or short) by hedging out the main company risks with a paired transaction.

Pairs trading can trade virtually identical classes of securities. For example, Berkshire Hathaway has two classes of common stock, with the smaller share equal to 1/30 of the larger share (there are additional differences in voting rights and convertibility is possible from the small shares into the large but not from the large shares into the small shares).

American depository receipts (ADRs) are shares that trade on U.S. exchanges backed by non-U.S., nondollar shares. The ADRs should closely track the common stock that backs each issue, adjusted for changes in currency exchange ratios. A pair-trading hedge fund can buy and sell these similar issues and create the currency hedge to remove the risk between the two issues.

Pairs trading can include risk arbitrage positions (see "Risk Arbitrage or Merger Arbitrage," following). Some pairs trading managers may find ways of creating hedges between stock and bond issues of the same company, in ways not much different from convertible bond arbitrage.

Equity pairs trading has been a low-risk strategy with attractive returns. Because of the tightly constructed individual transactions, returns are not correlated with stock or bond returns. Leverage of around 2:1 or slightly higher is typical of equity pairs trading.

Equity Market-Neutral Funds

Equity market-neutral funds combine issues into similarly behaving long and short portfolios within a country. Generally, the manager tries to create similar sector exposure, market capitalization, beta, and currency risk in the long and short portfolios.

The portfolios are not narrowly built of similar securities. For example, it would not be typical to buy one automobile manufacturer and sell short another manufacturer. Instead, portfolios are constructed with high-powered statistical models, so the long and short positions behave similarly in aggregate but differ in individual composition.

Often, equity market-neutral funds design trading rules around an overriding theory. For example, a manager may believe that small-cap stocks outperform large-cap stocks. This theory is translated into rigorously tested explicit trading rules. Successful strategies are generally implemented with little discretion or overrides.

Risk Arbitrage or Merger Arbitrage

Risk arbitrage (also called merger arbitrage) funds seek to profit from trades involving change of corporate governance. In the most common transaction, the fund buys stock in a company after a takeover has been announced. Shares of the acquirer are sold short. If the deal is completed, the long shares in the acquired company are exchanged for shares in the acquiring company. These shares are used to satisfy the short position in the issue. In some cases, the funds can unwind positions early if prices of the company shares reflect most of the profit potential.

Risk arbitrage is not arbitrage, despite any suggestion from the name of the strategy. The success of a particular trade hinges almost entirely on whether the announced deal is completed. It is difficult to hedge this risk. Instead, the traders must weigh the probability that the deal will be completed and the trade will be profitable against the probability that the deal will not be completed and the trade will be unprofitable.

Fund managers cope with these risks in different ways, which creates some inconsistency in performance between funds in this sector. Some managers invest in a large number of deals, perhaps using leverage to increase the diversification. Others invest in fewer deals but reduce risk by eschewing leverage. Some fund managers are more thorough about hedging major market risks than others. Some managers selectively hedge these risks. As a result, it is important for investors to review the performance of individual funds in addition to aggregate data on the performance of the strategy.

In addition to risks on individual transactions, the strategy depends on a steady supply of merger transactions. In the past, this activity has been cyclical, and the success of deals is more likely when regulatory and antitrust challenges are limited.

Risk arbitrage funds have had low correlations to bond returns and fairly low correlations to stock returns. Returns from risk arbitrage are fairly highly correlated with other hedge fund strategies. Risk arbitrage strategies are highly correlated with hedge funds classified as event driven. Like the event-driven strategies, funds classified as risk arbitrage have offered attractive risk-adjusted returns.

Event-Driven Strategies

The strategy of risk arbitrage is often included in a broader category called *event-driven* strategies. This classification includes strategies involving merger, acquisition, divesting, liquidations, bankruptcies, restructuring, and other corporate events. Some funds invest in a variety of strategies; other funds specialize in one or several related strategies.

The strategies rely on fundamental research (see Chapter 5) to appraise the deals quickly. Often, the team of analysts is given considerable input into the portfolio decision making. In some funds, the traders/portfolio managers take on the responsibility of doing the analysis.

Investments are usually made when there is considerable uncertainty about whether the deals will occur or when they will occur. Usually, however, the fund managers have fairly complete details about how the deals will occur because the Securities and Exchange Commission (SEC) requires extensive and timely disclosure.

Event-driven strategies have fairly high correlation to stock returns compared to some hedge fund strategies but low correlations to bond returns. These funds have produced moderately high returns. Because the volatility of returns in these strategies has been moderate, these funds have offered excellent risk-adjusted return.

Convertible Bonds

Fund managers buy convertible bonds or convertible preferred stocks that have debt, equity, and óptions characteristics. Usually, convertible bond hedge funds are long the convertibles issues. It is often difficult and risky to sell short convertible issues because they are small and illiquid. The funds combine hedges in the underlying common, nonconvertible debt, options on the common, futures and options on fixed-income products, and futures and options on broad equity indices.

In the closest variation to pure arbitrage, the manager seeks to hedge fixed-income risk, default risk, sensitivity to the stock, and perhaps even changes in volatility. It is generally not possible to create true arbitrage positions. Instead, the manager attempts to build a portfolio relatively immune to these risk factors.

In other funds, managers are long convertible securities and short the underlying common, in order to remove the effect of changes in share price from the net asset value. The funds remain long the options and hope to benefit from future price changes. These funds make money when markets are volatile and they are able to rebalance their position profitably. These funds lose money when the implied volatility of equity options declines.

In still other cases, managers select stocks they want to buy or sell and use convertible issues to create the exposure. For these funds, the limited downside protection inherent in the convertible security is combined with leverage to create the opportunity for substantial upside. These funds attempt to select the best performing stocks and do not hedge their exposure to the stock prices. Because convertible issues are most common in the high-yield market and also to the new issue market, their performance often depends on the performance of these sectors.

As a group, convertible bond arbitrage funds are among the lowest risk hedge fund strategies, despite carrying leverage up to 10:1. They generally have very low correlation to aggregate stock and bond returns. They are sensitive to credit spreads, benefiting when credit spreads narrow and default risk is declining and suffering when spreads widen. The group is also vulnerable to declines in option volatility (some funds more than others) and generally profit from higher volatility.

Fixed-Income Arbitrage

Fixed-income arbitrage includes trades between the cash and futures markets, yield curve strategies, credit and default strategies, and synthetic money market instruments using foreign issues and forward currency exchange rates.

Like most strategies, some of the fixed-income arbitrage strategies are arbitrage-like in their behavior. The ability to make money in pure arbitrage trades requires very high leverage because the profit per trade is generally very small. The successful fixed-income arbitrage funds that have kept positions very close to arbitrage must seek out opportunities worldwide as more established markets have gotten too efficient to provide fair returns.

Many fixed-income arbitrage funds actually make substantial bets on a variety of risks. Many of these funds "buy the curve" (buy shorter maturities and sell short longer maturities) or "sell the curve" (sell short the shorter maturities and buy longer maturities), hoping to profit from changes in the spreads between the sectors. Funds may also buy lower-quality fixed-income instruments (both domestically and internationally) and hedge the interest rate risk but remain exposed to changes in the spread between default-free rates and the instruments they own.

Fixed-income arbitrage funds have very low risk when compared with other hedge fund strategies. Not surprising, they have the lowest returns. They have the highest leverage of all major hedge fund strategies (30:1 or higher), which may be problematic with tax-exempt investors (see Chapter 10 concerning unrelated business taxable income). They are almost uncorrelated with broad stock and bond indices (with a weak tendency to do better when rates decline). They are somewhat more correlated to other hedge fund strategies because many hedge fund styles are sensitive to changes in credit spreads.

Mortgage Arbitrage

Mortgage-backed bonds are complicated instruments that resemble a bond paired with a short position in an embedded call option. The instruments traded start out as mortgages. Freddie Mac, Fannie Mae, and the Home Loan Bank pool the mortgages into pass-through securities. These securities are then reengineered into collateralized mortgage obligations (CMOs) and real estate mortgage investment conduits (REMICs).

Homeowners almost universally have the right to prepay their loans at face value without penalty. This right resembles a call option. For the same reason, most mortgage-based securities are callable securities. The complicated structures of CMOs and REMICs are designed to divide that risk of call (or prepayment in the mortgage vernacular) among investors in a way that makes the collection of instruments more valuable.

These deals often create some securities with very little option risk and other securities with amplified risk. The low-risk issues are easy to sell and are priced similar to other types of low-risk debt securities. The remaining securities are difficult to sell. Mortgage hedge funds are important owners of these risky issues, sometimes called "toxic waste."

These funds identify undervalued and overvalued issues. The most difficult instruments to hedge are attractively priced. The funds seek to eliminate sensitivity to changes in interest rates. Often, mortgage arbitrage is included in the funds categorized as fixed-income arbitrage.

Emerging Markets

Emerging market funds invest in securities of smaller, less developed economies. Funds can specialize in equity or fixed-income positions or they can create balanced positions. The way the funds manage their currency exposure can have a significant effect on the net returns.

Emerging market hedge funds are not market neutral. These funds are very sensitive to economic and political factors that affect all emerging markets. Most funds also track the broad market indices (Standard & Poor's 500 Index and other world equity indices) closer than many other hedge fund strategies.

Emerging market investments tend to be fairly volatile. A variety of economic and political events can significantly affect the prospects for these instruments. Also, there typically is not an organized lending market for these securities (see Chapter 7), so it is difficult to sell short most issues. Most instruments do not have a futures contract that reasonably tracks these issues. As a result, buyers are generally not able to hedge risk. Market makers cannot cushion change in demand for the issues by inventorying or selling short issues to investors.

Distressed Securities

The distressed securities manager buys stock or bonds of companies in or nearing bankruptcy. These securities are usually bought at large discounts from face value or earlier price levels. The strategy relies on being able to buy securities with enough profit potential to offset the obvious risk of loss. Buyers theorize that prices are low (and future returns are high) because most investors cannot or will not invest in distressed securities.

Distressed securities hedge funds are exposed to the risk of default, which they usually do not hedge. Not surprisingly, the funds tend to perform well when credit spreads narrow and perform poorly when spreads widen. Most funds contain unhedged fixed-income securities and therefore benefit when benchmark rates decline and suffer when rates rise.

The investments are illiquid and funds generally own the securities for years. As a result, the strategy is vulnerable to liquidity pressures if the style should move out of favor with investors. Therefore, these funds usually force longer commitments from investors.

Distressed securities funds have been a low-risk strategy, based on the volatility of returns (perhaps half as volatile as stock market returns). Performance in the sector has been moderately high, providing an attractive risk-adjusted return. Some investors believe that distressed securities funds and other styles that have substantial investments in illiquid instruments may be more volatile than the reported performance indicates. There is a tendency to carry these illiquid instruments at cost or the lower of cost or market, so volatility may be understated somewhat.

Global Macro Funds

The global macro group of funds has been one of the most visible hedge fund styles. Traders make investment decisions based on broad economic (especially international) factors. The funds can invest in stocks, bonds, currencies, and commodities. The funds seek to profit from directional moves in their positions. Although the funds may have long and short positions in a variety of assets, the positions may not be designed to hedge each other.

Macro funds invest in liquid, efficient markets. Most investments are limited to bonds, stocks (including equity index products), and currencies. They profit by making concentrated directional bets in these markets.

The definition of the global macro strategy is confused by some large funds, such as Tiger Investment Management, that primarily make levered stock selection bets. In addition, Soros Fund Management introduced international trend trading into a strategy that began as a U.S. stock selection strategy. Sometimes macro trading and stock selection are considered twin strategies that together define the global macro category. Other investors argue that Tiger was never a global macro fund and that Soros funds reflect multiple strategies.

Leverage in this sector is typically between 6:1 and 10:1. This ratio is higher than many equity hedge fund strategies and is particularly significant considering the outright nature of most of their positions.

Global macro hedge funds have had some of the highest returns of all hedge fund strategies. They are among the most volatile strategies of hedge funds. They have had higher correlations to stock and bond returns than most other hedge fund strategies (because of outright long positions in stocks and bonds). Their correlations are still low enough to make them valuable diversifiers in a conventional stock/bond portfolio. Global macro funds are also added as a way of increasing the overall return on a conventional portfolio.

Futures Funds

Futures funds commodity pools behave much like global macro funds. Most futures funds seek profits from directional moves in the positions they hold (long and short). Many of these futures funds use technical analysis to select positions to buy and sell.

Some futures funds focus on a single asset class, such as currency or fixed income. More often, these funds try to develop a consistent trading strategy that can be applied to many or most of the actively traded futures contracts. The funds that use a variety of instruments are less likely to be correlated with stock and bond returns. As a group, their performance tends to be fairly uncorrelated with underlying markets.

Commodities funds do not consistently buy options. Yet, as a group, they tend to act as if they did own substantial investments in options. These funds tend to perform best when volatility is high and perform less well when markets are quiet.

FUNDS OF FUNDS

Funds of funds are hedge funds that invest in other hedge funds instead of making direct investments in securities. Funds of funds contain between $75 billion and $85 billion under management currently and should grow in excess of 25 percent per year[1] and comprise more than a quarter of all hedge fund assets.

A fund of funds offers several advantages over a direct investment in a hedge fund. Typically, these pools invest in 15 or more managers (perhaps many more managers). Diversification can lower the riskiness of the investment without lowering the return. Although some investors have the resources to create diversification themselves by splitting their investments between multiple funds, the minimum investment levels make this impractical for many investors.

Fund of funds managers may be able to make investments not available to individual investors. As long-term investors with successful funds, they may have money invested with funds closed to new investment. The fund of funds may have the ability to increase that investment even while the individual funds are closed to new investment. The fund of funds is in a better position to evaluate new funds and enter before the funds get too large to be effective.

Finally, many hedge funds have long lockup periods. The fund of funds may be more likely to be given special permission to exit before lockup periods have expired. More importantly, the lockups on individual funds matter less because the number of funds creates many more opportunities for liquidity. Often, fund of funds managers do not need to liquidate positions when investors withdraw because they have other investors entering at the same time.

A fund of funds should have adequate diversification. Typically, no single fund should comprise more than 5 percent of the assets in the fund of funds. The fund of funds should define a particular style and then stick with that strategy. The fund of funds must have a way of dealing with lockups and minimums. Frequently, they get preapproved borrowing authority to create liquidity when investors withdraw.

Selecting Funds to Consider

The fund of funds must consider many variables when building its portfolio. Many fund of funds managers begin by identifying the strategies they will invest in and the proportions in the portfolio. A fund of funds may limit its investments to only market-neutral strategies, only equity strategies, only U.S. assets, or other ways. This initial decision will greatly affect the investment characteristics of the final product.

Perhaps the most important variable influencing the choice of fund is the historic returns of the funds considered. Generally, funds that have had the highest returns are preferred, if the fund of funds manager is convinced that the performance is repeatable. Managers may seek out funds in a particular strategy that have recently done poorly based on an expectation that the strategy will do better in the future. The level of fees may influence which funds are selected because differences in fees may translate into differences in net return for funds using similar strategies.

Fund of funds managers consider the risk that the investor experiences. Less risk is better than more risk, but there are many ways to define risk. One important measure of risk is the volatility (or standard deviation) of return. Numerous variations on the standard deviation exist. Downside deviation distinguishes large and variable losses (which are undesirable) from large and variable gains (which are desirable). Managers incorporate other measures of risk (drawdown, probability of loss, size of largest monthly loss, length of consecutive losing months, etc.) to design a fund of funds with less risk.

Fund of funds managers pay close attention to correlation of the returns between the funds. By selecting funds that are uncorrelated, the fund of funds manager gets more risk reduction from diversification. The manager also has some ability to control how correlated the fund of funds portfolio will be to stock and bond indices. A fund of funds with a low correlation to broad market indicators is more desirable to potential investors.

The fund of funds conducts a due diligence review of all funds in the portfolio. Due diligence involves any factor that may predict future losses. The process involves a thorough review of performance, especially various measures of risk. Perhaps more important, the review seeks to identify a dangerous lack of controls, signs of fraud, and funds that do not do what they say they do. Fund of funds managers seek out funds where key partners have made a substantial investment in the fund. For some managers, this consideration is the most important. Managers prefer funds that completely disclose positions to investors (transparency). With the benefit of this information, the fund of funds can confirm that it does not have excessive concentration in individual issues (summed across separate funds). The manager can also confirm that the fund is adhering to its strategy. In practice, most funds resist providing detailed position information.

The manager must consider several portfolio issues. Lockups on individual funds constrain the liquidity of the fund of funds to its investors. Incremental investments are allocated to cope with lockups, rebalance the portfolio, and provide flexibility in the future against lockup restrictions.

Capacity constraints at individual funds may influence position sizes. The fund of funds may overallocate to funds that will soon close to new investment. The manager must anticipate capacity limits with its managers and seek out new capacity by adding additional managers in advance of a critical need to invest more in that strategy.

Determining Fund of Funds Portfolio Weightings

The simplest weighting scheme would put equal money in each fund. This scheme is not ideal for a variety of reasons. It may not be possible to increase the size of particular funds that are closed to new investment. Minimum investment amounts may dictate that cash inflows be directed to a small number of funds. Lockups may require liquidation from a small number of funds. It also may not be possible or desirable to weight the individual investments the same and achieve the desired portfolio weights.

It is possible to select the weightings to achieve one or more objectives: maximize return, minimize risk, minimize correlation to stock and bond indices, maximize Sharpe ratio, minimize drawdowns, or others. In practice, the manager will probably trade off these objectives.

The manager can develop heuristic rules. These rules are developed from historical data and allow the manager to attempt to improve returns or lower risk. The rules aim to make the fund of funds portfolio more consistent over time.

A sophisticated portfolio strategy is called *portfolio optimization.* This technique, also called *Markowitz programming,* uses mathematical models to find the portfolio weightings that best trade off risk versus reward. The method gets the maximum benefit from diversification.

In practice, the portfolios selected either with heuristic rules or mathematical models are impossible to implement. Varying returns month to month causes weights to increase for some portfolios and decrease for others. Minimum investments rules prevent weightings from precisely matching model allocations. Lockups prevent precise reallocation. Business relationships may warrant maintaining an allocation even when the model has divested.

It is not clear that a portfolio would perform best if the weightings could precisely match the model weightings. Most models (1) give too much weight to what has happened and too little to what could happen and (2) do not deal with correlations that appear to be low under steady market conditions but become high when markets are in disarray. (This shift in correlations is what made the collapse of Long Term Capital Management possible. See Chapter 16.) Models may also be too quick at allocating profits out of winning strategies to rebalance.

DIFFERENT BUT THE SAME

Classifying hedge funds into styles is imprecise at best. Within a particular strategy, differences in techniques, strategy, the universe of assets, and even the personalities of the traders create considerable variation in performance.

Despite these differences, many—if not most—of the funds in a particular strategy respond similarly to a short list of factors: interest rates, stock returns, credit spreads, and market volatility. As a result, these classifications can be used (with some caution) to help identify potential hedge funds for investment.

NOTE

1. According to Freeman and Company as quoted in Susan L. Barreto, "Hedge Fund of Funds Boom Building Momentum," *The Alternative Edge,* May 21, 2001, page 1; available at http://www.hedgeworld.com/news/alt_edge.

CHAPTER 4

Types of Hedge Fund Investors

Hedge fund investors are usually classified into a small number of categories: individuals, endowments and foundations, pension funds, and corporate investors. There can be significant differences in investors within as well as between categories. These differences are valuable to marketers of a particular strategy. A financial institution that wants to build a hedge fund to cross-market with its existing product lines should understand the characteristics of its client base to select the right type of fund.

This chapter briefly explores the major types of hedge fund investors. Freeman and Company has assembled industry data from a variety of sources, and some of those data are presented as Table 4.1. As the table demonstrates, hedge funds get the largest share of their investment from high net worth (HNW) individuals; individual investments make up more than 83 percent of hedge fund assets. Endowments, foundations, corporate investors, and public funds each make up approximately 4 percent of the balance.

Individuals are the largest category of investors in the United States, with an estimated $12.5 trillion assets under management (AUM) (more than four times larger than any other category), and also have a fairly high (2.5 percent of their wealth) allocation to hedge funds. In comparison, endowments and foundations have a much smaller pool of AUM ($267 billion and $259 billion, respectively), but an estimated 5 percent of those assets are invested in hedge funds. Although corporate assets and public funds are substantial ($2.3 trillion and $3 trillion, respectively), their commitment to hedge funds has been small.

TABLE 4.1   U.S. Demand for Hedge Fund Products ($ billions)

Client Type	Allocation 2000 (%)	Allocation 2005, Estimated (%)	Hedge Fund AUM 2000	Hedge Fund AUM 2005, Estimated
HNW individuals	2.3	4.0	$287.5	$734.7
Endowments	5.0	10.0	13.4	39.2
Foundations	5.0	10.0	13.0	38.1
Corporate	0.5	1.2	11.4	40.3
Public funds	0.5	1.0	15.1	44.5
Life insurance	0.1	0.3	3.2	14.1
Other insurance	0.1	0.3	0.9	3.9
Taft-Hartley	0.0	0.1	0.0	0.5
Total			$344.5	$915.3

Source: Organization for Economic Cooperation and Development, Nelsons, AM Best, Freeman & Co. estimates.

The data in Table 4.1 predict an overall growth of 8 percent in all money under management across all types of investors. All groups are expected to commit a larger portion of their assets to hedge funds by the year 2005, with the resulting growth of hedge fund assets predicted to approach 22 percent per year. The largest percentage increases are expected from the investors with the smallest commitment, with individuals still expected to own more than 80 percent of the hedge fund assets.

It is difficult to generalize about the characteristics of the many individuals who have invested in hedge funds. With that warning, the following section describes characteristics of individuals who invest in hedge funds. Later sections contrast individual investment attitudes with those of endowments, foundations, pension funds, and other institutional investors.

INDIVIDUALS

Individuals are most likely to perceive risk as the chance of losing money. In contrast, institutions are more likely to accept the academic view of risk as the standard deviation of return (or another statistical measure). Most hedge funds are committed to delivering absolute returns, meaning they are not concerned with generating returns attractive relative to a benchmark; instead they try to earn high returns and avoid losses. Attention to absolute return does not mean that losses are unacceptable, but the potential for losses must be justified by the potential for gains. Further, the losses in stock and bond indices are not used to justify losses in the hedge fund. This objective is very appealing to most individual investors.

Individuals have been quicker to invest in hedge funds than all other types of investors. Private placement requirements ensure that most individual investors in hedge funds are wealthy with a high annual income. They should be knowledgeable investors and have the financial wherewithal to lose their investment in hedge funds.

Hedge funds may impose other restrictions. Because of limits in the number of investors,[1] hedge fund managers often refuse small investments, thus simplifying compliance and reporting.

Certain institutions closely resemble individuals and may actually make hedge fund investments legally as individuals while acting more like institutions. The best example of such a group is called a *family office*. A family office is a group of investors with an affiliation (often close relatives) who join together to manage their personal investments. Typically, the family office hires professionals to run money for several members of the office. The arrangement resembles a privately engaged trust officer. The stereotypic family office includes all the grandchildren of a particular 19th century industrialist. Despite the name, family offices might be made up of co-workers (Microsoft millionaires, for example), friends, or others.

Many family offices are interested in hedge funds because they appreciate the way low correlation allows diversification to lower risk. Other family offices are interested in raising the return of the overall portfolio.

For tax reasons, family offices generally have not put large portions of client money into hedge funds. Family offices might seek to maximize after-tax returns and hedge fund returns tend to be primarily short-term gains, taxed up to 40 percent at the federal level (and higher with state income tax rates included). In contrast, a traditional equity portfolio can be taxed at 20 percent or less and that gain can be deferred indefinitely.[2]

At one time, the typical individual investor in hedge funds was looking for very high returns and was willing to tolerate extreme volatility to get those returns. In the early 1990s, much of the growth of hedge funds came from individuals investing in global macro funds (see Chapter 3). These funds were capable of making 30 or 40 percent per year or higher and were able to lose nearly as much.

Most individuals interested in hedge funds today are unwilling to accept returns that are much more volatile than broad market indices (Standard & Poor's 500 [S&P 500], for example). These investors will not hesitate to accept much lower returns (perhaps lower than stock market returns) in exchange for lower risk.

Individuals may be more willing than institutional investors to invest in very young hedge funds. A board of directors for an endowment or pension plan does not benefit financially if it makes a successful hedge fund investment, but the same board may risk lawsuits or even loss of jobs if hedge funds perform poorly. Boards are biased toward making conservative decisions and avoiding decisions that might be viewed as imprudent in hindsight.

Some individuals invest in hedge funds through a self-directed individual retirement account (IRA). The investor must have sufficient funds in the IRA or similar retirement account and must find an administrator willing to allow the investment. The tax deferral may make a hedge fund investment considerably more attractive to an individual in the maximum tax bracket because investors receive most of their return in the form of ordinary income with little or no opportunity to defer income and little income taxed at a reduced capital gains rate.

OFFSHORE INDIVIDUALS

Offshore individuals have never been subject to the 99-investor rule (see Chapter 10). Hedge funds often impose smaller minimum investments for offshore funds. Some offshore investors may prefer to invest in a pool to preserve the anonymity of their investment.

Offshore individuals frequently invest in hedge funds through private banks. In this case, the hedge fund manager may not know the true investor or investors. Instead, a single investment from a private Swiss bank may represent 5 or 10 individual investors.

Offshore funds are domiciled in places that have minimal taxes, but investors generally must report the income to their taxing authority. Because tax laws differ widely, the tax consequences differ widely (see Chapter 12).

Offshore individuals differ from domestic individuals. The money directed by European banks is run with a higher level of investment sophistication than U.S. individuals because of the professional representation provided by the private bank.

With hedge fund investments (and other types of investments), European investors are much more likely to invest in issues outside their local markets. There seems to be some tendency for this to carry over to hedge fund investments. That is, European investors are more accepting of non-U.S. hedge fund assets than are U.S. individuals. However, there is also a group of non-U.S. investors who are seeking out U.S. assets in their portfolios.

OFFSHORE INSTITUTIONS

Most offshore funds are located in countries that impose very little taxation on the assets or returns. In offshore areas, local tax codes do not impose double taxation of institutional income,[3] so the corporate structure is more common than the partnership.

Many offshore institutions resemble domestic funds of funds. These institutional investments can be commingled individual investments, investments made directly by financial institutions, or even industrial corporate funds.

The disclosure rules are much more lax in many areas outside the United States. However, investors in these regions typically demand much of the same disclosure that legislation and regulation requires in the United States.

A sizable block of money is invested in low or moderately risky offshore hedge funds run by U.S. managers. Although the hedge fund investments are more risky than money market instruments, these corporations or international financial institutions find these controlled-risk investments a convenient place to hold dollar-denominated funds.

ENDOWMENTS

Universities were among the earliest institutions to invest in hedge funds. Several prestigious universities committed aggressively to hedge funds and experienced notable success. This early success has created a positive attitude about hedge funds and other alternative assets.

Endowments have not escaped the losses associated with many well-publicized hedge fund losses. These events slowed the movement of endowment money into hedge funds. Endowments are now more likely to use hedge funds to increase diversification and reduce risk and less as a source of excess return.

The endowment return is not taxed by state and federal income taxes, and therefore these institutions get no benefit from a reduced capital gains tax rate. There is no disincentive to invest in hedge fund instead of common stock; however, tax-exempt institutions are exposed to unrelated business tax income (UBTI). Consequently, endowments are likely to favor hedge fund strategies that employ less leverage. Moderately levered equity strategies are less vulnerable to UBTI than fixed-income arbitrage or convertible bond arbitrage strategies that employ significant leverage. See Chapters 10 and 12.

Endowments tend to have a longer-term horizon than other hedge fund investors (although time horizons tend to be longer for all investors when performance is good than when performance is poor). That longer horizon should make them more tolerant of short-term swings in net asset value. Although an endowment may not increase commitment to a hedge fund experiencing losses, it is less likely to liquidate to second-guess short-term performance. As a result, endowments may be somewhat more likely to invest in strategies involving illiquid securities (private placements, venture capital, real estate, and emerging markets) that may require a lockup of funds.

Spending plans limit an endowment's tolerance for risk. Endowments generally spend most of their investment returns. Minor swings are not enough to force changes in spending plans or commitments; however, major losses could force an endowment to cancel programs or defer projects. Consequently, endowments are concerned that the losses they can experience be relatively small.

Except for a few institutions with very large investments in alternative assets, hedge fund investments generally reduce portfolio risk. Risk in the endowment portfolio can be lower in part because the typical hedge fund is less volatile than the S&P 500, a proxy for a major asset class in most endowments. Also, when correlations to stock and bond returns are low (most hedge funds have a correlation below 50 percent to stock and bond returns; many correlations are significantly lower), hedge funds provide diversification that reduces the risk of loss in the portfolio.

Most endowments hire consultants to recommend a hedge fund strategy. These consultants may pick the style of fund that works best with other assets in the endowment's portfolio, review managers following this strategy, and recommend one or more funds to the board of the endowment. Usually, the endowment relies on the consultant to conduct due diligence on the managers.

FOUNDATIONS

Foundations are tax-exempt organization-like endowments. They have made substantial investments in hedge funds perhaps because they also do not have the tax disadvantage that plagues individual high net worth investors. Foundations are also concerned about avoiding the UBTI. For this reason, they risk being taxed on returns from a highly levered strategy. Like endowments, they favor hedge funds with low leverage.

Foundations tend to be longer-term investors, though perhaps somewhat shorter than endowments. Foundations that actively solicit funds from potential donors find that they are more successful in fund-raising when performance is good.

Foundations also frequently rely on consultants to select a hedge fund strategy, select a manager, and conduct a due diligence review of fund managers.

In the face of recent losses in stock portfolios, both foundations and endowments have increased their investments in hedge funds at the expense of traditional stock and bond investments. In a study released in January of 2002,[4] a survey conducted by the Commonfund found that foundations and endowments were increasing their allocation to alternative assets (including hedge funds and private equity) by 9 percent and decreasing their investment in common stocks by about the same percentage. The study also showed these groups increasing their allocation to cash by 3 percent and paring fixed-income investments by a like amount.

PRIVATE PENSION FUNDS

Pension funds have been relatively slow to commit to hedge funds and their investments are small relative to the total pool of pension assets. Pension funds control a very large pool of assets, though, so their potential for investing in hedge fund investments is significant.

There are many types of retirement accounts, but the main two traditional pension funds are defined benefit plans and defined contribution plans. Defined benefit plans cover many more workers than defined contribution plans. A defined benefit plan promises the level of pension benefits regardless of the investment performance of the paid-in funds. The sponsoring employers bear all the risk and benefit of investment performance. With a defined contribution plan, the company makes periodic contributions to the plan and the level of benefits enjoyed by the employee depends on the investment performance.

Investing in a hedge fund requires a fair amount of investment sophistication and risk tolerance (at least according to the securities regulations). Many participants in a defined contribution plan would not qualify to invest directly in a fund. To expose them to the risks of hedge funds is risky for the trustees of a pension plan.

However, many corporations would definitely qualify to invest in a hedge fund. For a defined benefit plan, where the company experiences the effects of performance, a strong case can be made for increased investment in hedge funds.

When returns are high, the pension fund sponsor may discover that the increase in assets exceeds the increase in pension liabilities. Corporations have been able to avoid many pension expenses as actual cash expenditures have not been needed. The reduction in pension expenses has led to increased earnings at many companies.

Following several years of negative stock returns, many corporations find they must again include an expense for future pension requirements. This increased expense has come at a time when corporate earnings have been under pressure for many reasons. It is not a convenient time to have increases in pension costs.

It remains to be seen whether hedge funds will be able to attract this new money into their funds. Hedge fund returns generally remained positive when stock prices declined in 1999–2001. Pension fund trustees have seen the value of diversification. Meanwhile, pension trustees are assuming a more conservative attitude that may bias them away from alternative assets.

Hedge fund managers may be reluctant to accept major investments from pension plans. As described more completely in Chapter 10, hedge funds risk being classified as pension funds themselves if more than 25 percent of the hedge fund comes from retirement accounts. Presently, pension fund investments are small enough that few hedge funds are burdened by this rule. Further, it is unlikely that this rule is responsible for the small amount of pension fund assets directed to hedge funds. Nevertheless, managers should be careful if they have substantial pension assets.

Pension funds are more sensitive than endowments and foundations to short-term losses because performance can have an impact on a sponsoring corporation's reported earnings. Endowments and foundations tend to have longer investment horizons than pension funds. Pension funds have more to gain by making hedge fund investments (especially in funds with low correlations to stock and bond returns), but they have nevertheless been slow to invest in hedge funds.

Pension fund investors tend to be very conscious of the level of management and incentive fees. In traditional, unlevered, long-only investing, there is little persistent difference between money managers before accounting for fees. The managers with the lowest fees tend to provide the highest net returns. Perhaps for this reason, pension fund managers have had trouble committing to pay the level of fees frequently charged by hedge fund managers.

STATE PENSION FUNDS

State pension funds are sometimes discussed separately from private pension plans. Many states run large pension pools for state employees. Many state plans have made very visible investments in hedge funds, CTAs, and other alternative assets.

Public-sector funds have generally run lower exposure to stocks (30–40 percent) than private-sector funds (50–60 percent).[5]

State funds are more likely to invest in a funds of funds than to invest directly in one or more hedge funds. The diversification provided by investing in 6 to 10 or more funds reduces the risk of poor performance. The fund of funds manager is responsible for performing due diligence on the individual investments.

CORPORATIONS

Corporations have made significant investments in hedge funds. The investments are small relative to the capital structure of most corporations but remain one of the four or five largest sources of hedge fund capital.

Corporations may invest in hedge funds for a variety of reasons. One corporation may seek to reinvest capital until it is needed for plant or equipment. Another may simply use hedge funds as a fairly low-risk way of increasing the returns. Others may want to put additional assets on the books to cushion other risks the corporations face. Relative to the powerful factors that can influence corporate earnings, hedge fund returns are a fairly predictable class of assets.

INSURANCE

Life insurance and property/casualty insurance companies make investments as a major part of their business, yet Table 4.1 shows only moderate investments in hedge funds by life insurance companies. Life insurance companies sell insurance and annuity products that earn a fixed-income return. These products, including guaranteed investment contracts (GICs), are essentially corporate debt borrowed from policyholders. Insurance companies make investments that should return more than their fixed-rate commitments so that they can profit from the difference.

Insurance companies are able to allocate some money to hedge funds, but the investment would reduce their permissible investments in common stock and other higher-risk investments. Insurance companies could benefit somewhat from the diversifying benefits of hedge funds but the magnitude of this investment is small because regulations limit the riskiness portfolios and regulators perceive hedge funds as risky investments. Also, insurance companies do not routinely mark securities positions to market. The unrealized gain or loss on a stock or bond position held as a long-term investment can be deferred. Hedge funds report results to investors monthly or quarterly.

Property/casualty insurance companies make substantial investments. These insurance products are priced to account for the risk of loss due to claims offset against the investment return that can be made between the time that premiums are received and damages are paid to policyholders. Regulations favor an allocation predominantly to short-term fixed-income securities.

Growth forecasts for this group are probably way too low. Recently life insurance companies have been selling insurance policies and annuities offering hedge fund returns that shelter much of the return from income tax. Offshore reinsurance companies create insurance products, derivative securities, and engineered securities that seek to (1) offer the chance that returns will be taxed at the long-term capital gains rate rather than the ordinary rate; (2) delay taxation; and (3) create loss limits for investors.

Reinsurance companies have become major fund sponsors. Investors who invest directly in a hedge fund face a punitive tax situation for most hedge fund investments. Most hedge fund returns are taxed at the taxpayer's short-term rate. For corporations, this also creates a second layer of taxation on the company results.

Reinsurance products have been designed to let investors enjoy tax deferral of investment returns and perhaps convert the investment performance from ordinary income to capital gain for individual investors.

FUND OF FUNDS

As the fund of funds data in Table 4.2 reveal, individuals are much more likely to invest directly in hedge funds than in funds of funds. Because individuals comprise so much of the hedge fund total, they still constitute more than half of the fund of funds assets. The share of hedge fund business channeled through funds of funds is 23 percent.

Many individual investors find it difficult to diversify their hedge fund commitments into several different funds. Funds frequently impose a minimum investment requirement of $1 million or more. For example, if an individual wants to invest no more than 10 percent of a portfolio in hedge funds, the entire portfolio must be at least $10 million to satisfy the minimum and comply with the asset allocation decision. If the individual wants to invest in three funds to diversify, the entire portfolio for the individual must be at least $30 million. Alternatively, the investor could invest in a fund of funds that contains 10 or more fund investments and get substantial diversification.

TABLE 4.2   U.S. Demand for Fund of Fund Products ($ billions)

Client Type	In Fund of Funds 2000 (%)	In Fund of Funds 2005, Estimated (%)	Fund of Funds AUM 2000	Fund of Funds AUM 2005, Estimated
HNW individuals	15	18	$43.1	$132.2
Endowments	60	70	8.0	27.5
Foundations	60	70	7.8	26.6
Corporate	60	70	6.9	28.2
Public funds	70	80	10.6	35.6
Life insurance	50	50	1.6	7.0
Other insurance	50	50	0.4	2.0
Taft-Hartley	100	100	0.0	0.5
Total			$78.4	$259.7
Market share of hedge funds			23%	28%

Source: Organization for Economic Cooperation and Development, Nelsons, AM Best, Freeman & Co. estimates.

Individuals and institutions also invest in funds of funds to get the benefit of due diligence and manager selection from the fund of funds manager. Fund of funds managers usually have research departments that conduct a thorough due diligence review of all potential investments. Fund of funds managers also tend to informally share information about individual managers, so it is much less likely that fund of funds managers will invest in inappropriate or fraudulent funds.

Investors with smaller amounts to commit to hedge funds have the most to gain from the diversification created in a fund of funds. Large investors can achieve some of this diversification by investing in more funds directly. Less sophisticated investors have more to gain from the portfolio management performed by the fund of funds manager. There is a tendency for new individuals who invest in hedge funds to be somewhat less affluent than existing individual investors (this is less true for institutional investors). It is reasonable to predict that fund of funds market share should rise for individual investors.

According to the Freeman and Company estimates, institutional investors are expected to increase their hedge fund investments faster than individuals (up to 35 percent per year versus 22 percent). Fund of funds are expected to capture a larger portion of all groups. As a result, growth in fund of funds assets will range from 25 percent annually for individuals to nearly 38 percent for the institutions that have the least hedge fund exposure now.

Faster growth is anticipated in the types of customers that have invested through funds of hedge funds. In addition, funds of funds should increase their market share for all types of individuals. As a result, this group should represent a higher percent of all hedge fund assets, rising to 28 percent by 2005. This increased importance enjoyed by the fund of funds managers means that they will be responsible for nearly one-third of the growth of assets under management in the hedge fund industry.

NOTES

1. Although the 99-investor rule has been substantially relaxed, hedge funds often impose minimum standards higher than required by law.
2. In fact, capital gains tax can be avoided completely if gains are not realized in the investor's lifetime. Congress recently passed a series of changes that phase out the estate tax and also eliminate the ability to avoid capital gains taxes at death. The changes are complicated and may make hedge fund investments more attractive for some taxpayers.
3. The U.S. corporate income tax would tax returns to individuals twice if U.S. investment pools were organized as corporations.
4. See Susan Barreto, "Commonfund Study Finds Investors Taking on New Asset Allocations," *The Alternative Edge,* November 11, 2001, page 2; available at http://www.hedgeworld.com/news/alt_edge.
5. Maginn, John L., and Donald L. Tuttle, *Managing Investment Portfolios: A Dynamic Process*, 2nd ed., Warren, Gorham & Lamont, 1990, page 4-3.

CHAPTER 5

Hedge Fund Investment Techniques

Hedge funds use a variety of techniques to produce returns for their investors. This chapter reviews a broad range of techniques including technical analysis, fundamental analysis, and several quantitative and statistical techniques. These techniques are used in equity, debt, commodity, currency, futures, and options markets in a number of ways.

Whole books have been written on these techniques. Readers interested in a particular topic should read more about the technique before building an investment strategy around techniques described in this chapter. The goal of this chapter is to explain the techniques in sufficient detail to allow the potential investor, a marketing specialist, a lawyer drafting organizational documents, or an auditor reviewing transactions to understand the businesses they are working with.

This chapter begins with a review of ways in which hedge funds are classified because they are often categorized according to their investment techniques. The chapter provides a review of many technical trading tools, followed by fundamental investment techniques and various arbitrage transactions. Finally, we review several specific methodologies and trades commonly used in hedge funds: dividend capture, earnings momentum models, earnings surprise models, volatility forecasting, and nonparametric methods.

In Chapter 1, we noted that there are estimated to be nearly 6,000 hedge funds. These funds invest in a wide variety of instruments based on many investment strategies. It is not possible to determine the exact number or characteristics of the funds because there is no central location to collect the information.

In the United States, most funds do not register with the Securities and Exchange Commission (SEC). Many funds do not register with the Commodity Futures Trading Commission (CFTC) or the National Futures Association (NFA), which handles the actual registration. Even the Internal Revenue Service (IRS) gets information on funds only if they have U.S. investors even if U.S. managers run offshore funds.

Similarly, no non-U.S. or worldwide organization has complete information. However, many funds report considerable information to hedge fund data services. This information varies in quality from data provider to data provider. Generally, the data services do not validate any of the information. Most organizations allow the individual investment managers to voluntarily report data. Finally, a fund may provide data to one or more data providers but usually not to all the data purveyors. Surprisingly, a single fund's performance may vary slightly when two or more data providers carry a fund's performance, usually because one service incorporates revisions and another does not. The services also have slightly different ways of calculating performance.

FUND CLASSIFICATIONS

There are many ways to categorize hedge funds. The simplest manner classifies hedge funds according to the types of assets they buy and sell. For example, a hedge fund could be classified as an equity, debt, currency, or futures fund. Because more than half of all hedge funds are considered equity funds, this group can be subdivided into equity sectors. Hedge funds can be classified as technology, large-cap, mid-cap, small-cap, micro-cap, value, growth, opportunistic, or in some other shorthand way of indicating positions.

Funds may be classified according to the place of origin for the securities they buy and sell. Certainly, the categories of U.S. or European are too large to be useful. Other categories include Asian, Pacific Rim, Russian, Eastern European, and Latin American. These funds may invest in a variety of instruments in these regions (including debt and equity), so the classification is not very descriptive. What they generally have in common is a deep knowledge of economics, credit risk, politics, and other factors that affect securities in those regions.

The trading tools of the funds can be used to categorize the funds (which is why this discussion on classification appears in this chapter rather than in Chapter 3). One type of fund makes trading decisions based exclusively on *technical* analysis of data, including a wide variety of models and techniques that base trading decisions on the pattern of historical prices, yields, or exchange rates. Another type of fund makes decisions based entirely on *fundamental* factors such as company information, industry information, and aggregate economic information. A third type of fund, called a *macro fund,* bases investment decisions primarily on national and international economic data and political information.

Funds generally are easy to categorize into fundamental, technical, or macro styles. Other funds combine these factors to improve returns or reduce the chance of loss. *Discretionary* funds make investment decisions based on more than one type of information. Funds may also be called discretionary if they primarily follow fundamental, technical, or macro data but override the models from time to time for subjective reasons.

The way the manager structures the investment decision-making process represents an additional way to categorize the funds. Within the funds categorized as fundamental, individual funds may be top down or bottom up. An example of a bottom-up fund is one that begins by making fundamentally based forecasts of individual company results. Valuation of individual issues depends primarily on these individual forecasts. The composite of all the valuation results provides a forecast for individual sectors and overall market returns. In contrast, a top-down process starts with macroeconomic assumptions that drive aggregate stock market assumptions and valuation. Individual company forecasts, if any, are made relative to the aggregate market forecast. Macro funds are frequently top down and equity funds are often bottom up.

Within a top-down or bottom-up organization, individual decisions can be based on quantitative models or qualitative means. Quantitative models can vary tremendously, but they attempt to represent past market actions numerically (using fundamental or technical data) as a basis for forecasting future market actions. In contrast, a qualitative fund may operate by committee to form a consensus estimate. As before, funds differ markedly in the degree to which they follow the decisions that derive from these models. Funds sometimes describe themselves as either discretionary or nondiscretionary. These investment processes are often developed without regard to marketing considerations but can have a significant effect on marketing efforts.

Finally, hedge funds have been divided into a category that might be called *true* hedge funds in contrast to others that only resemble hedge funds. A fund that buys distressed securities or a short-only equity fund may do little or nothing to alter the pattern of return on those assets. Some hedge fund participants argue that such portfolios of alternative assets are not truly hedge funds. Because hedge funds are, themselves, alternative assets, it is a distinction that may matter little to potential investors.

TECHNICAL INVESTMENT TECHNIQUES

It is not possible to give complete coverage to the many methods of technical analysis without expanding this section into a complete book on the subject. Several excellent books[1] are available and the reader is encouraged to read more about these techniques.

Technical models generally fall into one of two types. One group of models seeks to identify trends in place in particular securities or groups of securities. This group is always positioned incorrectly when the trend ends or reverses. Another group of models seeks to predict when trends are about to reverse. Not surprisingly, traders often combine techniques from both categories to improve results.

Academic theories generally hold that patterns in past prices, yields, exchange rates, or returns cannot predict future prices, yields, exchange rates, or returns. Alternatively, if they could be used profitably, the models would become so popular that markets would immediately reflect those forecasts. In either case, investors should not expect to earn returns above the level generally available to that group of assets.

Technical models assert that trends last longer than would be expected for truly random returns or that the techniques can improve the chance for success in making buy and sell decisions. Success using the models also requires that the market has not adapted the models to the extent that prices have already adjusted to the information derived from the models.

Most trending techniques begin with a visual presentation of data. Levels are generally plotted from low to high on the vertical (y) axis. For daily charts (one data point per day), the closing price is frequently used. For charts spanning multiple days, the date axis (x-axis) is usually compressed, so weekend days are removed from the axis. Figure 5.1 shows a typical price chart.

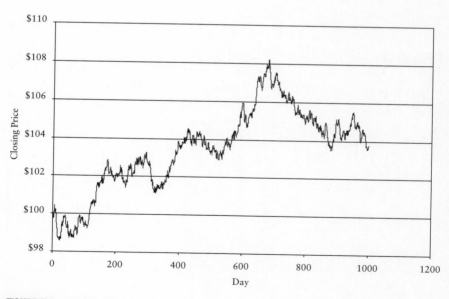

FIGURE 5.1 Daily Line Chart

There are several ways that additional data can be represented on the same chart. A bar chart draws a vertical line for each data point (day or intraday subperiod). The line extends from the high to the low value. A horizontal line attached to the left side of the bar shows the opening value (not shown here). A horizontal line attached to the right of the bar shows the closing value (see Figure 5.2).

The same information can be represented with a figure that resembles a candlestick. Because of this appearance, the charts are usually called *candlestick charts*. Although popular in many parts of the world, the technique is usually associated with Japanese traders. Figure 5.3 shows part of a Japanese candlestick chart.

Technical analysis can try to identify prices that represent support or resistance. Support is a level where buyers tend to buy and stop a price decline. Resistance is a level where sellers tend to sell and stop a price rise.

There are a variety of psychological reasons why this pattern of trading occurs. Often, support and resistance are predicted where

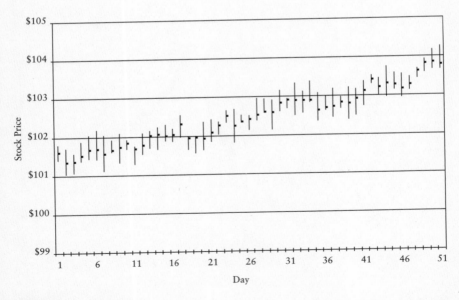

FIGURE 5.2   Bar Chart

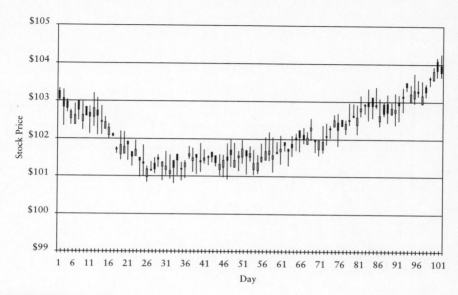

FIGURE 5.3 Candlestick Chart

trading has previously occurred. At these prices, traders who had profitable trades begin to lose money. Traders who had losing trades can unwind and break even.

In practice, these support and resistance levels are updated to reflect a previous upward or downward trend. A chart (see Figure 5.4) may predict resistance (support) by extending a line connecting two or more high points (low points) on a trend. Figure 5.4 shows a line chart with daily closes, support, and resistance. Support and resistance can also be added to bar charts utilizing intraday data.

If these local highs and lows occur with high volume, the support or resistance is considered stronger and more likely to act as a barrier when approached from above or below. Also, if three or more points can be connected, the support or resistance is considered stronger.

It is frequently possible to draw both support and resistance lines bracketing a previous trend. When the support and resistance lines are parallel or nearly parallel (called a *channel*), traders are comfortable buying or selling to join in the trend.

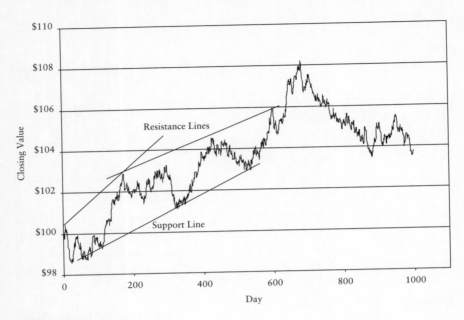

FIGURE 5.4 Support Resistance

Point and figure charts are a much-simplified method of representing prices (or yields or currency exchange rates) over time. The technique is believed to trace back to Charles Dow, who created the Dow Jones indices. Because the technique predated computers, the detail of information preserved was greatly reduced.

Like most charts, it begins with an x-axis that represents time from left to right. Prices are displayed on the y-axis. However, it records only that a particular high price has been attained, omitting much of the short-term swings. Each time a new high is established, another box on the graph paper is filled. Once an upward trend is deemed over, a new column is begun with a new symbol for the downward trend (see Figure 5.5).

Point and figure charts were designed to record prices of individual stocks during the trading day. They were not meant to track broad market indices or macro data such as interest rates and cur-

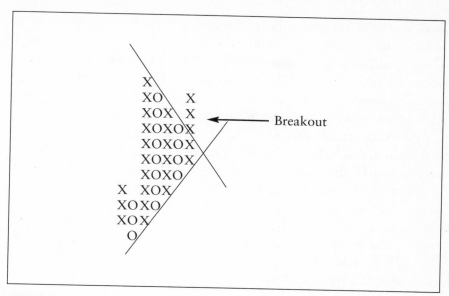

FIGURE 5.5 Point and Figure Chart

rency exchange rates or even long-term trends in daily closing prices (although they have been used for these purposes).

In addition, because the *x*-axis measures only consecutive upward and downward trends, it is really not a measure of time. The data can accumulate quickly if trading is active and prices are changing or slowly if markets are not active or are staying within a range.

The point and figure charts are read much like bar charts or candlestick charts. Support and resistance lines are drawn, although the location of the lines can differ from other methods because the *x*-axis differs. A variety of additional patterns are believed to provide confirmation of signals or increased confidence in signals.

Stochastic describes a technique designed to measure the extent to which a trend is nearing an end. The technique assumes that markets close near their daily highs when a solid upward trend is underway. Likewise, markets should close near their daily lows when a solid downward trend is occurring. Several indicators measure this assumption. The indicators can range from 0 to 100. Values above 80 indicate the trend upward is still strong and predict that purchasing is likely to be profitable. Values below 20 indicate the trend downward is still strong and predict that selling is likely to be profitable. Although primarily used as contrary signals of overbought and oversold conditions, the indicator is sometimes used to signal or confirm a trend when the statistics are near the extreme values.

Moving averages can also be used to detect an upward or a downward trend. A simple moving average sums a certain number of prices and divides by the number of points summed. This average moves up slower than the underlying series when prices are rising. The average also moves down slower than the underlying series when prices are declining. Therefore, it can be used to identify trends. When the most recent price is above the average, a rising trend is underway. When the price is below the average, a declining trend is occurring. The method is successful if trends persist longer than would be expected of random data.

Traders use a variety of methods to calculate a moving average. More days can be accumulated to make the index slower to react to new data. This slower indicator may be less likely to generate false buy and sell signals when prices are trendless. A weighted average can put more emphasis on recent data and less weight on earlier data. A geometric average combines the value with multiplication instead of addition. The harmonic average uses the inverse of the data, which can be used in conjunction with the standard present value mathematics (see Equation 5.1).

$$\text{Average}_{\text{harmonic}} = \frac{1}{\dfrac{1}{N}\displaystyle\sum_{i=1}^{N}\dfrac{1}{X_i}} \tag{5.1}$$

An important weighted average is the exponentially weighted average. Each successive average is equal to a weighting of the previous average, which incorporates information from all the data back to the beginning of the series, and the latest data point. If the weight for the latest data point is α (between 0 percent and 100 percent), the updated average (μ) is:

$$\mu_i = (1 - \alpha)\mu_{i-1} + \alpha X_i \qquad (5.2)$$

In this equation, the new average (μ_i) is a weighted combination of the previous average (μ_{i-1}) and the latest data point (X_i); the weights are α and $1 - \alpha$, which sum to 1 or 100 percent.

While the most recent data point has a weighting of α in the average, the previous point has a weight of $(1 - \alpha) \times \alpha$. For example, if $\alpha = 10$ percent, the updated average equals a 90 percent weighing of the most recent average and a 10 percent weighting of the most recent data point.

The weight for each older data point is smaller than the previous. The data point before that has a weighting of $(1 - \alpha) \times (1 - \alpha) \times \alpha$. By assigning a value for α close to 1, or 100%, the exponentially weighted average resembles a moving average over a short interval. By picking a weight for α close to 0, the exponentially weighted average resembles an average of a long range of data points.

Sometimes, two moving averages are used together. Trends are identified with a long-term average (using a larger number of points in the average). Timing (especially exit points) is determined by the shorter average. For example, starting from no position, a trend is identified when the price moves above (for an upwardly trending market) or below (for a downwardly trending market) the long-term average. Probably, the price was already above or below the short-term average. The long or short position is established and held until the price touches the short-term average and before the price returns to the long-term average. By combining two averages, the trader hopes to avoid the whipsaw losses of trading in a trading range but also to exit a major trend closer to the extreme high or low price.

A second class of models seeks to identify points to enter positions running counter to a major trend. These models are called countertrend models or contrary indicators. These models attempt to make money by identifying extreme points where purchases and sales are more likely to be profitable.

One major contrary indicator is called the *relative strength indicator* (RSI), an index that averages the gains and losses over an interval as shown by Equation 5.3:

$$RSI_N = 100 - \left(\frac{100}{1 + \left[\dfrac{\dfrac{1}{N} \sum\limits_{i=1}^{N} \Delta Price(+)_i}{\dfrac{1}{N} \sum\limits_{i=1}^{N} \Delta Price(-)_i} \right]} \right) \qquad (5.3)$$

In the equation, positive price changes (gains) are accumulated separately from the negative changes (losses). The ratio of the two averages gives an indication of the strength of the trend. This ratio can range from 0 to an unbounded upper value, and it is converted to an index ranging from 0 to 100.

When the index gets above 70 to 80, the market is called overbought and is deemed more likely to decline. When the index gets below 20 to 30, the market is called oversold and is deemed more likely to rise. Traders change the number of days included in the average to see which variation best predicts opportunities to trade counter to a trend. Traders may incorporate different time periods for different assets.

Various measures of sentiment are used to construct contrary indicators. Commercial surveys such as the Bullish Consensus report published by Market Vane report the percentage of the survey group that expects higher prices for a variety of futures contracts. It is possible to create both trend-following and countertrend strategies from the information. According to the contrary theory, when everyone believes prices will go higher, there is no one left to become bullish, so prices are much more likely to decline. Similarly, when everyone believes prices will go lower, there is no one left to become bearish, so prices are much more likely to increase. Either the probability of a directional movement or the size of potential movements up or down makes a speculative position attractive.

Traders attempt to measure bullish and bearish sentiment by tracking the size of a short equity position. They also compare the open interest in calls versus open interest in puts. There are several theoretical problems with these indicators. First, for every open option position, there is a long and a short. It is not clear why larger gross positions should be a predictor of direction. Second, large numbers of options and short interest in the underlying issues can be part of an arbitrage strategy, which should offer no information about customer sentiment.

Whether these sentiment indicators *should* work is much less important than whether they *do* work. It is important to test the indicators for the markets that will be traded.

Many traders believe that, after a trend has reversed, there will be a tendency for the reversal to stop at predictable points. For example, if a stock has risen 10 points and is currently going down, this theory might predict an increase in buying when the stock has lost half (5 points) of the 10 point gain. That level is called a 50 percent reversal.

The 50 percent (1/2) reversal is popular because people (and presumably the traders of that stock) are attracted to natural points. Another example of such a point of reversal is derived from a mathematical series called *Fibonacci numbers*. A Fibonacci series is built by adding two contiguous numbers to get the next number in the series. Fibonacci series are named after the early Italian mathematician Leonardo Pisano (c. 1170–1250), who was nicknamed Fibonacci. Starting with 0 and 1, the next number is also 1 (0+1) followed by 2 (1+1), 3 (1+2), 5, 8, 13, and so on. The ratio of consecutive Fibonacci numbers converges on the number .618:

$$.618 = \lim 1, \frac{1}{2}, \frac{2}{3}, \frac{3}{5}, \frac{5}{8}, \frac{8}{13}, \frac{13}{21}, \frac{21}{44} = 1, .5, .667, .625, .615, .619... \quad (5.4)$$

This ratio shows up frequently. It apparently describes the proportion of height to width on ancient Greek architecture. It shows up as a proportion found in the human body and other species. For this reason, it seems logical to see the ratio show up in securities markets. In particular, when a trend is reversing, many traders believe there is a tendency to stop the reversal at 61.8 percent or 38.2 percent (100 percent – 61.8 percent).

Elliot waves are based on the belief that major moves are caused by real supply and demand forces. However, there is consistent overreaction due to psychological forces. The techniques were designed to be used on major indices, but they have been applied to individual issues.

The theory holds that bullish market moves called *tidal bull waves* are divided into five subwaves (up then down, up, down, and up) overlaid on the upward trend. Each of these subwaves is divided into five additional subdivisions of alternating up and down swings. In contrast, the corrective bear wave is subdivided into only three cycles. Those three patterns are subdivided into subwaves (three up and five down).

To apply the theory, recent price changes are interpreted as being one of these major or minor waves. Different Elliot wave analysts may interpret past patterns differently. Accuracy of prediction is measured by the performance results.

FUNDAMENTAL INVESTMENT TECHNIQUES

Fundamental techniques also challenge the efficient market hypothesis. However, instead of looking for patterns in prices, these techniques analyze a variety of data for the companies, the security, the economy, and other data.

These models can try to time the market, buying when securities are undervalued and selling when securities are overvalued. These techniques can be used to form judgments on broad aggregates, sectors of the market, or individual securities.

This section first describes fundamental equity analysis and trading. Bond-related issues follow.

The simplest fundamental model compares the market value of a security with the book (or accounting) value for the company. This technique applies primarily to common stocks. It is very intuitive to believe that a stock is attractive if the market price is below the book value and unattractive (or attractive to sell short) when the price is above the book value.

As a trading model, this rule is much too simple. Most sectors trade consistently above or below their book value. More stocks trade above book value than below. These differences arise in part because of accounting rules that create differences between the book value and the market value. For example, tax and accounting rules require companies to treat research and development costs as expenses on the income statement rather than assets on the balance sheet. Depreciation rules can value physical assets above or below fair market value.

Even within a sector, book value can be a misleading indicator. It may be necessary to adjust for the accounting differences between companies and between industries for the indicator to be meaningful. Nevertheless, it is the foundation for strategies such as the Dogs of the Dow strategy, which holds that there is a tendency for the Dow stocks with the highest yield and the lowest ratio of price to book value to outperform other Dow stocks.

Dividend discounting (and variations) treat stocks much like bonds. In practice, the periodic cash flows could be dividends, earnings, or cash flow (earnings with noncash expenses added back). The model can be configured for any type of cash flow, but users are generally very opinionated about which method works best.

The general formula (for simplified annual cash flows) is:

$$\text{Present Value} = \frac{CF_1}{1+r} + \frac{CF_2}{(1+r)^2} + \frac{CF_3}{(1+r)^3} \ldots + \frac{CF_\infty}{(1+r)^\infty} \quad (5.5)$$

The cash flows (CF) are forecast from fundamental accounting information. The discounting rate (r) is selected according to the riskiness of the particular issue (usually the capital market line based on the issue's beta[2] and the risk-free rate). Analysts may derive point estimates for the early cash flows, then predict growth rates for later cash flows.

A simple model assumes that a single growth rate (g) applies to all cash flows. The formula given as Equation 5.5 becomes:

$$\text{Present Value} = \frac{CF_1}{1+r} + \frac{CF_1(1+g)}{(1+r)^2} + \frac{CF_1(1+g)^2}{(1+r)^3} \ldots + \frac{CF_1(1+g)^{\infty-1}}{(1+r)^\infty} \quad (5.6)$$

When the cash flow is defined as after-tax earnings and a constant growth rate is used, the formula becomes the price/earnings ratio (P/E):

$$\text{Present Value} = \text{Price} = \frac{\text{Earnings}}{r - g}$$

$$\frac{\text{Price}}{\text{Earnings}} = \frac{P}{E} = \frac{1}{r - g} \tag{5.7}$$

From this overly simple model, it is clear that the P/E of all stocks should not be equal. Rather, the ratio should reflect the riskiness of the stock (and hence r, the risk-adjusted discounting rate) and the expected growth in earnings. In addition, the P/E of a particular stock or all stocks should change along with market interest rates and earnings growth forecasts (which can vary immensely over an economic cycle).

Many strategies select stocks based on the P/E. Frequently these strategies account for risk and growth potential in some manner. Like the price-to-book strategies, the P/E methodology is still powerful when efforts are made to cope with the shortcomings.

One of the most popular methods of stock selection involves earnings momentum. Although it is possible to portray this strategy as a way of generating cash flows, earnings momentum usually focuses more on the trend in earnings growth over time than on how that trend feeds back into pricing. Instead, these models drive fairly short-term trading strategies.

Contrary investing is a form of fundamental decision making. The idea behind contrary investing is that issues that are out of favor become attractive notwithstanding the risks that investors seek to avoid. Similarly, companies that have everything going well for them may become overvalued if investors pay too much for the issues.

Although contrary investment can take the form of knee-jerk reaction to good or bad news, it also takes the form of Dogs of the Dow or simply buying low P/E stocks. To be successful, investors must be convinced that the current pattern of success or failure will reverse. Fundamental analysis is a key tool for contrary investors.

Fixed-income traders base trading decisions on forecasts of changes in interest rates and changes in the shape of the yield curve. The yield curve is the (imaginary) line derived from graphing yield on the *y*-axis versus maturity on the *x*-axis Changes in interest rates are driven by changes in the rate of inflation. Because market interest rates are forward looking, the bond market responds to changes in the buyers' forecasts of future inflation. Forecasting inflation may be possible over a short period (although market participants will not agree on the way inflation is measured). Forecasting inflation far into the future is much more difficult because many of the events that will determine future inflation have not yet happened.

Another key determinant of interest rates is the central bank (the Federal Reserve in the United States). The central bank has considerable ability to affect short-term rates. Changes in long-term rates reflect investor confidence in the central bank to responsibly determine policy.

The aggregate flow of funds affects interest rates. The real rate of interest (the amount the rate exceeds inflation) rises or falls when the borrowing by the government, private companies, and individuals does not match the savings in the economy. The incremental cost for corporations and municipalities to borrow (relative to default-free governments) depends on forecasts for defaults by those issuers.

The yield curve can be described as the general level of rates, the slope of the yield curve (how rates in the 10-year maturity compare to yields in the 5-year sector, for example), and the shape of the curve. At times, the curve is flat. Other times, there is a notable difference between short and long maturities. These changes may be the result of changes in inflation expectations. Often, the changes reflect evolving views on the future course of central bank policy.

Many factors can influence yields and yield spreads. For example, when property/casualty insurance companies lose money (following a big hurricane, for example), insurance portfolios may sell municipal bonds that are sheltered from income tax and buy comparable corporate bonds that are not sheltered from tax because the insurance company does not anticipate paying taxes for several years. Such moves are large enough to influence spreads between fixed-income sectors. Similarly, demand by corporations or homeowners may drive spreads wider if issuance exceeds investor demand.

Changes in spread may reflect changes in the likelihood of bankruptcy or default or changes in the estimate of how much would be recovered in the event of bankruptcy or default. This view of default as the driving force for determining spreads is the basis for Creditmetrics™, discussed in Chapter 13.

One form of fundamental research in fixed income involves credit research on corporate and municipal bonds. Bond markets generally reflect this credit risk in the yields on specific securities. Fundamental analysis seeks to more accurately predict actual loss experience. Analysis can also predict which issues are likely to be perceived as better (worse) credit risks in the future and position accordingly. These models are driven by macroeconomic data, company financial results, and sector forecasts. Some analysts use a nondiscretionary mathematical system to predict changes in bond prices likely to occur because of changes in the market's perception of risk. With the creation of credit derivatives, hedge funds can employ this research in many additional ways.

The mortgage market comprises a major portion of the debt market. A large portion of single-family home mortgages is transformed into debt securities. Most of these securities are extremely unlikely to cause loss of principal because the underlying loans are secured by the value of the houses and Fannie Mae, Freddie Mac, and the Federal Home Loan Bank guarantee the payments.

The timing of the payments is not certain. Most homeowners have the right to repay mortgage loans without penalty. When rates decline, the borrower can repay the loan and borrow at a lower rate. This repayment works to the disadvantage of the mortgage security holder. Changes in the timing of repayment significantly affect the attractiveness of the mortgage-backed securities.

To make matters more complicated, many of the mortgage loans have been divided and recombined into complicated mortgage derivative securities. Some instruments are less sensitive to these changing factors. Other securities are extremely sensitive to the changes.

Mortgage investors have extensive research departments to follow macroeconomic news and housing statistics and translate this information into trading decisions in the mortgage-backed sector. The level of interest rates, macroeconomic data, credit spreads on alternative investments, and the rate volatility ultimately affect the value of mortgage securities.

NONDIRECTIONAL TRADING STRATEGIES

Many trades that are described as arbitrage are actually market-neutral trades. In contrast, pure arbitrage involves the simultaneous buying and selling of the same good. In the pure form, nothing is left unhedged. Nothing can go wrong. There is very little arbitrage profit in the market, but a lot of nondirectional trading is called arbitrage.

One classic arbitrage involves buying wheat in one village and selling it in another for a profit. The only thing necessary to complete the transaction is to transport the grain, presumably at a known cost.

A slightly more complicated version involves buying gold in England and selling it in the United States. In addition to transporting the commodity,[3] the transaction would require at least one exchange of currency, and possibly two if the trader preferred to hold neither dollars nor pounds sterling. It is only slightly more complicated, however, and the trade can still be accomplished without assuming substantial risks.

In addition to the location arbitrages just described, it is possible to arbitrage across two time periods. For example, for many commodities, it is possible to sell for delayed (forward) delivery. If the prices permit it, an arbitrage trader can buy the good, finance short-term ownership, and redeliver at a later time with a certain profit.

A third, related, arbitrage involves buying a commodity or security and selling a futures contract. Eventually, the commodity or security is delivered into the futures exchange to satisfy the futures obligation. Like the forward transaction, the trade primarily involves financing costs, storage cost, perhaps transportation costs, and other incidental amounts.

Some futures contracts introduce uncertainty when futures can track similar but not identical assets. Grain delivered in Toledo, Ohio, may not be a perfect substitute for grain delivered in New

Orleans. Differences in sulfur content and specific gravity create distinct markets for crude oil from different regions, which may be deliverable into a single futures contract. Bond futures allow a basket of issues to be delivered versus the future.

There are many transactions where a physical transformation is possible that tightly links two or three separate assets. For example, in a trade called the soy bean crush, a soy bean processor can buy soy beans and sell soy bean oil and soy bean meal, the major finished products. Although the processor may incur costs to accomplish the conversion, the costs are known and potentially could be hedged, too.

A second type of product arbitrage involves crude oil and the finished goods that can be derived from the crude oil. For example, an oil refiner can buy crude oil and sell gasoline and heating oil. While a variety of products can be produced from a barrel of oil, the hedge removes substantially all the risk between the three commodities.

A third example of commodity arbitrage involves natural gas and electricity. Natural gas and electricity have been deregulated in many areas. Where that is true, a trade called the "spark" is possible. Here, the electricity producer buys natural gas and sells electricity. Assuming the power generator has the proper equipment, the ability to transmit power to potential electricity buyers, and the ability to take delivery of the gas, it can create a nearly riskless trade because the costs of production and the yield are known in advance.

There are several nearly perfect arbitrage trades in the option market. To be a perfect arbitrage, the options involved must be European options that can only be exercised on the final day of expiration. American options can be exercised at any time until expiration. The early exercise alternative means that there is some uncertainty of the timing of the cash flows in the arbitrage.

A conversion involves a call, a put with the same strike price and expiration date, and a position in the underlying security. For example, a long call with a strike of X combined with a short put with the same strike is equivalent to a forward purchase at the price of X. If the underlying price is above X on the expiration date, the owner of the call will exercise the call. Below X, the owner of the put will exercise the right to sell. Whether the market trades higher or lower, the long call/short put combination will become a long position at expiration. To turn the combination into an arbitrage, the trader needs only to sell short the underlying asset.

For the same reason, a short call and long put acts like a short position in the underlying asset. Above the strike, the call owner will exercise the call, changing the option position into short in the underlying. Below the strike, the owner of the put will exercise the put, also creating a short position. To transform the option position into an arbitrage, the holder of the option spread should buy the underlying asset.

A box spread resembles two conversions. Suppose the trader is long a call and short a put, each with the strike of X_1. The trader is also short a call and long a put with the strike of X_2. Like the conversion just described, the trader will buy the underlying asset at X_1 and sell the position at X_2. The trades occur on the same day, so the only remaining exposure is the time value of money on the spread between the two strikes, which is a very small effect. In fact, even that risk can be hedged with interest rate futures if the size of the position is large.

Dividend capture represents another strategy that closely resembles arbitrage. Companies declare dividends with an effective date in the future. For example, a company may declare a dividend on May 1 payable to the holders of record on May 15 to be paid on May 31. On May 15, buyers and sellers of the stock know the holder will receive the previously declared dividend and that anyone buying the stock on May 15 or later will not receive the dividend. Note the cutoff date is when trades settle after the ex-dividend date. The trade date associated with dividend capture occurs several days before.

There is every reason to expect the stock to decline by the amount of the dividend (on average) from the close prior to May 15 to the open on May 15. However, the stock tends to decline somewhat less than the dividend. Dividend capture purchases stock immediately prior to the dividend record date and sells it immediately after, profiting when the stock declines by less than the full amount of the dividend.

A variety of cross-sectional trades resemble arbitrage to greater or lesser degrees. In any case, many of the strategies seek to make money independent of the level of the market.

In the bond market, yield spreads provide an opportunity to trade relative value. Corporate bonds, mortgage-backed bonds, foreign bonds, bonds from emerging economies, and junk bonds yield more than U.S. Treasury securities. Municipal issues gain a valuable exemption from income taxation. In each case, the increased return compensates for the risk of default, the risk of decline in value if the issuer's credit deteriorates, prepayment risk or early call, and illiquidity. Hedge funds can buy these issues (perhaps with leverage) and earn the incremental income. They can also buy undervalued issues (and in some cases, sell short overvalued issues) to profit from expected changes in valuation.

Hedge funds can buy fixed income assets to make money if rates rise or decline. That type of trade was described in the section describing fundamental analysis under the descriptions of trading by technical and fundamental traders. In addition, bond investors can create somewhat more complicated positions that benefit by a steepening yield curve (yields on short issues declining more than yields on longer issues or yields on short issues rising less than yields on longer issues), widening of yield curve spreads (yields on short maturity issues rising more than yields on longer issues or yields on short issues declining less than yields on longer issues), or buy or sell mispriced sectors.

Option traders can create a variety of positions that are not sensitive to the price of the underlying asset. These trades are not arbitrage in the narrow sense of the word because they do not involve buying and selling the identical asset. For example, a long position in an option on one underlying asset can be combined with a short position in an option on another underlying asset. If the prices of the two underlying assets move fairly closely together and if the trader also carries neutralizing positions in the underlying assets, the trade will perform much like an arbitrage.

A position long or short an option can be hedged with a neutralizing position in the underlying asset. For example, a long position in a put (which loses money if the market rises and makes money if the market declines) can be combined with a long position in the underlying asset (which makes money if the market rises and loses money if the market declines). The trader must be careful to carry the appropriate size position in the underlying asset. This amount is calculated from the option delta. As a result, the technique is called *delta hedging*.

Delta hedging is not an arbitrage trade. Changes in the level of volatility (a key determinant of the price of the option) would affect results. Also, the hedge in the underlying asset must be adjusted frequently.

An option trade can create a position that makes money if option volatility rises and loses money if volatility declines (or vice versa). This is not an arbitrage. It can be a strategy that makes or loses money independent of the underlying asset. Many of these kinds of trades can be included in a market-neutral hedge fund.

For this strategy to work, the trader needs to accurately forecast changes in volatility. Volatility forecasts start with measurements of historical volatility in the underlying asset. There is a strong tendency for options prices to rise (as measured by volatility) after markets have been volatile. Similarly, there is a strong tendency for option prices to decrease (as measured by volatility) after markets have been quiet.

Converting these strong relationships into workable trading models is no simple feat. Simple tools track historical volatility over short and long periods and derive point estimates of fair value from these results. See Figure 5.6.

As of February 20, 2001, this asset had historical price volatility of 16.46 percent for one month, 21.64 percent for two months, and 23.12 percent for three months. A trader might assert that a two-month option should be priced at 21.64 percent on the presumption that the period forthcoming should look something like the previous two months, all other things being equal. Alternatively, the trader may forecast volatility of 16.46 percent, arguing that data beyond one month old are not timely enough, considering the contrasting information from the recent week. Finally, the trader may adapt a forecast from the foregoing information and incorporate adjustments to account for ways the future period will differ from the recent past.

FIGURE 5.6   Historical Volatility of S&P 500 Index (based on daily price changes)

A quantitative variation on the preceding methodology uses advanced statistical techniques to get precise (but not necessarily more accurate) forecasts. One popular family of model is called *generalized autoregressive conditionally heteroskedasticity* (GARCH). This model relies on the level of volatility being somewhat persistent. Using only previous volatility information, the model tries to incorporate recent results, recent trends, and some tendency toward a long-term level. When these indicators show contradictory forecasts, the model attempts to balance the inputs consistent with previous option pricing.

Many stock traders attempt to make money from investors by identifying relative value. The simplest strategy involves buying a stock and selling another stock in the same narrow industry group. The return from the strategy relies on correctly identifying undervalued and overvalued companies. Risk is managed two issues at a time (although there usually are many issues in the portfolio).

Other traders construct a portfolio of long positions and a portfolio of short positions. The success of the strategy also depends on the trader's ability to identify undervalued and overvalued stocks. With this portfolio approach, however, the trader seeks to make the portfolio of long positions in aggregate behave like the portfolio of short positions in aggregate.

Another variation on this long/short portfolio approach puts less emphasis in making the long and short positions track closely. Instead, the trader identifies whole sectors of the market to buy or sell. The long positions do not track the short positions as closely, but the portfolio is substantially hedged to changes in the level of the broad market aggregates. Tiger Fund carried long positions in value stocks and short positions in high-technology companies. While the residual risk is considerably higher, the potential for return is higher, too.

Another major category of trading is sometimes called *mean-reverting* trading. It is often difficult to distinguish which type of strategy a fund employs. Many of the types of positions described in this section are also created with models that track relationships over time. For example, traders follow the spreads between different bonds or different maturities. There usually is no objective fair level for these spreads. Instead, traders track the spreads and forecast future levels for the spreads. These forecasts become the basis of trades.

This methodology can support trading between sectors in the stock market, stocks versus bonds, and individual issues. Certainly some applications are more plausible than others. Following the tremendous losses within Long Term Capital Management in 1998, this type of trading moved out of favor.

Earnings momentum models monitor the growth rate of earnings. These models were mentioned in the preceding discussion of technical analysis. The same models can be used to construct market-neutral positions. Momentum strategies seek to buy companies where earnings growth is accelerating (or very fast and not decelerating) and sell short companies where earnings growth is weak. If the manager correctly identifies companies that accelerate earnings growth, the fund benefits directly, because the share prices will reflect the higher earnings. Perhaps more important to an earnings momentum trader, the price of the stocks held long may rise faster than rise in the price of the short stocks.

Another form of time series trading is called *earnings surprise*. Earnings surprises occur when companies report earnings materially higher or lower than consensus forecasts. Although prices react quickly to surprise earnings announcements, there appears to be some persistence in the price reactions beyond the initial spike. Academic studies have identified a tendency for the stock to continue to go up or down faster or further than the market for several days or longer.

Earnings surprise trading tends to produce a return that has lower correlations to the market than might be expected from an outright position in the stock, in part because positions are held for a fairly short period and in part because the earnings surprise can motivate short sales. It is also possible to improve the hedge with futures or derivatives, making the strategy significantly more nondirectional.

Options trades frequently are based on the assumption that future changes in price will resemble previous price changes. As a general rule, options traders are not particularly interested in the direction of the underlying asset. Instead, the volatility of the instrument is extrapolated from past experience.

NONPARAMETRIC INVESTMENT TECHNIQUES

Many investment strategies (including fundamental, technical, and nondirectional or arbitrage strategies) rely on statistics to determine relationships and, eventually, trading rules. This broad group includes most of the methods described in this chapter on techniques. Included in this group are averages of spreads (fixed income), regression models (used everywhere), Garch models (short-term forecasts of many factors, especially volatility), and even most definitions of risk (including standard deviation, VaR, Sharpe ratio, semivariance, and credit risk analysis, which are described in Chapter 13).

The techniques are inherently sound logically and tend to produce decent results. The techniques do not all assume that data follow a normal distribution, but many do rely on that assumption. That assumption is good enough for many assets (especially for short time intervals) but implausible for others.

Nonparametric investment strategies make no assumptions about the underlying processes driving investment relationships. These techniques may rely on no assumptions about the distribution of prices or returns. Instead, they rely on a variety of methods to identify the issues to buy and sell.

For an example of a nonparametric strategy,[4] rank the potential investments on several factors, then pick outliers to buy and sell. For example, suppose you ranked all actively traded common stocks by the price/earnings ratio (P/E). Using this ranking, divide the entire universe into three to five groups. Separately sort the best group (lowest P/E) and the worst group (highest P/E) again on an additional criterion (and ignore all the issues in the middle groups). Suppose the second criterion is dividend yield. With this additional sort, divide each list into three to five groups. Determine the best issues (highest dividend yield) from the stocks in the low P/E category and buy these issues. Determine the worst issues (lowest dividend yield) from the stocks in the high P/E category and sell short these issues.

The criteria can be based on fundamental or technical data. The data can be discontinuous or even nonnumeric. The data may apply standard financial market data in new ways. Some hedge funds spend considerable effort to generate original data (the number of empty parking spaces in a Home Depot parking lot, whether there is a line of individual investors waiting to bid a Treasury auction at the Federal Reserve window, the daily ticket count [ignoring whether they are purchases or sales] at a retail investment house, etc.).

There are many reasons to adopt nonparametric techniques. First, many examples of nonparametric methods produce excellent investment returns. One explanation for the success of nonparametric strategies is that nonextreme data points may not be predictive, but extreme data points might be. By focusing on outliers, nonparametric methods may be able to extract information from data undetected with standard statistical methods. Second, the returns from these decision rules are not very correlated to traditional investment portfolios. Perhaps low correlations should be expected out of strategies that are fundamentally different from decisions based on conventional statistical analysis. Finally, these investment techniques are fairly easy to market to investors because of their uniqueness and intuitive appeal.

NOTES

1. P. J. Kaufman, *Trading Systems and Methods,* Wiley, New York, 1998. John J. Murphy, *Technical Analysis in the Financial Marketplace: A Comprehensive Guide to Trading Methods and Applications,* Prentice Hall, Englewood Cliffs, NJ, 1999. Robert D. Edwards, John Magee, and W. H. C. Bassetti (editors), *Technical Analysis of Stock Trends,* 8th ed., AMACOM, New York, 2001.
2. Beta is a measure of risk relative to a broad universe of stocks. See Chapter 13.
3. In addition to transportation costs, it may be desirable to acquire theft insurance. The transaction may also necessitate storage costs.
4. This example is for discussion purposes only and has not been tested as a trading strategy.

CHAPTER 6

Hedge Fund Business Models

This chapter explores the typical forms of business organization, including partnerships and corporations. Two or more of these building blocks are combined to form the business that may include a management company, one or more onshore investment funds, and one or more offshore investment funds. Several of the more typical structures used to form a hedge fund business and *pro forma* issues and assumptions unique to hedge funds are also presented.

TYPICAL BUSINESS STRUCTURES

Corporation

The familiar corporation is called a *C corporation*. This corporation resembles an individual in many respects. It exists as an entity distinct from the owners, is taxed as a separate entity, and generally survives beyond the lives of the individual owners.

A simple C corporation is represented by Figure 6.1. Although stylized, the boxes represent the value of the assets of a corporation, which must equal the sum of its liabilities and equity. If the assets decline in value, the equity holders (common stock) receive all of the loss because the liabilities must be repaid before the equity holders have a claim on the assets. Then the stylized balance sheet would be shown as Figure 6.2.

If the assets decline further, it is possible that the liabilities will exceed the assets and the shareholders will lose the company to the

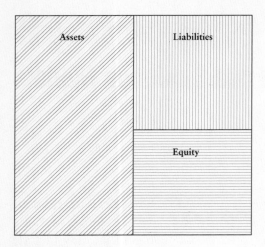

FIGURE 6.1   Simple C Corporation

holders of the liabilities (lenders). The lenders can lose some or all of their investment if the assets are not adequate. However, neither the equity investors nor the lenders can lose more than their investment.

A C corporation can have an almost unlimited number of share-holders. If the number of authorized shares is insufficient, the board

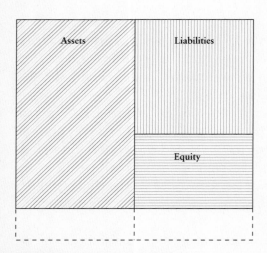

FIGURE 6.2   Stylized Balance Sheet

of directors can vote to authorize more shares. Further, the company can have several classes of shareholders. In addition to a special kind of equity called *preferred stock,* the company can create shares that have special voting rights, have no voting rights, receive income only from a division, or differ from the standard common stock in additional ways.

Figure 6.3 demonstrates how corporate income is often taxed twice. In the figure the tax is represented as a reduction from earnings before interest and taxes (EBIT) rather than as an expense to emphasize how it reduces the potential return. The revenue and expenses are reported to the U.S. government (and most state governments). Corporations pay up to 35 percent of their net income in corporate income tax. If a corporation earns $100 but pays 35 percent or $35 in taxes, it has $65 to distribute to investors. When the company pays out the $65 to investors, they pay up to 39.6 percent or $25.74 in federal income taxes (39.6 percent of $65). The investors retain only $39.26, an effective tax rate of 61 percent.[1]

A corporation can postpone the second tax event indefinitely by refraining from declaring dividends. This does not avoid the second taxation (paid by the investor) but postpones the payment. (For some investors, the retained earnings may be taxed as a capital gain.)

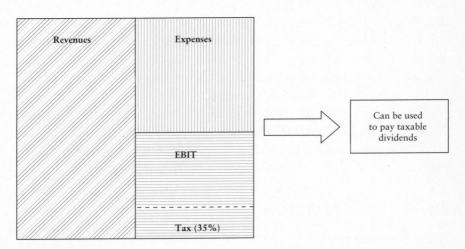

FIGURE 6.3   How Corporate Income Is Often Taxed Twice

Because the investor has use of the funds that will someday be payable, the sting of the tax is reduced by the ability to "borrow" the payment interest-free from the taxing bodies.

Partnership

A partnership is a business entity but is not taxed as a business entity. Instead, the net income is declared in the returns of the investors.[2] For this reason, a partnership is often described as a "flow-through entity." In fact, all the characterizations of the income (short-term gain or loss, long-term gain or loss, tax-exempt income, Treasury income, Section 1256 income, passive losses, etc.) are preserved when they are reported on the investors' income statements.

Partnerships must file tax forms with the U.S. government and the states where its investors are domiciled. This filing includes an enumeration of the partner ownership percentages. This breakdown is reported to investors on the form K-1, which is used for completing the investors' tax return.

The advantage to this business structure is that the investors pay tax only once on money earned by the partnership. Investors in the maximum bracket retain 60.4 percent of income (1 − 39.6 percent),[3] some 50 percent higher than the worst-case corporation that immediately pays out income as dividends.

The disadvantage of the partnership structure is that the partners are jointly and separately liable for the obligations of the business. The losses can continue until each investor runs out of money. Only then are the lenders at risk for loss.

The requirements for being a partnership are fairly easy to satisfy. There must be at least two investors. The partnership can allocate income and expenses to the partners according to whatever rules the partners choose. The allocation does not need to be equal.

General/Limited Partnership

A simple modification to the partnership structure allows the partnership to create two (or more) classes of partners. A general partner (one or more investors) assumes the same responsibilities as the partners in the simple partnership described in the previous section. However, this structure allows some partners to invest as limited partners. These investors cannot be asked to invest more than their paid-in amount.

The general/limited partnership (also called a limited partnership or LP) is taxed exactly like the simple partnership. Income and expense items are allocated to all investors on the partnership tax return. This information is conveyed to all partners via the K-1 forms. General and limited partners must declare these amounts on their tax returns.

Like the simple partnership, the allocation must follow complex rules. The allocation is not required to be equal among partners. It should not be arbitrary and must be disclosed to partners as they enter the business. Changes in the allocation require the approval of the partners.

A general/limited partnership must have at least one general partner and one limited partner. The entity can have multiple general partners and many limited partners. The rule that limits hedge funds to no more than 99 investors is a requirement to avoid registration with the Securities and Exchange Commission (SEC). The partnerships themselves are not bound by these limits. The general/limited partnership is the most common structure for the pool of investment funds that make up a hedge fund.

Subchapter S Corporation

The subchapter S corporation (or S corp.) combines the tax features of a partnership with the limited liability of a corporation. It can be thought of as a general/limited partnership that has no general partners. Like a partnership, the S corp. files a tax return that reports income and expenses but does not lead to a tax liability for the business. The S corp. distributes the income items with a K-1 form. This business also preserves the characteristics of the income items.

Several limitations make the S corp. unusable for some companies. There can be no more than 35 investors but as few as 1 owner.

And there can be only one class of shares (even preferred stock counts as a class). All owners must be individuals, not businesses. If these limitations are not important, the S corp. is one of the two preferred structures for a management company of a hedge fund.

Limited Liability Corporation

A limited liability corporation (LLC) closely resembles an S corporation. This fairly new structure has approval in most but not all states. Like the S corp., the LLC is a flow-through tax entity. Investors in an LLC enjoy liability limited to their paid-in investment.[4] The LLC must have at least two but may have many investors. A limited liability is one of the two structures commonly created to assume the general partner responsibility. Many people believe the LLC will completely replace both the partnership and the S corporation.

Nested Structure

The prospect of unlimited liability for a partnership creates a potentially large risk factor. However, the general partner does not need to be a person; it can be another business entity. While that entity is liable for any losses of the partnership, up to the entire net worth of the general partner's capital, the amount of capital that must be committed to this business unit is fairly small.

For example, if an individual creates an S corporation with $100,000 and makes the S corporation the general partner of a limited partnership, losses to the investor are limited to the $100,000 at risk in the S corporation. The structure is illustrated in Figure 6.4.

Domestic Limited Partnership Structure

The typical hedge fund organized in the United States for U.S. investors is a limited partnership (LP). In Figure 6.4, the actual investment fund is the LP. It frequently has no employees. It is funded by investments from limited and general partners. In addition, the fund hires a management company to make investment decisions. Al-

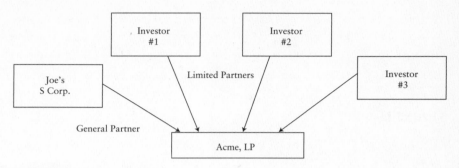

FIGURE 6.4 Nested Structure

though the management company can be an additional business unit, in this example, the S corporation serves as both the management company and general partner. The S corporation carries most or all employees engaged in running the hedge fund and is paid management and incentive fees by the fund.

The decision to hire the management company is almost never an arm's-length transaction. Instead, the management company organizes the hedge fund, markets the fund, and conducts all the necessary functions for the benefit of the fund.

A slightly more complicated structure appears in Figure 6.5. This kind of structure is typical when the sponsor has more than one fund. This model allows the sponsor to separately capitalize each fund. The general partner of each fund is protected from claims from other funds. In addition, a single company that hires the staff can service all the funds. The assets of the investment management company are not exposed to the risk of loss from any of the hedge funds.

Offshore Hedge Fund

The offshore hedge fund (Figure 6.6) is typically a corporation. The fund is located in a country that levies few or no taxes, so the penalty of double taxation is minimized. Fund administration is much simpler as a corporation than as a partnership. Because the partnership

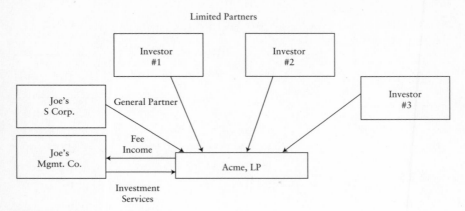

FIGURE 6.5 Domestic LP Structure

treats each position as if the individual partners owned it proportionately, every change in ownership creates complications for all the
partners. In contrast, the corporation carries the cost basis for all assets. Net income does not flow through unless dividends are declared.
When these payments are made, the characterization of the payments
at the corporate level is not carried through to the investors.

This structure is subject to considerable variation. Instead of having a separate business, the management company may invest in the
fund. An investment by the sponsoring organization is not necessar-

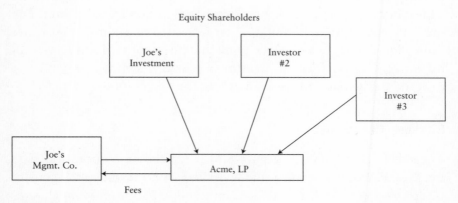

FIGURE 6.6 Offshore Hedge Fund

ily required by regulations in offshore domiciles but is generally expected by investors.

Mirrored Structure

A hedge fund sponsor may wish to market a fund to both U.S. and offshore investors, typically accomplished by running two nearly identical funds. The domestic limited partnership would receive money from U.S. investors. The offshore corporation would accept investments from all other locations. The two funds are run identically, with proportionately identical positions in both funds.

In practice, it is very difficult to maintain mirrored funds. Each time flows are allowed into and out of one of the funds, the proportion in the domestic fund changes relative to the offshore fund. Money coming into a fund dilutes the positions. To keep the funds tracking each other, positions must be moved between the accounts.

Consider the following example (see Figures 6.7, 6.8, and 6.9). A fund manager has $10 million invested in Fund A, a domestic limited partnership, and $20 million invested in Fund B, an offshore corporation. The manager buys 30,000 shares of XYZ common stock and allocates 10,000 shares to Fund A and 20,000 shares to Fund B, pro-

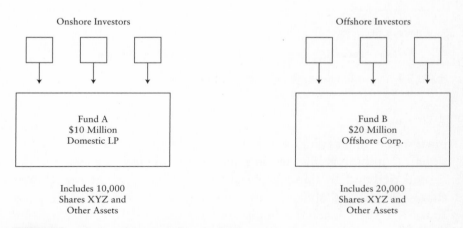

FIGURE 6.7 Mirrored Funds Before Cash Flow

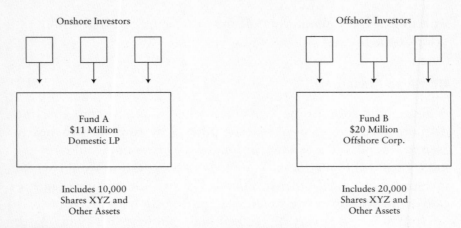

FIGURE 6.8 Mirrored Funds After Cash Flow (not rebalanced)

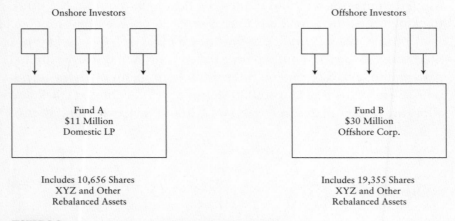

FIGURE 6.9 Mirrored Funds After Cash Flow (rebalanced)

portional to the capital in the two funds. At month's end, an additional $1 million is invested in Fund A and no change is made in the capital of Fund B. Fund A should now own 11/31 of the 30,000 shares (or 10,656 shares) and Fund B should own 20/31 (19,355 shares). To rebalance the funds, 645 shares of XYZ can be sold by Fund B to Fund A. As long as the entry is made at the month-end closing price, there is no effect on either fund's performance and subsequent changes in value will impact the two funds identically.

It would also be possible to buy 1,000 additional shares of XYZ common on the open market. After the rebalancing, Fund A would have 11,000 shares as part of its $11,000,000 invested and Fund B would have 20,000 shares as part of its $20,000,000 invested. This re-weighting maintains the balance between the domestic and the offshore fund and does not permit the asset allocation to change due to fund flows. However, unless the additional shares can be bought at exactly the month-end closing price (not higher or lower), this rebalancing will cause the return in the two funds to diverge slightly.

For many types of assets, it is not possible to transact between funds. Futures regulations require that all such transactions occur on the floor of the exchange in the presence of the traders. All traders on the exchange floor are free to participate in either the purchase or sale. If the number of contracts sold does not equal the number bought or if the price of the sale or the price of the purchase differs from the settlement price, performance between the funds can diverge. It is likely that an effort to transfer futures positions through open-outcry trading will lead to differences in performance between funds.

Many private placements and most derivative securities have very limited ability to resell or assign positions. For these kinds of positions, it may not be possible to rebalance.

Master-Feeder Hedge Fund Structure

The solution to the problem of keeping two funds tracking is to eliminate one of the funds. Offshore investors do not want to invest in U.S.-based hedge funds because they will likely be exposed to tax withholding on their returns. The U.S. investors do not want to invest in offshore funds because it complicates their tax returns. The solution is to create the offshore and domestic funds as before, but the offshore fund carries all the positions. The domestic fund has a single asset, which is an investment in the offshore hedge fund. The structure appears in Figure 6.10.

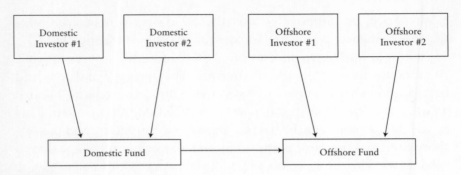

FIGURE 6.10 Master-Feeder Structure

Exchange-Traded Funds

It is often a surprise to U.S. hedge fund observers that offshore investors can simply buy into a hedge fund on an exchange in Luxembourg or Ireland. In the United States, hedge funds are almost universally created as private placements exempt from registration under the Securities and Exchange Act of 1940 and the Investment Company Act of 1933. To avoid registration requirements, these investments cannot be made available to the general investing public. Outside the United States, securities regulation is much less restrictive.

SETTING UP THE BUSINESSES

The business of running a successful hedge fund is one of the most profitable forms of money management. To establish a new fund, the manager must deal with a variety of organizational expenses. To facilitate planning, the following sections include estimates for many of the cost and revenue items. These items can vary greatly by the region of the country (salaries and rents), number of employees (determined by fund style and investment philosophy), and other factors.

To create both a management company and a domestic fund, the businesses themselves need to be established. Individuals can set up both organizations without the assistance of a lawyer[5] for a couple hundred dollars in filing fees (each). Indeed, anyone who can follow instructions on government forms could set up the entire business without consulting a lawyer.

Nevertheless, it is extremely important to consult a lawyer and an accountant at the early stage. There are many decisions to make. Should the management company be an S corporation or an LLC or something else? Should the management company also be the general partner? Where should each business be domiciled (the state where each business is legally founded even if the business will not have any other presence in that state)? What happens to the founders of the partnership if things go well? Or poorly? What registrations are necessary to comply with state regulations? (These issues are discussed in Chapter 10.)

Typically, the management company is organized first. It is often located in the home state of the founders for simplicity. The business must be set up first because it will be a general partner in the fund.[6]

Once the management company has been set up, the partnership can be created. There must be at least one limited partner. At the early stage, this investment can be just a small one from one of the founders as an individual.

Domestic funds are frequently organized in Delaware because of the reputation of the Delaware Chancery and the way the state handles bankruptcy proceedings and hostile takeovers. It is easy to exaggerate the benefits of organizing in Delaware when these features are not important. While every state has made strides to make doing business in the state easy, a cottage industry has developed to assist in setting up new Delaware businesses. As a result, it is at least as easy to set up a business in Delaware from a distance as in your home state.

Both companies must select a professional to receive official documents from the state and other parties. These documents may just be forms for renewing registrations or may involve legal notices and subpoenas. This address of record can be your lawyer or accountant. When the business is domiciled outside your business area (e.g., in Delaware), it is convenient to hire a firm specializing in statutory representation. For a small fee, these companies handle the paperwork.

The cost is almost always cheaper than fees charged by your lawyer or accountant. An example of a firm providing statutory representation is CT Corporation, which has offices in many major cities.

It is not substantially more complicated to create an offshore fund than a domestic fund. However, the tasks are different and much of the work must be done offshore. Generally, it costs at least $10,000 more to create an offshore fund than a domestic fund.

Frequently, the decision of where to set up a fund will determine where to look for legal and accounting advice for creating an offshore fund. To create a fund in a Caribbean domicile, a lawyer in the region will generally be familiar with local requirements, will operate on local time zones, and will have access to forms and documents that should facilitate registration of the new fund. The local expert should have business contacts that will facilitate assembling the package of services necessary to conduct business.

The business structure for an offshore fund need not reflect the requirements of U.S. tax law. For example, a fund can be (and usually is) structured as a corporation without having to suffer double taxation on income. The fund is not limited to business structures authorized by U.S. commercial code and sanctioned by the Internal Revenue Service (IRS). In addition, the provisions of the U.S. commercial code will probably not control bankruptcy events offshore. Lawyers with experience in this field can guide these decisions.

Although disclosure documents for offshore funds face considerably less stringent requirements than U.S. entities, the documents created for U.S. use provide the model for offshore hedge fund documentation. In practice, the scope of documentation is ultimately driven by the demands of potential investors.

With foreknowledge of the likely sources of investment, an offshore fund and documents can be designed to accommodate special tax provisions. Documents can be drafted in more than one language. The domicile can be selected for the convenience of these investors (time zone issues, etc.).

It is important to distinguish the tax situation of offshore investors, who legally and legitimately can avoid U.S. taxation, from illegal tax avoidance. The U.S. investor must declare and pay taxes on any income, whether earned within the United States or outside. All U.S. citizens must declare when they move funds outside the United States and laws require banks to report transfers to the U.S. Internal Revenue Service. To the extent that U.S. citizens are able to export investment funds outside the United States (and outside the reporting requirements for financial institutions that force investors to honestly report income), any income not reported constitutes tax fraud.

Non–U.S. investors who invest in an offshore fund generally must report income and pay taxes on hedge fund returns. These investors would be subject to double taxation if the hedge fund were organized in a location that also assessed taxes. By locating in a "tax haven," these investors pay tax only to their home country.

The founders must turn to a competent lawyer and accountant in drafting three key documents: the partnership agreement, the risk disclosure document, and the subscription agreement. The partnership agreement defines the rights and obligations of each partner, including provisions for entry and exit from the fund, rights to transfer partnership interests (if any), and whether the partners can use their partnership assets as collateral. This document authorizes the general partners to act on behalf of the limited partners. It documents how performance will be reported, how performance will be calculated, how fees will be calculated, how results will be allocated to investors, how a general partner can be replaced, bankruptcy provisions, and more. It is important to work with the lawyer and accountant to make sure the partnership agreement complies with the designs of the founders and complies with accounting and reporting requirements.

A risk disclosure document (or disclosure doc) replaces the prospectus in a private placement. The stated purpose of the document is to advise the investors in advance of all the risks that can affect the investment. The document enumerates risks that could apply to any private placement, partnership, and/or illiquid investment. Generally, the lawyer drafts these provisions without significant input from the founders of the fund. The disclosure document also lists risks that are specific to the particular fund. The founders should assist the lawyer drafting the document to ensure that specific risks are described completely and clearly.

The purpose of the risk disclosure document is not to educate the potential investor of the investment characteristics. On the contrary, this document predominantly enumerates the bad things that could happen. It is important to resist the temptation to edit out risks that seem extremely remote. The probability of these things occurring is not a consideration (unless the probability is clearly, unambiguously zero).

In other words, the real purpose of the risk disclosure document is to protect the fund sponsors. This is not a jaded view of the process. It is the sponsor's responsibility to mention the risks that could plausibly affect results. It is the investor's responsibility to consider those risks. It is the responsibility of investors, not the sponsors, to conclude that dire risks are remote enough to warrant investment despite those risks.

The alternative to complete disclosure is not an attractive situation for the fund sponsor. Suppose that the sponsor discovered that the language in a risk disclosure document discouraged investment in the fund. In drafting a friendly sounding replacement, the firm risks being sued by investors if undisclosed risk events occur at the same time that an investor loses money. It may be enough that the events look like they caused the loss, even if the cause and effect are not clear. It is as if the fund gave away calls on its performance—the investor wins if the fund provides a fair return and is compensated for losses if they should occur.

The subscription agreement is primarily a disclosure by the investor to the fund. The investor declares he/she has read and understands the risk disclosure document and documents that he/she is a qualified investor (income rules, net worth rules, has sufficient investment knowledge and sophistication and loss tolerance).

In addition to the subscription agreement, the fund generally requires each investor to complete and sign a survey with general descriptive information (age, contact information, education, current job), information to confirm that a hedge fund is an appropriate investment (previous experience with private placements, knowledge and sophistication, income, wealth), and information that could affect fund activities (being an officer or director of a company the fund might invest in, large positions in publicly held companies, being an ERISA[7] entity, working for an NASD [member firm, etc.]). In lieu of a signed survey, companies may maintain these data in internal records. The manager should rely on the lawyers to develop adequate procedures.

DEVELOPING *PRO FORMA* REVENUE AND EXPENSE FORECASTS

To create a fund and management company, the founders will need to make fixed, up-front expenditures and underwrite both fixed and variable continuing expenses. Revenues will derive from the fees charged for managing the funds.

The cost of creating two domestic business units, including the documents necessary to accept investments, will run from $6,000 to $30,000. The lowest figure assumes that an experienced lawyer drafts the documents. Frequently, the most qualified lawyers (almost inevitably at high-priced, prestigious law firms) will complete the job for the smallest expense and sooner because they can rely on language that they have already drafted and know the business and legal issues in advance. The $6,000 figure also assumes that the founders or a local attorney create the business units instead of relying on expensive, prestigious law firms for this service. The high figure reflects inefficiency in going to a less-experienced lawyer, significant custom work, and particularly complicated structures and provisions.

It should be said that spending $6,000 to create the package is not necessarily "better" than spending $30,000. If the fund is successful, the initial investment will not be material. If business relations or outside considerations warrant it, the higher figure may offer the best value. For example, if a mutual fund manager decides to open a hedge fund, the legal staff of the manager might get tremendous advantage from using their existing outside counsel, even if the legal bills pay to train the outside counsel about hedge funds. From the point of view of the entire organization, the incremental legal fees might be very well spent.

An estimate for salaries in the first year can vary tremendously. Founders may be willing to work without salary and may be able to assume minor clerical responsibilities while the scale of business is small. It may be cheaper to outsource many services at least while the fund is small. For the purposes of the example in this section, we assume $300,000 in out-of-pocket costs for the first year of salaries.

Rent for office space can differ substantially from region to region and between city and suburbs. Many hedge funds have started in a home office. Others have benefited from free or discounted office space in the office of friends who have an unoccupied desk or two to spare. For our example, assume first-year rent equal to $30,000.

Many investors in start-up hedge funds understand and even respect cost-saving strategies during the first year or so of operation. After that, however, investors rightly worry if a fund does not have the success to carry the legitimate cost of running the business.

Most of the revenue of the management company will come from management and incentive fees. In this *pro forma* analysis, we assume that the fund will collect 1 percent of the assets under management as a management fee and 20 percent of the net return (not subject to a hurdle rate) as an incentive fee.[8]

The total expense previously given for salaries did not include a provision for bonuses and support staff that may be discretionary or contractual. For this demonstration, we assume that total compensation (including the base amount of $300,000) along with the remaining variable expenses constitutes 15 percent of net trading profits (or approximately 75 percent of gross revenue).

Figure 6.11 shows the net income to this management company. The fund would get to a breakeven (including fairly competitive compensation if the founders are the trading staff) at about $9 million under management. For this breakeven, assume the fund returned 15 percent, that expenses tended to consume 75 percent of gross revenue (management and incentive fees), and that expenses were at least $350,000.[9]

Actual calculations will differ greatly, but for our assumed business, the break-even target for assets under management is very attainable. Perhaps more important, the returns to increasing assets lead to nice profits even with moderate growth targets. With $100 million under management, the management company will receive $4 million in fees, most of which could actually be compensation for the founders.

LIMITS TO INCREASING SCALE

Figure 6.11 implies that the profits can grow without limit. In a world where multibillion-dollar hedge funds are mentioned frequently in the press, the potential for profit seems vast. It is important to remember that the average hedge fund is only $100 million.[10]

There is academic evidence that the industry does not enjoy the benefits of return to scale overall. Return to scale means that a busi-

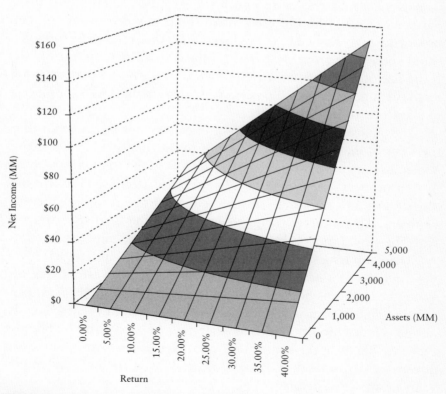

FIGURE 6.11 Hedge Fund and Net Income *Pro Forma*

ness gets more profitable the larger it gets. In the consumer software market, where the marginal cost for a copy of tax software or a word processor is very small, the profitability of a company is determined almost completely by the units sold. Some economists believe that the natural structure of these businesses is a monopoly.

The existence of thousands of distinct hedge funds discourages the conclusion that the hedge fund business is (overall) like the software industry. In addition, statistical evidence shows a tendency for large hedge funds to decrease in size after a period of excellent returns.[11] The logical explanation for this behavior is that there is a limit to the size a fund can be without limiting returns. The ability of a strategy to be expanded is called *scalability*.

When a fund gets large enough that the returns begin to decline, management may choose to return some of the capital to investors, particularly when hurdle rates make the firm's revenue more than proportionately related to the return. To see this, consider a fund that should be able to return 10 percent, subject to a 5 percent hurdle rate. If the size of the fund has driven down the return to 8 percent, profits to the fund are only 20 percent below attainable levels, but incentive fees are 40 percent lower.

The choice of optimal size for a fund may not be determined on the basis of maximizing the net profit to the management company. When insiders have substantial investments in the fund, any sacrifice in return affects them doubly. When returns decline, incentive fees also decline. In addition, the insiders suffer a lower return on their investment. This incentive helps to ensure that the fund sponsors will scale the size of the fund to the best interest of the fund investors.

There are issues associated with the optimal fund size that favor the founders of a new fund. Many fund of funds investors seek out young hedge funds because they believe that hedge funds often provide the highest return in the second through the fifth years. The situation is much more complicated than this, of course, in part because there are biases in the hedge fund data. Nevertheless, this marketing advantage can provide an entry for growth on the basis of several years of attractive returns.

ONSHORE ADMINISTRATION

Administration includes all those functions performed by (or for) the management company other than investing. This includes ticket writing, safe keeping of securities, making and taking delivery of securities, receiving money from and disbursing money to investors, paying expenses, corresponding with investors, marketing, accounting, and governance of the business.

Most of these functions for a domestic hedge fund are provided by the manager of the hedge fund directly or, on the direction of the management company, are outsourced. In any case, the services are almost universally performed within the United States. This behavior is very predictable and reinforces the legal basis for saying that the manager and the fund are U.S. businesses subject to the laws of the United States.

OFFSHORE ADMINISTRATION

When creating an offshore fund run by a domestic (U.S.) manager, it is important that the IRS consider the principal office of the fund to be offshore. This requires that a manager not provide the preponderance of services within the United States. Over the years, many court cases have helped define what is possible to administer within the United States and still qualify as an offshore fund. The concept is known as a safe harbor. The manager who follows guidelines that derive from previous court cases can be reasonably assured that the IRS and the U.S. Tax Court will consider the fund an offshore entity.

The following so-called 10 Commandments are rules promulgated by the U.S. Treasury [under IRC § 864-2(C)(ii)] for ensuring that the offshore office is considered the principal office:

1. Communication with investors—including provision of monthly statements of accounts, investment reports, annual financial statements, and all other reports, financial or otherwise—must be conducted from outside the United States.

2. Communications with the general public must originate from outside the United States.
3. Soliciting investments into the fund must originate outside the United States.
4. Accepting and processing investments must be done outside the United States.
5. Both accounting and corporate records must be maintained offshore.
6. The fund's books must be audited offshore.
7. Disbursements (including payment of dividends, fees, salaries, and other expense of the fund) must originate offshore.
8. The fund's net asset value per share must be published offshore.
9. Board and shareholders' meetings must be held offshore.
10. Fund investments must be redeemed offshore.

In 1997, Congress passed laws greatly relaxing the provisions of the "10 Commandments" as part of the Tax Report Act of 1997 (TRA '97). Refer to legal and accounting advisors to ensure that offshore investors will not be subject to withholding tax by the United States.

MISCELLANEOUS TAX ISSUES

Several special tax issues affect hedge funds. Hedge funds must pick a tax year. It would be convenient to have a year-end that does not correspond with the calendar year-end.[12] At year-end, banks and broker-dealers must publish a balance sheet. There is considerable pressure to temporarily pare down assets and liabilities. This unwillingness to lend translates into unpredictable and often high cost of borrowing over year-end (the so-called turn of the year or just "turn"). In addition, if the fund could arrange a tax year out of cycle with other financial institutions, it would be in a better position to exploit price anomalies at year-end. At a minimum, the fund would be able to accomplish its own manipulation when there is less pressure on financing and spreads.

Unfortunately, the IRS requires a valid business reason for selecting a business year that differs from the calendar. Window dressing (making changes in positions to make your statements more desirable) is not a valid reason in the eyes of the IRS.

Every business must declare whether income and expenses are to be recognized at the time that cash is transferred or whether the items accrue. Nearly every business must use the accrual basis for timing of the recognition of these items. This generally means that an income or expense should be recognized as soon as the event is known with reasonable certainty and the amount of the item can be reasonably estimated.

An S corporation, however, must use the same basis as its investors, because it is a flow-through tax entity. Because corporations cannot own an S corporation, an S corporation is inevitably on a cash basis. That means that the fund must be careful in making distributions to a management company that is structured as an S corporation. If the fund accrues an item due to the management company (the management and incentive fees, for example) but does not pay the amounts until the next period, the books of the two organizations will disagree.

A hedge fund needs to distinguish short-term gains, short-term losses, long-term gains, and long-term losses. In addition, if the fund takes positions in futures and other eligible commodities, it must keep a separate accounting of those gains and losses. These assets are called Section 1256 assets and receive a blended treatment that assumes 60 percent of the gains (or losses) are long term and 40 percent of the gains (or losses) are short term. It is necessary to calculate Section 1256 short-term gains, Section 1256 short-term losses, Section 1256 long-term gains, and Section 1256 long-term losses. Under certain circumstances, these 1256 amounts may be reclassified for tax purposes.

The tax code requires that investors declare certain types of transactions as *identified straddles*. With an identified straddle, both (all) assets are valued at each tax period and unrealized gains and losses are recognized for tax purposes. These identified straddles require additional contemporaneous record keeping.

In lieu of identifying straddles one at a time, a hedge fund can declare that all trades are potentially part of a mixed straddle. The fund can avoid identifying specific straddles by making a mixed straddle election at the time the fund is created. With the mixed straddle election, all positions are marked to market for each tax period.[13] All unrecognized gains and losses for the entire position are recognized for tax purposes.

NOTES

1. In general, the investors keep $(1 - \text{tax rate}_{corp}) \times (1 - \text{tax rate}_{individual})$.
2. These investors may be individuals or other business units.
3. The residual is reduced further by state taxes.
4. Some investment structures use contracts that commit investors to invest additional amounts. This provision is typical in venture capital funds and tax shelters. These investors enjoy liability limited to the committed amounts.
5. Better yet, under the advice and direction of your lawyer but without help in filing.
6. If the founders want to have a separate business for both the management company and to serve as the general partner, it will probably be advisable to create both units before the partnership is created.
7. ERISA stands for the Employee Retirement Income Security Act of 1974. NASD refers to the National Association of Securities Dealers. These issues are discussed in Chapter 10.
8. Although there is market pressure to include a hurdle rate in the fee structure, 98 percent of the funds followed by the Hennessee Group do not include a hurdle in their incentive calculation. See *Barron's*, July 31, 2000.
9. Management fees of 1 percent of $8,750,000 are $87,500. Incentive fees are $8,700,000 × 15% × 20% or $262,500. The gross revenue is $87,500 plus $262,500 = $350,000.
10. There are no figures regarded as reliable at this time.
11. "High Water Marks," *Working Paper*, Goetzmann, Ingersoll & Ross.
12. Japanese year-end is March 31 and has problems similar to December 31.
13. This tax period is generally at least as frequently as partners can enter or exit the fund because of the requirements of tax allocation.

CHAPTER 7

Creating Leverage

Outside the hedge fund industry and the broker-dealer community, most people view leverage as a mysterious, even suspicious technique. Most individuals do not buy investments with borrowed money and even fewer sell short issues they do not own. Institutions are frequently forbidden from using leverage. As a result, few investors know much about the basic techniques used to create leverage. This chapter explores the most common methods used in securities markets. Chapter 11 reviews the specialized accounting entries needed to account for leveraged transactions.

Most hedge funds use leverage as part of their trading strategy. The amount of leverage is generally fairly small. For example, in a recent survey,[1] more than 30 percent of hedge funds claimed they used no leverage and 54 percent said they maintained leverage at two times capital or less. Nevertheless, that means more than 70 percent of hedge funds use leverage to some degree. For certain strategies (most arbitrage strategies, for example), leverage is essential. Prior to the collapse of Long Term Capital Management, leverage of 100:1 or higher was routine for fixed-income arbitrage funds. Even today, these funds can run positions 40 times their capital.

Very similar techniques are used to create leverage in the securities and commodities markets. This chapter discusses techniques in the equity markets and fixed-income markets and then explores alternative ways of creating leverage using derivatives, including futures, options, and swaps.

THE EQUITY LOAN MARKET

On a trade-by-trade basis, equity hedge funds have considerable ability to lever an equity portfolio. In practice, the amount of leverage prudent for most equity trading strategies is much less than the maximum leverage possible. In addition, several regulations severely limit the amount of leverage possible in a hedge fund investing in stocks.

Owners of stock can borrow against the value of the stock at rates below the broker call rate. In a typical transaction, the owners will sell the position to a lending counterparty for approximately the fair value of the position, then buy the position back at a later time for an amount that repays the implicit loan plus interest. This is the so-called cash-driven market because the primary object of the transaction is to borrow money. The transfer of shares to the lender collateralizes the loan.

Three very similar structures are used to accomplish this lending: securities loans transactions, repo transactions, and sale-buyback transactions. The three structures are similar, but differences exist on how title to the securities is carried, how dividends are handled, and how the transactions are handled under bankruptcy.

For example, suppose a trader owned $51 million in a stock and agreed to borrow $50 million for a week at 5 percent interest. The trader could sell the position for $50 million and buy it back one week later for $50,048,611.11.[2]

The rate of interest charged is called a *repo* (short for repurchase agreement) rate. Originally, financing transactions were deemed to be true sales of securities to the lender of money. The original holder of the securities prearranged to buy the securities back for a price equal to the loan balance plus interest.

The sale and repurchase agreements proved to be inadequate protection in the event of bankruptcy.[3] The Uniform Commercial Code was revised to recognize the secured claim for repo loans. In addition, hedge funds and dealers routinely exchange a master agreement prior to trading that spells out each party's rights in the event of default. The master agreement is usually based on the model document created by the Public Securities Association (PSA) or the International Securities Market Association (ISMA) for this purpose.

Lenders in the stock loan market typically demand 102 percent collateral on loans secured by domestic stock loans (potential leverage of 50:1) and 105 percent collateral on international issues (potential leverage of 20:1).

The trader can also finance a short position, the securities-driven market. Revising the previous example, the trader could buy (borrow) $50 million worth of stock by providing $51 million in cash as collateral. The financing is repaid by a sale back to the counterparty at the original price plus interest on the position. In practice, the loan of securities can be collateralized with cash, other securities, or a bank letter of credit.

For a short loan secured by cash collateral, the rate of interest is called a *rebate*. This rebate is paid to the trader who borrowed the securities as interest on the cash placed on deposit with the lender of the stock. This rebate rate is somewhat lower than prevailing interest rates, meaning that the lender of the stock is borrowing money at a below-market rate. By reinvesting the cash collateral at prevailing rates, the lender earns a net fee for lending securities.

A very large portion of the stock available to be lent resides at State Street Bank, Northern Trust, Barclays, Citicorp, J.P. Morgan Chase, and Wells Fargo. These institutions control the shares as custodian or master trustee for a variety of pension funds, trusts, mutual funds, and hedge funds, although individual portfolio managers are increasingly handling their own stock loan or assigning the task to independent brokers. Although the rebate rate is generally within 10 to 25 basis points (100 basis points equals 1 percent) of prevailing interest rates, stock rebate rates can actually become negative.

It is generally not difficult or expensive to borrow shares of most companies. If shares are difficult to borrow, the rebate rate is low and the stocks are called *special*. Suppose you bought one issue worth $10 million and sold short a related issue also worth $10 million. For purposes of illustration, assume that you can borrow the entire $10 million to pay for the long position and can borrow shares to settle the short position with cash collateral exactly equal to the proceeds of the short sale. If the repo rate is 5 percent and you carry the long position for one month, you will pay $41,667 in repo interest.[4] If the rebate rate paid to you on your cash collateral is 4.90 percent, you will earn $40,833 in rebate interest,[5] for a net cost of $833 to carry the position for a month.

If your short position is special and you only get paid 2.5 percent, your rebate interest will be only $20,833.[6] The net cost of carrying the position increases to $20,833. This cost is 25 times higher than the net cost of carrying the positions with a 10 basis point spread in the financing rates.

Traders should anticipate these financing costs as part of the profit expectation on trades. The $20,833 represents about 0.10 percent of the value of the $20 million worth of securities carried. This sounds insignificant, but if the entire portfolio is levered 2:1, the special would cost the fund 2.53 percent per year.[7] Since hedge funds charge a flat 1 to 2 percent management fee, the fund would need to earn 3.5 to 4.5 percent just to break even. The comparison gets worse for higher leverage.

The shares of initial public offerings (IPOs) can be expensive to borrow, especially if the price of the shares is trading below the IPO price or dramatically above. Small issues and heavily traded issues tend to be more special. An IPO becomes less special at the end of the 30-day lending restriction imposed by the syndicate and when the insider lockup provisions end (usually 180 days after pricing).

Securities of companies involved in mergers may also be expensive to borrow if risk arbitrage traders carry substantial short positions in the issues. The acquiring company is usually special and the acquired company is not special. Small acquiring firms tend to be more special than large acquirers. Generally, the costs of financing these positions are not a major factor in the profitability of the trades.[8]

Most stock loans are executed overnight or open. An open trade is booked without a stated end date. Either the borrower or the lender can close the trade at any point. The rate is reset every business day and the rebate accumulates. Term stock loans are sometimes used for dividend plays and some merger arbitrage applications.

The U.S. Federal Reserve Bank, through Regulation T (Reg T), requires broker-dealers to hold initial margin equal to 50 percent of the value of the trade. The rule applies to the way broker-dealers manage customer accounts, not to investors, so a U.S. investor could find offshore broker-dealers that could extend greater leverage. To prevent this, the Federal Reserve Bank's Regulation U basically says that the same rules also apply to domestic investors. It would appear that hedge funds are limited to leverage of 2:1, consistent with the leverage found in most equity hedge funds.

After the transaction, the New York Stock Exchange (NYSE) and National Association of Securities Dealers (NASD) both require all investors to maintain margin at least equal to 25 percent of those positions. This margin requirement forces margin calls on days when the share prices decline. Also, dealers and brokers are free to assess higher margin than required by NYSE and NASD rules.

Broker-dealers are granted partial relief from the margin provisions. They must meet initial margins of 15 percent on long positions and 30 percent margins on short positions. They have maintenance margin of 10 percent. Some hedge funds have registered as a broker-dealer to increase leverage. Leverage of 5:1 or higher[9] is possible.

A hedge fund can get greater relief from Reg T and exchange margin requirements if its prime broker allows the hedge fund to carry the positions in a joint back office (JBO) account. The rules allow a parent broker-dealer to assess prudent levels of margin for its affiliates.[10] The hedge fund creates a relationship, often with preferred securities of nominal value so as to technically qualify as a subsidiary. The prime broker or clearing broker then carries the position on its balance sheet and must comply with margin limits on the aggregate positions. The broker is free to assess whatever margin percentage, or haircut, it feels is adequate, often 5 percent of the value of the positions or less.

Offshore hedge funds are outside the jurisdiction of Reg T and Reg U if they limit their financing to offshore broker-dealers. These broker-dealers can be offshore subsidiaries of U.S. broker-dealers. Most broker-dealers maintain business organizations in several locations to legally skirt these and other regulations.

The offshore hedge fund can have strong ties to the United States. Many U.S. management companies have established offshore funds, domiciled in countries with favorable tax laws. The day-to-day management may take place within the United States, if this foreign fund has hired a U.S. management company to run the investments. Some of the money may even come from U.S. investors, especially if the master-feeder structure is used to organize the U.S. and offshore investors into a single fund.

It is easy to avoid initial and maintenance margin rules by substituting derivative positions for actual shares. A total return swap is a customized derivative trade that replicates the performance of a leveraged long or short position. One party pays the other a short-term rate of interest on an assumed principal balance. The second party pays the first a return equal to the performance of a particular stock or group of stocks (dividends can be included or omitted in the contract). The transaction replicates a levered position in the underlying stock financed at the agreed upon rate. Actual principal amounts are not exchanged. Generally, no margin is required for the trade and the transaction does not appear on either party's balance sheet (see Chapter 11 for accounting and reporting requirements for derivative securities).

Investors and traders must abide by a locate rule that is part of Reg T. This rule requires a short seller to locate securities to borrow before the short sale is transacted. For small stocks with limited trading volume, this precaution is prudent. For blue chip issues, it is merely a formality but puts a record-keeping burden on the short seller and the security lender. In addition, Reg T prohibits anyone from borrowing a security for any purpose other than for making delivery on a short sale. The intention of this rule is to limit manipulation.

Assume a buyer agrees to pay $10.25 for 1,000,000 shares of stock. The purchase price equals $10,250,000 ($10.25 per share times 1,000,000 shares). The lender agrees to lend $10,000,000 if collateralized by the stock purchased.

Stock transactions are generally settled three days after the trade date. Financing may not be arranged until the day of settlement. Prices may have changed since the purchase three days previous. For example, if the value has risen to $11, it would be possible to borrow $11,000,000 (if no excess collateral or haircut is required), more than the cost. However, other positions may be financed for amounts less than the trade price. As a result, it is important that the buyer can afford to finance something less than the price paid.

Under stock loan financing, the true owner of the stock is no longer registered as the holder of record on the position. The holder of record becomes the lender of cash when the owner delivers the stock to the lender. In fact, the lender likely will redeliver the securities to a third party who may redeliver the position to yet another trading partner.

Figure 7.1 shows the change in registered ownership when the true owner uses a position to collateralize a loan with a broker-dealer. Then the broker-dealer delivers the stock to a third party (perhaps a short-term investor who owns the position merely as collateral securing a short-term loan to the dealer).

On the ex-dividend date, the corporation notes the holder of record and eventually pays the dividend to the holder of record on the payment date. Although the retail short-term investor will show up as the holder of record, the true owner is the levered buyer of the stock. As a result, the retail short-term investor must pay the dividend amount to the broker-dealer who, in turn, must pay the dividend to the true owner.

On the ex-dividend date, the value of the stock declines by the amount approximately equal to the dividend. The lender will want to reprice the financing trade to reflect this new value for the collateral.

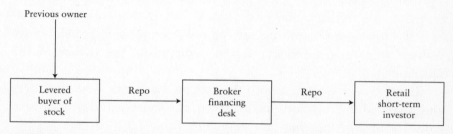

FIGURE 7.1 Trail of Registered Shares for Levered Stock Purchase

Typically, the trade is closed out and reopened for a new, lower principal balance. The borrower must repay part of the principal balance with the income from the dividend payment. The dividend payment occurs a couple of weeks later, but the cash approximately nets out.

The lender of shares loses the right to vote shares when the shares are transferred to the borrower. The borrower delivers the shares to the buyer of the shares, who acquires the right to vote the shares. The company still has the same number of shares outstanding, but the long holders own more than the entire issue (offset by the size of the short positions). Votes are rationed to the long holders who retain title to their shares.

The holder of record sometimes gains other advantages that are not reimbursed in the stock loan market. The holder of record may be able to reinvest dividends at a favorable price in a dividend reinvestment plan (DRIP). Traders can get favorable tax treatment of dividends in some countries that do not apply to substitute payments. These advantages seem to increase the volume of stock lending to buy voting rights or transfer cash flows to those who may have a tax advantage in receiving the actual payment.

Short positions are financed much like long positions. A trader sells a stock short for settlement 3 days later. On the day of settlement, the financing desk seeks an owner of the security who will lend the shares. The transaction usually occurs as a stock loan.

For example, suppose the trader sold 250,000 shares of stock at a price of $98. The buyer will pay $24.5 million ($98 per share × 250,000 shares). To secure the loan of the shares, the short-seller may negotiate to deliver $25 million cash to secure the stock loan. The lender of the security will get to invest the cash and earn interest on the amount. The lender of the stock must pay interest on the collateral. However, the interest rate paid will be somewhat below prevailing short-term interest rates to compensate the owner of the securities.

If one trader executed both the purchase and sale described here and financed the positions as described, the sources and uses of cash would approximately net out, as seen in Table 7.1.

TABLE 7.1 Source and Uses of Cash for Long/Short Position

($10,250,000)	Cost of long purchase
10,000,000	Borrowing of cash
24,500,000	Proceeds of short sale
(25,000,000)	Collateral on stock loan
($ 750,000)	Net cash required to settle trades

In the foregoing example, the trader was able to control approximately $35 million in securities (worth $34.75 million) for $750,000 of cash actually employed. The leverage on these trades is approximately 46:1. While the transactions are realistic, it is not realistic to assume that the entire capital base can be levered to such an extent. Rather, such leverage is possible on these trades because the trader has sufficient capital available that the financing counterparties will require very little excess collateral (margin). For the fund as a whole, it is generally not possible to exceed leverage of 2:1.

Repo interest is calculated on an ACT/360-day basis (interest is calculated using the actual number of days financed and the convention that a year has 360 days) for both stock and bond positions. To calculate interest amount, multiply the repo rate by the repo balance and divide by 360 (the assumed number of days in a year) to get the daily interest charge. The amount of repo interest due is equal to the daily interest amount times the actual number of days that the money is borrowed on that repo transaction. Interest on interest is not included in the total. Also, because there are either 365 or 366 days in a year, financing rates are about 1.5 percent higher than the indicated rate.[11]

The equity loan market developed first in the United States following the development of the repo market for government bonds (described in the following section). Most other countries have had an equity loan market for less than 10 years, usually following legislation enabling the market to exist. The equity loan market does not exist in many jurisdictions outside of G-7 countries and other European markets.

THE FIXED-INCOME REPO MARKET

The U.S. Treasury market (including Treasury bills, notes, bonds, and strips) is one of the most efficient markets in the world, because it is easy to create and maintain levered long and short positions in the issues, which makes it easy for traders to buy or sell mispriced issues.

The government repo market is a secured borrowing arrangement like the stock loan market where bonds owned are pledged as collateral backing loans of cash.

When a buyer agrees to purchase a bond for a price, that amount is usually quoted net of accrued interest. In other words, if a buyer agrees to pay $101 (per $100 face amount), the actual price paid equals 101 percent of the face amount plus accrued interest. Assume the accrued interest is an additional $.50 per $100 face amount. For a $10,000,000 purchase (face amount), the seller and buyer implicitly agree to exchange the bonds versus $10,150,000 (101.5 percent of the $10,000,000 face amount).

Nearly all government bond trades are settled on the next business day. Financing is typically not arranged until the day of settlement. Prices may have changed since the purchase on the previous day. For example, if the value has risen to $102 (including accrued interest), it would be possible to borrow $10,200,000, more than the cost. However, other positions may be financed for amounts less than the trade price. As a result, it is important that the buyer can afford to finance something less than the price paid.

The amount borrowed on a repo can vary from the current value because one counterparty may demand excess collateral, also called a *haircut*. For example, a 1-point or 1 percent haircut in the previous example means that the client can only borrow 100.5 percent of the face amount. In fact, haircuts of 1/8 or 1/4 of a point (per $100 face amount) are much more typical. Such minimal excess collateral makes it possible to borrow hundreds and perhaps even thousands of times as much as the capital committed to a particular trade.

In fact, leverage in the fixed-income market is generally one of the highest allowed in any securities market. However, it is not possible to lever the entire portfolio to this extent. In practice, leverage of 25 to 30 times capital is about all the counterparties will provide.

When a trader borrows money secured by a bond position, the transaction is called a repurchase agreement or repo. The interest rate is called the *repo rate*. When a trader borrows a bond collateralized by cash, the transaction is called a *reverse repurchase agreement* (usually shortened to reverse repo or reverse). The interest rate is called the *reverse rate*.

Like the equity loan market, bonds that are expensive to borrow are called *special issues*. The added expense of borrowing a short issue that is special is that the reverse rate is substantially below the repo rate. This means that the short-seller gets paid less interest on the collateral posted to borrow securities than is paid to finance the long positions.

The U.S. Treasury tries to maintain a regular schedule of auctions. Notes and bonds are generally sold quarterly, so fixed-income investors frequently must buy issues in the secondary market. Dealers maintain active markets in the recently issued bonds. Because of this active trading and because the issues are often used in arbitrages and as hedges against mortgage and corporate bond positions, these recent issues are usually the most expensive to borrow.

Most U.S. Treasury issues are not special, although securities lenders will charge a modest spread whenever a trader borrows a particular issue. The most actively traded issues, especially the most recently issued notes and bonds (called the *current issues*), are frequently special and can remain special for extended periods.

REPRICING FINANCING TRANSACTIONS TO REDUCE CREDIT EXPOSURE

Altough repos and reverse repos are priced very near to the value of the bonds at the time the financing is arranged, the value of the collateral changes as stock or bond prices change. It is important to actively reprice these financing transactions to minimize credit exposure to financing counterparties. Suppose you had the financing positions at current valuations in Table 7.2. The trader has borrowed $25,000,000 cash and delivered securities currently worth $26,100,000 to Dealer A. This trader has an unsecured exposure to Dealer A equal to the $1,100,000 difference on this bond. In contrast, the trader has also borrowed $15,000,000 from Dealer B, collateralized by securities currently worth $14,800,000. The trader has no credit exposure to Dealer B (but Dealer B has a $200,000 exposure to the trader). On the third issue, the trader has also borrowed securities worth $29,000,000 on a reverse repo collateralized by $30,000,000 of the trader's cash. On Bond 3, the trader has an additional $1,000,000 of credit exposure to Dealer A. The trader may ask Dealer A to reprice his financings because the net exposure ($1,100,000 plus $1,000,000) is large enough to justify the effort to reprice.

Frequently, financing counterparties will have several financing trades with different credit exposure. It is standard industry practice to net all the financing exposures. Credit committees generally establish the maximum exposure a firm will tolerate before repricing, but $500,000 is a common threshold. It is also industry practice to reprice all the issues whenever the repricing limit is reached.

The trader will not ask Dealer B to reprice that repo even if the $200,000 difference grows to $500,000, because it is in the trader's interest to retain the excess collateral. Also, if Dealer B fails to reprice repos when required, the trader benefits by having an attractive source of capital and leverage.

As indicated earlier, a dealer may require a haircut of a hedge fund looking to borrow money (repo) or securities (reverse repo).

TABLE 7.2 Financing Positions

Issue	Repo Balance ($)	Current Value ($)	Exposure ($)	Counterparty
Bond 1	25,000,000	26,100,000	1,100,000	Dealer A
Bond 2	15,000,000	14,800,000	(200,000)	Dealer B
Bond 3	(30,000,000)	29,000,000	1,000,000	Dealer A

Similarly, a money market mutual fund may require a broker-dealer to post excess margin on a repo trade. This excess margin (or haircut) can differ for longer and shorter issues. Because longer maturities can change in value more quickly than shorter maturities, they are more risky as loan collateral. It is typical to charge a larger haircut on these trades. It is also typical to charge a larger haircut and higher borrowing rate for agency bonds, mortgage-backed bonds, and corporate bonds.

FINANCING MORTGAGE-BACKED SECURITIES

Although it is possible to repo a mortgage security, traders of mortgage pass-through securities have an alternative to the repo market called the *forward* or TBA[12] market. Mortgage pass-throughs are sold on the basis of the original face amount, adjusted by the amount of this balance previously repaid. Every month, the amount outstanding declines, depending on both the scheduled amortization of principal on the underlying mortgages and prepayments. Until the updated balance is known, it is difficult to settle purchases and sales. As a result, dealers and customers have become accustomed to trading for forward settlement dates.

In addition, the process of loan origination creates mortgage securities that do not even exist for several months. A lender first commits to the homeowner, who may not borrow the money for 8 weeks. Then the mortgage is delivered to Fannie Mae or Freddie Mac and converted into a pass-through security (another week or so). As a result, lenders need to sell forward 2 or 3 months the loans they originate.

A forward market has developed to accommodate this need. Traders can buy and sell mortgage pass-throughs and avoid the repo market altogether. Policies on margining these forward trades differ from dealer to dealer and on a case-by-case basis even with a single dealer. Frequently, a dealer will ask for no margin for its most creditworthy customers. When margin is required, it is typical to post securities instead of cash. Because of these differences, it is not possible to say how much leverage is available in the mortgage forward market, but it is comparable to repo leverage.

CREATING LEVERAGE WITH FUTURES

The amount of leverage provided by futures differs from contract to contract. Each exchange determines the margin for its contracts. The exchanges change margin from time to time, especially when the contracts are extremely volatile. Exchanges usually offer a reduced margin for hedgers and exchange members. Margins on spreads between futures can also be substantially less than margins on outright positions.

Table 7.3 lists major futures contracts at the time of this writing with the value of the underlying position, the margin required for a speculative position, and the implicit leverage.

The leverage possible with stock index futures and financial futures corresponds roughly with leverage possible with the underlying cash instruments. In general, hedge funds must run leverage well below the amount of leverage possible with either cash or futures in-

TABLE 7.3   Futures Contracts

Contract	Underlying Value ($)	Spec Margin[a] ($)	Leverage
30-Year	100,000	2,363	42:1
10-Year	103,750	1,620	64:1
5-Year	104,000	1,080	96:1
2-Year	205,750	945	218:1
Eurodollar	960,000	600	1,650:1
Muni bond	102,625	1,350	76:1
S&P	312,750	21,563	15:1
Dow	218,500	6,750	32:1
Nasdaq	179,700	33,750	5:1
Russell	248,000	28,350	9:1

[a]The margin listed is the amount required for an outright long or short position, a so-called speculative position. Hedgers receive somewhat lower margin and commensurately higher leverage.

struments. It is interesting to note that there is little correspondence between the effective leverage and the level of risk involved with these contracts.

Transaction costs in the futures markets may be less than the underlying markets. In some markets, such as the government securities market, trading costs are lower in the cash market. With the dramatic decrease in equity commissions, the cost advantage for futures has declined substantially.

The Chicago Mercantile Exchange (CME), the Chicago Board of Trade (CBOT), and the Chicago Board Options Exchange (CBOE) have announced a plan to jointly trade futures on a single stock. The exchanges will begin by trading large, actively traded issues. The London International Financial Futures and Options Exchange (LIFFE) and the Nasdaq stock market have also announced plans to create an electronic exchange to trade single stock futures for U.S. and European investors.

Single stock futures are already allowed in Sweden, Finland, Australia, Denmark, Portugal, Hungary, Hong Kong, Canada, England, and South Africa. The contracts are moderately successful in Sweden and Portugal. In other locations, volume and liquidity are very limited. However, Reg T is a U.S. rule and may be a large enough difference to influence the success of the product in the United States.

Hedge funds that are not exempt from Reg T may enjoy a cost reduction if the futures are priced to the broker-dealer marginal cost. It generally costs about 10 basis points to carry a short position in the stock loan market (the difference between the general collateral rebate rate and the cost of financing long positions). Funds limited by Reg T have been able to bypass the regulation by substituting total return swaps for the short position in actual shares (also called *synthetic financing*). Such swaps generally cost the equivalent of 30 basis points. The fund will save money if the futures are priced below the cost of synthetically financing a short.

Single stock futures will probably not allow funds bound by Reg T to avoid these restrictions. The decision to allow single stock futures was complicated by an earlier agreement called the Shad-Johnson accord (subsequently incorporated into law by Congress) that

allowed the Commodity Futures Trading Commission (CFTC) to regulate stock index futures as commodities but granted the jurisdiction
of securities to the Securities and Exchange Commission (SEC). The
SEC was granted jurisdiction over single stock futures, and it appears
that somewhat reduced Reg T margin, insider-trading rules, and
uptick rules will apply to these futures. The SEC and CFTC have proposed 20 percent initial and maintenance margin on single stock futures.

CREATING LEVERAGE WITH OPTIONS

Exchange-traded and over-the-counter options provide an additional
opportunity to create leverage in an investment portfolio. Long positions in calls can substitute for a long position in the underlying asset.
Likewise, short positions in calls can substitute for a short position in
the underlying asset. In the same way, a long position in puts can be
used instead of a short position in the underlying assets. By the same
logic, a short position in puts can be used instead of a long position
in the underlying assets.

The option alternatives are not identical substitutes for a position in the underlying asset. It is relatively straightforward to convert
the option position into the current equivalent position by means of
a standard risk measurement device called the *delta* (discussed in detail in Chapter 13). The delta of an option measures how much a put
or call gains or loses along with changes in the underlying asset.
Using the delta, it is possible to construct an option position that
perfectly matches the changes in value of the underlying asset. This
option position, however, exposes the trader to changes in volatility,
erosion of the option premium, and sensitivity to interest rates not
present in a simple long or short position in the underlying asset.
Also, the characteristics of the put or call change as the value of the
underlying asset goes up or down and as the option approaches expiration. In order to maintain the same equivalent position in the underlying asset, the option position may need to be adjusted from
time to time.

These characteristics are not necessarily a disadvantage of using options instead of the underlying asset. Although position management is somewhat more complicated, the hedge fund can use calls or puts or a combination of calls and puts to create a pattern of returns that differs from the underlying asset by design.

It is relatively easy to create positions resembling a levered long or short amount of the underlying asset. Many factors affect how much leverage is possible with options, but it is often possible to create leverage equivalent to two times the fund's capital (either as long or short positions). In fact, spreads between two options (for example, long a call with a lower strike and short a call with a higher strike) can produce the same leverage, albeit over a more narrow price range.

CREATING LEVERAGE WITH SWAPS AND OTHER DERIVATIVES

Over-the-counter derivatives offer an easy way to create leverage and often simplify positions. The typical swap involves two counterparties. One party usually pays a floating short-term rate of interest to the second party. The first party receives a return that essentially creates a levered long position in the asset used to fix the second set of cash flows.

The cash flows in a swap can be summarized on the time line in Figure 7.2. The cash flows pointing downward represent the syn-

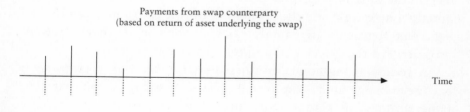

Payments from swap counterparty
(based on return of asset underlying the swap)

Time

Payments to swap counterparty
(based on London Interbank Offering Rate)

FIGURE 7.2   Total Return Swap Cash Flows

thetic cost of borrowing the money to buy and hold the asset. These amounts can vary as interest rates go up or down. The cash flows pointing upward represent the synthetic return of owning the asset. They are drawn randomly in the figure to illustrate that these cash flows are uncertain at the time the swap is initiated.

Although these returns are drawn as positive numbers (to keep the figure clear), the return can be negative, requiring the holder of the swap to pay both the interest payment and a payment equal to the loss. Note that in practice the cash inflows and the cash outflows are netted and one party makes the net payment to the other. Note, too, that the swap emulates the payment for the purchase of the asset plus an equal loan amount, exactly netting these initial payments. For the same reason, no final cash flows are required to liquidate the position and repay the loan.

BEST PRACTICES

The President's Working Group on Financial Markets[13] believes that reducing leverage by hedge funds and other financial institutions would reduce the collective risk in the financial markets. This preference has not been accepted by the hedge fund industry as a best practice. Instead, it represents a harbinger of best practices at some point in the future.

The amount of leverage possible is limited by the effect leverage has on the volatility of returns (which directly affects investors and potential investors) and the perception of risk by trading and financing counterparties. Hedge funds should adopt a degree of leverage appropriate for the assets used and the strategies employed.

A good starting point for a best practices level of leverage for a particular hedge fund is the degree of leverage in funds employing the same strategy. It is admittedly difficult to construct a list of peer hedge funds, given the variety of strategies, mix of strategies, and differences in investor preferences.

In general, lenders are biased toward lower leverage because they benefit little from the leverage of their counterparties but face increased risk. Fund managers are biased toward excessive leverage (see Chapter 16). This tension has the effect of imposing a de facto best practices level on individual funds.

The Basel Committee on Banking Supervision recommended[14] that hedge funds should not rely on the liquidity of securities markets to reduce leverage in times of crisis. Under these conditions, typically uncorrelated markets can be correlated. The liquidity of the underlying markets can disappear as many levered financial institutions all seek to reduce holdings in similar issues. Operationally for hedge funds, this might mean limiting positions in certain types of securities, maintaining a cushion of margining capacity, or buying out of the money puts on these types of instruments.

A hedge fund industry group proposed that managers and investors should use risk-based measures of leverage rather than traditional accounting measures.[15] One measure divides the hedge fund's value at risk (VaR) measure (see Chapter 13) by the equity in the fund. This type of measure can account for the difference in the risk of assets in the context of the strategy employed.

NOTES

1. Produced by Van Hedge Fund Advisors, Inc. as of 12/31/97 and presented to Congress in a speech by Steven A. Lonsdorf.
2. $50 million plus $50 million $\times$ 5% / 360 $\times$ 7 interest ($48,611.11).
3. For more information, see "Disturbances in the U.S. Securities Markets," Hearing before the Subcommittee on Securities of the Committee on Banking, Housing, and Urban Affairs of the U.S. Senate, May 26, 1982.
4. $10 million $\times$ 5% / 360 $\times$ 30 = $41,666.67.
5. $10 million $\times$ 4.90% / 360 $\times$ 30 = $40,833.33.
6. $10 million $\times$ 2.50% / 360 $\times$ 30 = $20,833.33.
7. Assume you had $100 million in capital and carried gross positions (long and short) of $200 million. If you had long and short positions equal to $100 million, the repo expense would be $100 million $\times$ 5% /

360 × 365. Rebate interest would equal $100 million × 2.5% / 360 × 365. The net interest expense equals $208,333, which is 2.53% of the assets under management.

8. Geczy, Christopher C., David K. Musto and Adam V. Reed, *Stocks Are Special Too: An Analysis of the Equity Lending Market,* draft June 30, 2001.

9. If the fund puts all its assets in long positions, the maximum leverage would be 1/.15 = 6.67:1. If the fund carries short positions equal to the long positions, the leverage is 0.5 / 0.15 + 0.5 / 0.30 = 5:1.

10. Section 220.7(c) of Regulation T.

11. 365/360 = 1.0139, so interest costs are about 1.4 percent higher than the indicated rate. 366/360 = 1.017 or about 1.7 percent higher than the indicated rate.

12. TBA is short for "to be arranged." The original TBA market allowed different mortgage-backed issues to be substituted with a crude mechanism to adjust the price. Once the Federal Housing Administration and the Veterans Administration stopped posting a current rate, the delivery option called TBA disappeared but the name survives as a synonym for a forward trade.

13. *Hedge Funds, Leverage and the Lessons of Long Term Capital Management,* President's Working Group on Financial Markets, April 1999, page 29; available at http://www.ustreas.gov/press/releases/docs/hedge fund.pdf.

14. *Banks' Interaction with Highly Leveraged Institutions,* Basel Committee on Banking Supervision, January 1999, page 14; available at http://www.bis.org/publ/index.htm.

15. *Sound Practices for Hedge Fund Managers,* February 2000, paragraph 16; available at http://planethedgefund.com/articles/Sound_Practices.doc.

CHAPTER 8

Hedge Fund Business Plans

Writing a business plan is an effective way to organize the entrepreneurial tasks required to create a new business. When creating a hedge fund and management company simultaneously, either one business plan encompassing both entities or two separate plans can be prepared. The entities differ from manufacturing and conventional service companies. Consequently, their business plan or plans should reflect their unique needs.

This chapter reviews the components of a typical business plan and addresses how business plans may differ from the standard. It also covers how business plans can help cope with the interrelationship between the hedge fund and the management company.

PURPOSE OF A BUSINESS PLAN

A business plan provides a path for a company to follow. This plan is especially important to a new business that must make many strategic decisions and establish its basic components. In fact, it is important to any business to force consideration of key strategic issues, plan for the future, and react to changing conditions.

A business plan can be a means for communicating to investors or potential investors. For a new business, the plan may be a marketing tool to equity investors, lenders, and potential clients. For an established business, it may be a formal dialogue between management and an independent board of directors. For an existing business forming a new unit, the plan may formalize the request for support from senior management that is the source of capital.

The plan can be a device for communicating to personnel. It can motivate talented potential employees to take a risk in joining a new organization. Within an established organization, a plan can be a vehicle for a committee to speak in an organized manner. The plan can become a template where staff throughout the organization can provide input and communicate the whole in a document much more clearly than the sum of the parts (the parts are the countless related memos on a list of related topics).

The plan can develop managerial skill within an organization. The business plan requires managers to address key managerial issues facing an organization. Without the discipline of a business plan, time pressures can cause a company to muddle through without making key decisions that can make the difference between success and failure.

A business plan can save both time and money for an organization. By reviewing the present and considering the future, strategic decisions can be made at optimal times. The company can direct efforts to things that most affect the new business. It can avoid missed opportunities for growth. Finally, a plan should reduce the waste of both time and money on efforts not consistent with the strategic plans of the organization.

PARTS OF A BUSINESS PLAN

A typical business plan has a title page, a contents page, an executive summary, a description of the vision or mission of the company, a company overview, a review of the product or service, a market analysis, and a marketing plan.[1]

The vision section of a business plan starts with a careful look at the present situation and reviews short-term and long-term anticipated developments. The section may include a vision statement, which condenses the future of the business into concise language. The mission statement is a short explanation of how specific efforts directed toward a business will achieve the vision. Finally, the vision section of a business plan should articulate clear goals and objectives for the business.

The overview of the company should describe the business in legal terms. This section should include descriptions of individuals who will run the business. For the management and the board of directors, this section probably includes descriptions of specific individuals who have committed to join the new business or business unit. The overview can describe remaining staff in more general terms, listing the types of skills required and the expected staff size. If the company has business partners (joint ventures, strategic alliances, etc.), the overview may describe those relationships.

The product strategy section of a business plan describes the current or anticipated first products of the company. If the product requires a description, this section should include a description at the level of detail necessary to explain the key aspects of the product to readers of the plan. This section should describe research and development efforts, especially if they affect future products.

The market analysis section should describe the microeconomic conditions of the market for the product. It includes a definition of the market to focus on and excludes related products in a reasonable way. It also includes a description of the potential customers for the product, pricing and competition in the market, and a list of risks to companies in this market.

A marketing plan is a miniature business plan on the specific task of marketing the company's products. In addition to a thorough strategic review of marketing issues for the company, the plan addresses specific intentions for sales, distribution, and promotion of the products. The marketing plan may include plans for organizing the public relations of the company with investors and the media.

ORGANIZATION OF A HEDGE FUND BUSINESS PLAN

The founders of a hedge fund must create two companies. From the point of view of a traditional manufacturing company, the underlying company being created is the management company. The hedge fund itself is the product that the management company produces. The fund is the more difficult entity to create.

TABLE 8.1   Business Plan Contents Page for a Management Company (Separate)

1. Executive Summary
2. Vision
3. Company Overview
4. Product Strategy
5. Market Analysis
6. Marketing Plan

The management company organizes the fund, invests in the fund, and promotes the fund so as to create demand for its management services. Because the interaction between the two companies is complex, it makes the task of developing a business plan quite different from most other businesses.

Table 8.1 shows the contents for a business plan describing a management company. The contents page and the business plan for the management company include each of the sections typically found in a business plan. Table 8.2 shows the contents for a separate business plan describing a hedge fund. The contents page and the business plan for the fund also include the standard sections typically found in a business plan. Each of these plans would be written independently, perhaps by different authors, and not necessarily distributed to the same readers.

Creating Two Separate Plans

Because two businesses are being created, it may be desirable to create two separate business plans. Creating two plans has several ad-

TABLE 8.2   Contents of a Business Plan for an Investment Pool (Separate)

1. Executive Summary
2. Vision
3. Company Overview
4. Product Strategy
5. Market Analysis
6. Marketing Plan

vantages over a single business plan that addresses management issues of both the management company and the fund. First, the management plan may contain information and estimates that the founders should not share with potential investors, lenders, broker-dealers, and other readers of a plan describing the fund. In particular, a plan that discusses the high levels of profit possible from running a fund would make a poor marketing document to share with potential investors. Also, it is probably not wise to disclose to lenders a discussion of how the legal structure diverts default risk to creditors and away from the general partner.

A second advantage of drafting a separate business plan for each unit involves the flexibility to devote different emphasis to issues on each plan. Although the plans must cover many of the same issues, fund investors have different concerns than the owners of the management company.

Finally, in drafting a separate plan for the management company, the founders must focus on aspects of running a hedge fund often ignored by investment professionals who set up a fund. Typically, too little attention is devoted to issues surrounding the operation of the management company as a business. Like a doctor who devotes too little attention to running the medical practice, it is easy to focus so much attention on the fund that entrepreneurial issues are ignored. By drafting a separate plan for each business, key decisions can be addressed at an early time.

The key disadvantage of writing two separate plans is that they can be very duplicative because many of the same issues must be addressed in both. When many issues do not stand alone, it may not be practical to create separate plans.

Creating a Merged Business Plan

It is tempting to create a single plan that sometimes contains separate sections for the fund and the manager and other times discusses the businesses together. The single plan needs only a single title page and contents page, of course, but for all sections of substance, it could contain the part of the plan devoted to the management company followed by the part of the plan devoted to the fund.

Table 8.3 shows the same sections of the business plans appearing in Tables 8.1 and 8.2. However, the sections have been merged into a single business plan. This format could include separate sections for the management company and fund for the plan for each of the main sections (executive summary, vision, company overview, etc.). Alternately, the plan can address the key points related to both organizations in each major section. The key distinction for the structure shown in Tables 8.1 and 8.2 is that there is only a single plan for the two businesses. The fund sponsors may be hesitant to disclose all this information to potential readers of the plan.

In contrast, a merged plan would have two sections addressing the vision of each company, two sections giving a company overview of the fund and the management company, and so on. The advantage of this structure is that key issues are developed from the perspective of the fund sponsors and the fund investors. The document can develop this interrelationship as needed to tie the plans together.

There are several disadvantages to this layout. First, despite the similar section headings, the content of each section often differs substantially for the two businesses. Presenting them together makes it

TABLE 8.3   Contents Page for a Merged
Business Plan

1. Executive Summary (Management)
2. Executive Summary (Fund)
3. Vision (Management)
4. Vision (Fund)
5. Company Overview (Management)
6. Company Overview (Fund)
7. Product Strategy (Management)
8. Product Strategy (Fund)
9. Market Analysis (Management)
10. Market Analysis (Fund)
11. Marketing Plan (Management)
12. Marketing Plan (Fund)

easier to fail to fully develop the plan for the management company. Second, it is difficult enough to keep separate the many strategic decisions involved in the fund and its manager. By merging the discussion of these issues, it is harder to keep the issues separate. Third, it is harder to divide the work (the actual writing and the strategic thinking) among the founders. In contrast, if there are two plans, one or more founders can develop the investment product while others develop the management company. If that is the reality of the established businesses, it is easier to start the division of labor early. Fourth, it need not be the case that merging the two plans eliminates duplication of text. Because each section addresses the issues first from the perspective of the management company and then from the perspective of the fund, much of the content can be duplicative as each section develops a topic independently.

Creating a Unified Business Plan

It may be possible to merge and reorganize the two plans into an original layout that combines the advantage of separate plans with a merged document. Naturally, the unified plan would eliminate obviously duplicative sections (title page, table of contents, and perhaps the executive summaries). The actual layout may be topical (e.g., safekeeping, revenues, risk management, etc.), thematic, or chronological. Whether such a structure works would depend on the specific needs of each business.

Table 8.4 shows the contents of a unified business plan. In this example, some sections are combined for the management company and the fund. For other sections, the two business units are addressed separately. It is also possible to create more novel ways to organize the topics that may be useful in some situations.

If it works, a unified plan can eliminate much of the duplication present in two business plans. The organization of the plan could emphasize the interrelationships of the businesses. For example, the investment strategy at the fund business affects the resources needed (personnel, analysis, data, software, etc.) at the management company.

TABLE 8.4 Contents Page for a Unified Business Plan (some sections combined to minimize duplication)

1. Executive Summary (Management and Fund)
2. Vision (Management)
3. Vision (Fund)
4. Company Overview (Management and Fund)
5. Product Strategy (Management)
6. Product Strategy (Fund)
7. Market Analysis (Management and Fund)

There are disadvantages to producing a unified business plan. The structure of the plan may not force the authors to address key strategic issues. There may be insufficient interaction between the issues in each plan to justify an unusual report format. Finally, by creating a single document, management may be including data and points of view they do not want to share with investors or lenders.

WRITING A BUSINESS PLAN FOR A HEDGE FUND

To clarify the content of a business plan for setting up a hedge fund, the key sections of a business plan are discussed in the following text. For each section, topics relevant to the management company and the fund are treated separately.

Vision/Mission Section for the Management Company

The vision/mission section must address the kind of products the management company will sponsor. Will the manager run a single fund or multiple funds? If the manager anticipates multiple funds, will they be philosophically similar (all value-oriented equity funds, for example)? Alternatively, will the manager seek to develop unrelated products to offer a choice to investors (and an opportunity to diversify)? Will the various funds invest in stocks, bonds, currencies, or a mixture? Will the investment decisions be based on fundamental factors, technical analysis, or other factors? Will the company offer hedge funds or funds of funds (or both)?

The vision/mission section should address the question of how much of the noninvestment-related services will be outsourced. This question rises from a tactical decision to a strategic decision, because a decision to offer offshore mirrored or master-feeder funds requires substantial outsourcing. The amount of outsourcing may be a life cycle decision, where a manager outsources many functions until funds under management rise above a critical level. Finally, if a financial institution is managing the fund and jointly markets mutual funds, brokerage services, or insurance products, outsourcing may be more or less attractive.

Although a business must address both investment and marketing issues, the emphasis can differ widely. A fund of funds may succeed primarily on the strength of the marketing organization at the management company. In contrast, a highly visible investment manager may feel the only effective marketing tool is good performance. The mission/vision section should clarify how important investment returns and marketing are to the business's success.

Of course, a manager does not need to be consistent between funds when the management company runs more than one fund. Indeed, if a hedge fund manager adds a fund of funds, the reason may well be to exploit the marketing advantage of previous investment performance.

Vision/Mission Section for the Investment Fund

It is important to delineate the investment characteristics of the fund. Does the fund invest in stocks? Bonds? Currencies? Is the fund making directional bets or arbitraging narrow price spreads?

The target benchmark is a second key part of the vision section of a fund business plan. A hedge fund invested primarily in stocks can target U.S. or global equity return. An arbitrage fund may compare its performance to short-term interest rates. Many hedge funds can be described as absolute return strategies; it is only the return, not the return relative to a benchmark, that matters. Finally, once a fund defines a target benchmark, it is possible to compare the fund results to other hedge funds with the same benchmark. Performance indices on many different categories are published by several services that track hedge fund performance.

A statement of vision for a hedge fund should include a discussion of the source of returns for investors. This might include market timing, which can be implemented in a variety of ways (fundamental, technical, macro). Or return may derive from superior judgment of relative value. To an equity fund, this may involve equity analysis. To an arbitrage fund, it might involve superior methods for valuing exotic derivatives. A fund may also try to derive returns through financial engineering. For example, an equity manager may combine an efficiently priced investment in futures with an investment in highly attractive money market surrogates. Finally, the fund may seek to provide superior returns by investing in assets likely to provide superior returns (private equity, venture capital, real estate, etc.).

The vision for a fund (especially if the fund is not yet operating) should include expectations about transactions, an honest prediction of leverage in the fund, and perhaps the turnover rate, especially if the turnover is high.

Although specific methods may be proprietary trade secrets, the vision section should give some insight into how investment decisions are made, including the kind of inputs the manager considers relevant and who makes the investment decisions.

Finally, to fairly represent the investment characteristics of the fund, the vision should discuss current and future growth of the assets in the fund. Some strategies can be scaled up more effectively than others. Ways that a fund adapts to increasing fund size affect the returns to investors.

In addition to investment characteristics of the fund, the vision section of a business plan should address the focus of the fund. A fund may be focused entirely on investment issues and ignore marketing altogether. In fact, for a new fund, survival may hinge almost completely on performance in the first few years. Almost singular focus on performance may be appropriate for some new hedge funds.

When an experienced investment professional starts a fund, there may be insufficient attention placed on marketing, which may reflect confidence that the world will beat a path to this better mousetrap. It may cause the firm to devote too little effort toward marketing.

The vision section may develop strategies to reduce the fund's reliance on investment performance as a marketing strategy. This might include hiring additional staff to create a marketing effort or institutionalizing the investment knowledge in the staff (through training or software) to free up the senior management to run the business.

Company Overview for the Management Company

The company overview should describe the structure of the management company. Generally, the management company is organized as an S corporation or a limited liability corporation. The company overview should list the owners of the management company. When there are multiple owners, the plan should describe how the results will be distributed. Finally, the company overview should describe the capital paid into the manager. The capital should be adequate to pay organizational costs, salaries during the start-up period, and necessary expenses (rent, equipment, etc.).

The company overview should also describe the management of the management company. While the management company oversees the investments of the fund, this section should describe the general management of the manager. The manager typically hires and directs the staff to handle accounting, trading, and marketing functions.

Although the head trader is often the general manager of the management company, this is frequently not a good choice. Just as some doctors make good business managers, some investment professionals can effectively run the business. However, it usually makes sense to make sure the investment managers have sufficient time to ensure the best performance. In particular, in a period of crisis, it is best if the investment professionals can focus on the investment crisis and other staff can attend to investor contacts and dialogue with creditors.

The company overview should include a discussion of staffing. Often, the fund will have no employees; the management company will carry all the employees. The overview should establish that the manager will have adequate staff to complete accounting, trading, and marketing functions.

A company overview for the management company can list strategic alliances if those relationships are vital to the success of the company. For a hedge fund manager, one of the most important business partners is the prime broker. A shared back office may make operations affordable for a start-up company. The overview should describe joint marketing agreements, marketing agreements with broker-dealers, and independent marketing agreements with important third parties.

Company Overview for the Fund

The company overview should describe the structure of the business. Usually a domestic (U.S.) fund will be structured as a general/limited partnership or a limited liability corporation. An offshore fund is usually a corporation. The overview should identify the general partner and the location where the fund is domiciled. The description of the structure of the fund should disclose whether the fund is part of a mirrored structure or a master-feeder structure and whether it is a fund or a fund of funds.

The management section of the company overview should briefly describe the management company, including a description of key personnel in the management company, even though the service is contracted out.

The description of the management should depict the investment process and establish why it should lead to good performance. Does the process lead to repeatable results? Do the compensation schemes provide the right motivation to the management company? Some types of compensation may encourage excessive risk taking.

The company overview should include a discussion of the staffing at the management company. Although this staff is not part of the business organization described by the plan, the success of the fund demands that the staff is competent, can adequately handle the peak load of business, and can handle the range of assets the fund will employ.

Many types of strategic alliances should be described in the company overview. The plan need not describe basic services, such as Bloomberg or Reuters computer services, unless the product is fundamental to the strategy. For example, a fund might disclose an investment process that relies on ValueLine timeliness rating. The plan should describe less standard services (specialized derivative pricing software) when they are a necessary part of the business. The plan may disclose sources of portfolio account and other services if the information might affect investors' confidence in the fund.

Product Strategy at the Management Company

In practice, the manager provides a variety of services to the fund. However, the product that provides the revenue to the manager is the investment management. The manager may manage only one fund or multiple funds. The funds may be part of a mirror structure or a master-feeder structure. The manager may also run separate accounts, mutual funds, or commodity pools (futures funds). Finally, the hedge fund management may be an extension to another line of business (sales and trading at a broker-dealer, private equity underwriting, or mutual fund management).

Product Strategy at the Fund

The product strategy of the fund is also called an investment plan. This plan should be very thoroughly developed. Further, a manager running multiple funds can have substantially different investment plans for each fund.

The investment plan should contain a description of the investment philosophy of the fund. What are the sources of risk and return for the fund? How is the fund expecting to generate attractive returns? How much risk (measured in a variety of ways) is expected? How much risk will be tolerated? Will the investment decisions incorporate tax considerations?

The investment plan should also describe any analytical tools used in the strategy. Are they fundamental or technical techniques? Do they involve proprietary techniques or trade secrets?

How are investment decisions made in the fund? Are decisions reduced to rigid rules (a black box)? Are decisions downstreamed to individuals (sometimes called bottom-up investing) or made by an investment committee (sometimes called top-down investing)?

How has the fund performed in the past? If actual performance is not available, is it possible to create a hypothetical track record that fairly measures how the fund would have performed?

Market Analysis for the Management Company

The question of whether there is adequate demand for the manager's service is impossible to separate from the question of whether there is demand for the fund. Unless the founders can attract money into the fund, there will be no fees to pay for management services.

However, if the fund grows to sufficient size to be viable, it is still not clear that the world needs yet another management company. Although it is not a typical business model, it is possible to contract out the management services to other fund managers. This business model exists in the mutual fund industry. For example, Vanguard contracts for management services on some of its mutual fund products.

The practice exists in the hedge fund industry, too. A fund of funds manager invests in other hedge funds, rather than directly investing the money. There are differences, of course. With the fund of funds, the allocator gives up custody of the funds, may get little information about how the money is invested, and retains none of the brand identification with the fund.

In truth, the fund of funds business is different than Vanguard's contract management. Unless the practice develops, the demand for management services will derive from the demand for the manager's funds.

Market Analysis for the Fund

A discussion of the market for the fund should also include an analysis of growth in the sector. What are recent trends for growth? What is the potential size of the sector? Is the sector large enough to accommodate a new fund?

The market analysis should also discuss factors that affect risk and reward in the sector and for the fund. Fundamental (exogenous) factors determine much of a hedge fund's returns. These factors include stock returns, interest rates, credit spreads, and market volatility. What is the recent experience of investors in this sector?

The market analysis should describe existing funds within the sector. How large are the funds? Are they open to new investment? How much capacity exists in these funds for additional investment? How have individual funds and the sector performed recently? Are there barriers limiting new entrants in the sector?

Finally, the market analysis should describe investors in the sector. Are typical investors individuals, trusts, endowments, and pension plans? Are the investors domestic (U.S.) or offshore investors? What is the tax situation of the typical investor?

Marketing Plan for the Management Company

It may not be necessary to create a marketing plan for the management company because the manager creates demand for its services by creating demand for its fund(s).

The manager is required to carry an investment of at least 1 percent of the assets of the fund. In addition, the manager needs sufficient capital to underwrite organizational costs (both for the manager and the fund) and initial expenses (salaries, rents, office equipment).

Frequently, the manager does not need to turn to outside sources for this capital.

Sometimes, a new manager will go to an outside investor to get capital for these start-up costs. In return for this investment, the investor owns part of the management company and shares in fees paid by the fund. If this outside investment is important, a marketing plan for the management company may be necessary. It is not likely that the marketing plan will be shared with potential investors in the management company, however.

There are several potential sources of capital for a management company. For an existing company, the most common source of additional capital is reinvested fees and investment profits on earlier commitments. Like any start-up business, friends, relatives, and work associates can provide seed money to begin operations. If the start-up is conducted by an existing business, the business will likely provide the funding (and retain all or nearly all the ownership in the manager). There are also investors who resemble venture capitalists. In return for early investments in the fund, these investors demand ownership in the management company and/or a variety of favorable terms for fund investments into the future. While these investments are usually technically made into the fund, the management fees on the investment allow the start-up manager to hire staff and commence trading.

Marketing Plan for the Fund

A marketing plan must allow for different needs and opportunities. Many of the most desirable investors (in terms of fees that can be charged and whether they are committed to remain in the fund despite performance swings) will not invest in new funds.

A hedge fund often starts with adequate money to commence trading. When a group of traders organize a fund, they may have sufficient capital to also create a viable fund. If a business starts a fund, it also may provide capital to open the fund.

Fund sponsors not so lucky can turn to family and work associates. A money manager may be able to attract investors from previous employment. Some investors are willing to make early investments in a hedge fund in return for attractive terms.

A marketing plan must cope with the needs of these early investors. They will likely differ in risk tolerance, tax situation, and investment sophistication.

After a couple years of successful operation, a fund can seek investments from fund of funds allocators. This is an opportunity for converting good performance into tremendous growth in assets under management. Fund of funds managers seek out promising new managers to accommodate the growth they are experiencing in their own funds. Often, they have trouble scaling up their own businesses because their favorite funds are closed to new investment.

In return for making fairly early investments in hedge funds, the fund of funds allocators may ask for commitments allowing them preference in making additional investments. The allocator may get the first right of refusal whenever the fund accepts additional money. In other words, whenever the fund is willing to accept new investment, the allocator gets the right to provide the funds.

Some allocators believe that these years moderately early in the life of a fund are the best years to invest in those funds. In the very early years, organization costs are spread over too few assets. Performance may not be optimized because trading systems are not fully developed. And the chance of failure is high in the first year or two. Also, after the fund grows (described as occurring after year five or after the fund raises $100 million or $250 million), capacity constraints on a strategy limit the returns.

Marketing to fund of funds allocators requires sophisticated investment analysis of historical performance. Allocators are likely to respond to characteristics other than return. A low correlation to stock prices, interest rates, and other funds is especially desirable. However, these investors are somewhat more fee sensitive than other investors.

An established fund can market to individuals, family offices, endowments, and pension plans. Marketing at this stage used to mean finding larger investments, stickier funds, or better financial terms. In the past, funds at this stage usually had the maximum 99 investors, so the fund would raise the assets under management by replacing existing investors with more desirable new investors. A previous restriction that limited the number of investors does not apply to most hedge funds anymore. As a result, marketing efforts focus on adding desirable investors regardless of size.

Established funds can market through a variety of channels not available to newer organizations. For example, conservative financial organizations are willing to recommend the funds to trust, insurance, and brokerage clients. The funds can market to groups that require 5 or more years of historic performance.[2]

An established fund will migrate growth away from fund of funds allocators. This group is more sensitive to the level of fees, in part because they add a layer of fees on top of the hedge fund expenses. Fund of funds allocators also have a reputation, perhaps unfairly, for withdrawing funds quickly at the first sign of poor performance.

A new fund created by an established financial institution will have a marketing plan much different from a new independent fund. The fund will not likely have to market to get seed money to start the fund. The institution will likely have very specific ideas about the characteristics the fund should have to fit the package of products already being offered to its clients. If the institution has a consistent philosophy uniting existing products (value equity management, for example), it will likely make sure that the marketing literature for the fund is consistent with other marketing efforts.

A fund can use a variety of channels for marketing. Internal efforts represent one important channel. These in-house methods include direct mail, traditional networking, and industry conferences. Independent marketers can supplement these efforts. Fund of funds represent a second major channel for distribution. Finally, financial institutions, including high net worth brokers, insurance brokers, and traditional money managers, can offer clients hedge fund products (run by independent managers).

Hedge fund promotion differs significantly from most goods and services because the private placement rules used to create the hedge fund structure also prohibit advertising. Certainly, hedge funds cannot advertise their products, but hedge funds and their advisors interpret this rule differently. Some funds will not initiate a contact with any noninvestor. Merely publishing data on the fund may be construed as advertising. Most funds conservatively apply the rules to Internet postings, so most hedge funds offer little information without password access.

The funds get promotion from word-of-mouth advertising. An effective public relations effort will get business newspapers and trade publications to publish favorable news stories about the fund. Funds can encourage this publicity by writing journal articles, nurturing contacts with journalists, and speaking at conferences and other educational forums.

CONCLUDING COMMENTS

A business plan is a valuable tool for any entrepreneur setting up a business. The features of a business plan for a hedge fund differ somewhat from those of a standard business plan to reflect the unique nature of the hedge fund business. In addition to preparing a business plan at start-up, it is advised that the plan be revised frequently to reflect new information and changing details.

NOTES

1. See *Write a Winning Business Plan (Reference Guide to BizPlan Builder)*, Jian, Version 5.0a.
2. Organizations with a board of directors are routinely the most conservative about hedge fund investments.

CHAPTER 9

Performance Measurement for Hedge Funds

Hedge fund investors use many of the same performance measurements that are used to monitor traditional investments. Some of the key measures of risk in an unlevered portfolio yield misleading results for a levered portfolio (standard deviation, for example). In addition, other measures have been devised specifically to monitor the performance of a leveraged portfolio.

This chapter reviews many of the methods used to measure performance and risk used by investors. Other measures of risk based on the underlying characteristics of the individual positions can provide better measures of future risk. These methods are reviewed in Chapter 13.

RETURN

Hedge fund participants use many different definitions of return. It is important to understand how these measures differ to understand performance review.

The simplest definition of return is called *nominal return*. Nominal return measures the change in value divided by the investment:

$$\text{Nominal Return} = \frac{\text{Gain}}{\text{Investment}} = \frac{\text{Ending Value} - \text{Beginning Value}}{\text{Beginning Value}} \quad (9.1)$$

$$= \frac{\text{Ending Value}}{\text{Beginning Value}} - 1$$

The return is not converted into an annualized number and does not contain any other reference to return over time. As a result, it can be difficult to compare two nominal returns when the time involved in each case differs.

Sometimes, the 1 in Equation 9.1 is not subtracted from a return calculation.[1] This variation is called a *return relative*. For example, if an investment earned a nominal return of 10 percent, the return relative would be 1.10. This calculation is used repeatedly in some of the following calculations.

The next adjustment adjusts the nominal return to a 1-year time horizon. For this calculation, the nominal return is tied to a specific interval of time and the return is extrapolated to 1 year and is called *annualized return:*

$$\text{Annualized Return} = \text{Nominal Return} \times \frac{\text{Number of Days in Year}}{\text{Number of Days in Period}} \quad (9.2)$$

The return presented is analogous to simple interest, which is quoted on the basis of a year of returns but does not provide for any interest to be earned on interest paid during the year.

In practice, the units of time can be measured in days, weeks, months, fractions of a year, or other units. In addition, the time in the denominator over which the nominal return was earned can be greater than a year. In this case, the same formula reduces the nominal return by prorating a part of that return to a year's portion of the return. A nominal 5 percent return earned over a 6-month period becomes 10 percent annualized. Similarly, an 18 percent nominal return earned over 18 months is a 12 percent annualized return.

When annualized returns are earned successively over two or more periods, the amount received exceeds the gain predicted by the annualized return. For example, if a 10 percent annualized return is earned each year for 5 years and if each year's gains are available to be reinvested each year, the investor has 61 percent more value after 5 years, substantially more than the 50 percent predicted by annualized (uncompounded) returns.

The exact amount can be measured by multiplying together five of the wealth relatives at 10 percent:

Cumulative Wealth $= 1 \times (1.10) \times (1.10) \times (1.10) \times (1.10) \times (1.10) = 1.61$

The calculation of cumulative wealth is usually called *future value*. The type of return that assumes interim gains are reinvested is called *compound return*.

In the foregoing example, we assumed the investor started with $1 at the beginning of the 5-year period. In fact, we could have started with any value. However, when we start with $1, the wealth we calculate can be used as a convenient scaling factor. This scaling factor can be multiplied by any cash flow to generate the appropriate future value.

If we know that a payment of $1.61 will be made in 5 years, we can compare this cash with an immediate cash flow of only $1 (if we believe we will earn 10 percent per year). For a variety of reasons, we may prefer either the immediate $1 cash flow or the 5-year deferred payment of $1.61. From a purely mathematical basis, however, we should not care because we could convert the immediate $1 payment into the $1.61 payment simply by investing the money.

We call the immediately occurring equivalent cash flow the *present value*. For a cash flow that occurs in the future, the present value represents the amount of cash today that could be invested at prevailing rates to equal that amount. We can calculate the present value of any future cash flow if we know the size of the future cash flow, when it will occur, and what return can be earned between now and the cash flow.

The formulas for present value (PV) and future value (FV) of a $1 cash flow for annual compounding are given in Equations 9.3 and 9.4:

$$PV = \frac{1}{\left(1+\text{return}\right)^{\text{No. Years}}} = \left(1+\text{return}\right)^{-\text{No. Years}} \qquad (9.3)$$

$$FV = (1 + \text{return})^{\text{No. Years}} \qquad\qquad (9.4)$$

Frequently, investors are paid portions of their return more often than once a year. If investment intervals are shortened to 6 months, the method is called *semiannual compounding*. For example, we can separate the 10 percent return into 10 returns of 5 percent over 5 years:

$$FV = 1 \times (1.05)(1.05) \ldots (1.05) = 1 \times (1.05)^{10} = 1.63$$

We can use the future value factors to convert between different return methods. Using the future value Equation 9.3, solve for the missing return consistent with the future value:

$$(1.05)^{10} = 1.63 = (1 + r_1)^5$$

$$r_1 = 10.25 \text{ percent}$$

In other words, if we invested money at 10 percent paid in semiannual installments, we would end up with the same amount of money at the end of 5 years[2] as if we received 10.25 percent annually. We say the 10.25 percent annual return is equivalent to a 10 percent semiannual compound rate.

We can increase the compounding frequency to quarterly, monthly, or daily. As the compounding frequency rises for a given rate, our net gain rises because more of the return is available for reinvestment. However, the benefit to reducing the interval grows smaller and smaller. At reasonable interest rates, there is very little difference between daily compounding and compounding every split second of the day.

The mathematical equivalent to this extremely inconvenient compounding is called *continuous compounding*. The method is actually quite convenient. It is especially easy to move from nominal returns to annual without concern that the compounding frequency is inconsistent.

The present value and future values of cash flows using continuous compounding are described by the formulas given as Equations 9.5 and 9.6:

$$PV = e^{-rT} \qquad (9.5)$$

$$FV = e^{rT} \qquad (9.6)$$

where r refers to the continuously compounded return and T is the time between the cash flows, measured in years.[3]

The continuous compounding method is not used much in performance reporting; however, it is used extensively in derivative modeling. It is used almost exclusively in academic work involving interest rates and returns. Use of the continuous method for hedge fund performance will probably increase over time.

AVERAGING RETURNS

Regardless of how returns are calculated, it is frequently necessary to average them. The simplest method simply adds up the returns for each period and divides the sum by the number of periods, as shown by Equation 9.7:

$$\text{Arithmetic Average} = \frac{\sum_{i=1}^{N} r_i}{N} \qquad (9.7)$$

This method usually works adequately. It is also the average used on a variety of other statistical calculations (standard deviation and variance, for example). However, if you use this average to predict the future value of a cash flow compounded over more than one period, you will overestimate the ending value.

Period	Return (%)
1	5
2	10
3	15

In this example, an investment that earned 5 percent, 10 percent, and 15 percent in 3 years[4] would be worth $(1.05) \times (1.10) \times (1.15) =$

1.328. The arithmetic average of 10 percent invested for 3 years yields $(1.10) \times (1.10) \times (1.10) = 1.331$. The values are close, but the arithmetic average systematically predicts too much gain.

The alternative is to calculate a geometric average. A geometric average multiplies N values, then takes the Nth root of the product. In this case, we actually use the one-period return relatives (i.e., $1 + r$):

$$\text{Geometric Average} \neq \sqrt[3]{\left(5\% \times 10\% \times 15\%\right)} = 9.08\%$$

$$\text{Geometric Average} = \sqrt[3]{\left(1.05 \times 1.10 \times 1.15\right)} - 1 = 0.0992 \text{ or } 9.92\%$$

The convenient feature of this geometric return is that when 9.92 percent return is compounded for 3 years, it will produce the same future value as the investment that provided 5 percent, 10 percent, and 15 percent returns.

Fund data for one multistrategy hedge fund were used to calculate arithmetic and geometric averages of monthly returns January 1990 through February 2001.[5] The results are shown graphically in Figure 9.1. Because the monthly returns were relatively consistent, there was little difference between the arithmetic average (1.18 per-

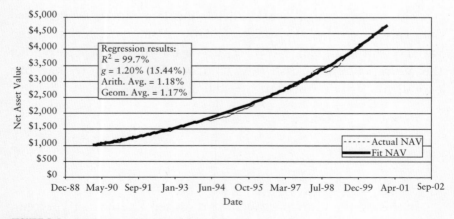

FIGURE 9.1 Hedge Fund A Net Asset Value

cent monthly) and the geometric average (1.17 percent monthly). However, for the newer, somewhat less consistent hedge fund, the estimates differ much more. The arithmetic average is 1.02 percent and the geometric average is 0.86 percent (see Figure 9.2).

A hypothetical example exaggerates the problem with using the arithmetic average. In Figure 9.3, the fund successively lost, then made 20 percent. Because each pair of months created a net 4 percent loss $(1 - 20\%) \times (1 + 20\%) = 0.96$, the hypothetical net asset value went down. The arithmetic average is a small negative return of -0.69 percent (because there was one more loss than gain), but the geometric average showed a much more plausible summary return of -2.70 percent.

There is a mathematical way to find the average return that is perhaps more failsafe than the geometric returns. The technique uses regression to find a return that best explains the net asset value (NAV) of the fund. To use the technique, first transform the NAV by taking the natural logarithm of each month's NAV. Then regress this trans-

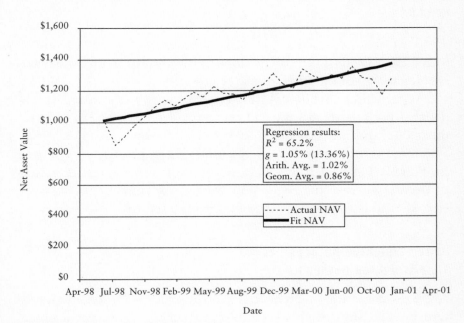

Regression results:
$R^2 = 65.2\%$
$g = 1.05\%$ (13.36%)
Arith. Avg. = 1.02%
Geom. Avg. = 0.86%

- - - - - Actual NAV
——— Fit NAV

FIGURE 9.2   Hedge Fund B Net Asset Value

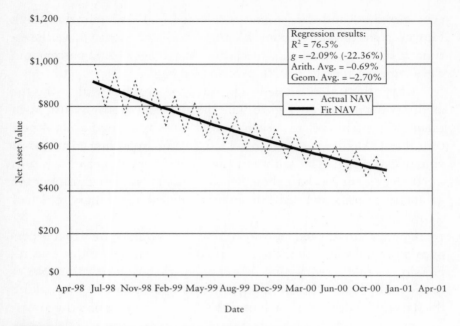

Regression results:
$R^2 = 76.5\%$
$g = -2.09\%$ (-22.36%)
Arith. Avg. = -0.69%
Geom. Avg. = -2.70%

------ Actual NAV
—— Fit NAV

FIGURE 9.3 Hypothetical Example for ±20 Percent Each Month

formed data against time.[6] The slope of the regression line is the natural logarithm of the fitted return relative.[7]

As the inset in Fund A (Figure 9.1) shows, the fitted return matches both the arithmetic and geometric averages. The fit of hypothetical returns is nearly unbiased by the additional loss in the series. The fitted return more closely resembles the geometric growth rate for Fund B (Figure 9.2). It is important to study the regression results to decide whether the regression weightings (sum of the squared errors) produce a better prediction of future returns.

Dollar-Weighted Returns versus Time-Weighted Returns

Average returns are sometimes called dollar-weighted or time-weighted returns. The time-weighted return is the same as geometric averages just described. The dollar-weighted return is the internal rate of return calculated on a series of cash flows.

To calculate the internal rate of return, set up an equation using the present value or future value formulas previously given. The equation may contain extra terms if there are multiple cash flows. The internal rate of return is calculated by trial and error to find a rate that makes the equation true.

The results of the calculations depend on the timing of the cash flows. For example, if an investor makes an additional investment just before a good period, he or she will likely outperform an investor who withdrew money at the same time.

STANDARDS FOR CALCULATING RETURNS TO INVESTORS AND DATA SERVICES SHORT POSITIONS

In general, the rate of return reported by hedge funds is the return defined in Equation 9.1. Although called nominal return earlier in the chapter, these returns (usually) monthly are compounded over 12 periods (or 4 periods if data are reported quarterly). The return is a bit more complicated if cash flows occur during the month. Also, both the leverage and derivative positions frequently found in hedge funds present special cases discussed in the following sections.

Calculating Returns on Short Positions

Returns on individual assets are calculated the same regardless of whether a hedge fund is long or short a particular position. By convention, the return on an asset makes the implicit assumption that the investor is long the asset in question. However, the effect on the portfolio is the opposite for a short position. For example, a common stock that has risen from 100 to 105 has risen 5 percent, but the effect on the portfolio is a 5 percent loss if the hedge fund is short the asset.

Calculating Returns on Levered Positions

Leverage can allow a hedge fund to control more assets by borrowing money (for long positions) or shares (for short positions). The hedge fund with leverage can make or lose money faster than a similar unlevered position.

The Association of Investment Management and Research (AIMR) Performance Presentation Standard[8] requires the manager to include the return calculated on the actual assets (including the amount purchased with borrowed money). The reporting convention followed in the industry is to look through the leverage, as if the asset were fully paid. One way to figure the return uses the amount actually paid plus any borrowings used to fund the purchase as the beginning value. The ending value is, of course, the value of the entire position in the next period. The leverage affects the weighting of the asset in the portfolio but not the return on the individual asset.

Calculating Returns on Derivative Instruments

Hedge funds frequently invest in derivative securities, including exchange-traded futures and options and over-the-counter options and swaps. Options are purchased for a small fee relative to the underlying position and create a situation similar to the foregoing levered cash market position.

Swap trades are usually initiated with terms that require no investment. Without making the foregoing adjustment to delever the position, any return on these derivatives would be infinite (positive for gains and negative for losses) because the beginning value in the denominator is zero.

Like the levered assets described previously, the manager should report a return figure that assumes the off-balance sheet assets are included in both the beginning and ending asset values. That amount to be added to the assets in each period is the margin (if any) plus the difference between the entire off-balance sheet amount and the margin already included in the accounting records. For purposes of return calculations on futures and other instruments that have a traded price, it is considered an acceptable approximation to treat the price as the value to use in both the beginning and ending values in Equation 9.1.

Returns on a Portfolio Involving Derivative Instruments

To see the problem this causes for a portfolio return, see Equation 9.8:

$$r_{\text{portfolio}} = \sum w_i \times r_i \tag{9.8}$$

where w_i represents the weight of each asset in the portfolio such that $\sum w_i = 100$ percent.

The returns in Equation 9.8 have not been adjusted to emulate a fully paid cash investment. If an investment is a derivative involving this division by zero, we are incorporating an infinite return in the average for the portfolio. The return on the portfolio is not infinite because the weighting for the derivative is zero.

The return is defined when the derivative positions are delevered. As a side benefit, the hedge funds are calculating returns consistent with the method used for unlevered portfolios.

COMPOUNDING FREQUENCIES

Hedge funds typically report data to hedge fund data providers monthly and that has become the default compounding frequency for hedge fund performance reporting. Usually, annual results are monthly compounded returns (consistent with the geometric average described earlier).

The compounding frequency can materially affect the reported results. Often, these hedge funds allow entry and exit to their funds quarterly or even less frequently. To complicate matters, the National Futures Association (NFA) permits the manager to figure performance for subperiods, if cash flows in or out of the fund may have materially affected performance[9] (and these subperiods are most likely unequal in length). Finally, in calculating drawdowns, no compounding is typically applied to the loss.

Using the continuous compounding method to compute returns solves most of the problems with ambiguity about equivalent returns.

There has been pressure to adopt this method for all performance numbers and it is likely to become a standard at some future point.

COMPUTING RETURN FOR NOTIONALLY FUNDED INVESTMENTS

Some partnerships allow investors to nominally fund a pool for an amount larger than the actual paid-in amount. For example, an investor may be allowed to commit to an investment of $500,000 but only pay in $250,000. Under this plan, the investor would be liable for an additional $250,000 and would earn returns as if the entire amount were used to purchase units or shares.

The NFA has not permitted this nominal capital to be used in calculating returns on the fund[10] because of the Commodity Futures Trading Commission (CFTC) requirements. The NFA favors including this notional capital and expects the CFTC to permit the NFA to change the standard to include the notional capital in the investment base.

STANDARD DEVIATION AS A MEASURE OF RISK

The standard deviation of returns is a common measure of risk in investment theory and practice. For many purposes,[11] the standard deviation is calculated using continuously compounded rates of return. This value is easily derived from NAV data. First calculate a return relative, then transform by taking the natural logarithm of the return relative:

$$r_{continuous} = \ln\left(\frac{NAV_i}{NAV_{i-1}}\right) \tag{9.9}$$

These returns are then used in the standard deviation formula (Equation 9.10) to get model inputs:

$$\text{Standard Deviation} = \rho = \frac{\sqrt{\sum_{i=1}^{n} \left(r_i - r_{\text{mean}}\right)^2}}{n-1} \tag{9.10}$$

For hedge fund performance, it is more common to avoid the transformation to continuous compounding:

$$r_{\text{discrete}} = \frac{NAV_i}{NAV_{i-1}} - 1 \tag{9.11}$$

This calculation implicitly assumes monthly compounded returns. Some fund managers may convert the monthly returns to annual and adjust the compounding frequency. As a practical matter, it is not necessary to subtract 1 to get the proper standard deviation because it does not vary, so it does not affect the measure.

SUBSTITUTES FOR STANDARD DEVIATION AS A MEASURE OF RISK

In using the standard deviation, investors are implicitly assuming that (1) the underlying distributions are normal and (2) it is appropriate to use the arithmetic mean in calculating the standard deviation. In fact, hedge fund returns are often not normal. There appear to be many more instances of extremely high and extremely low returns than would be expected with a normal distribution. Also, many hedge fund strategies are skewed to the left (many small positive returns and an occasional severe negative return).

Other methods produce better measures of risk. Downside semi-variance resembles the standard deviation (see Equation 9.12), except that only negative deviations are included in the calculation (doing better that the target is not perceived as risk). Also, instead of the mean, an arbitrary threshold, r^*, is used to separate successful months from unsuccessful months. The threshold can be zero (separating gains from losses) or the prevailing short-term rate or another rate defensible to the user.

$$\text{Downside Semivariance} = \frac{\sum_{i=1}^{n} \min(r_i - r^*, 0)^2}{n-1} \tag{9.12}$$

$$\text{Downside Deviation} = \sqrt{\text{Downside Semivariance}}$$

It may be desirable to measure the risk that a fund NAV falls below a target level. Some fund documentation requires managers to scale back positions after a predetermined loss amount and to close out all positions at a second threshold. Regardless of whether such a requirement exists, measures describing that potential are usual ways of measuring hedge fund risk. The statistic called *below target probability* (BTP) measures the likelihood of a loss below a particular target:[12]

$$BTP = \int_{-\infty}^{T} f(r)dr \tag{9.13}$$

In the equation, $f(r)$ is the probability of each return (or possible NAV levels) and T is the specified target level of returns. The probability function need not be a standard distribution (normal or lognormal distribution), so the measure can account for high probabilities for extreme events (fat tails) and returns that are skewed.

This measure only reports on the probability of a loss occurring in the relevant range but provides no information on the severity of the losses. The probability information can be used to weight the variance calculation, resulting in a statistic called *below target variance* (BTV) calculated as follows:

$$BTV = \int_{-\infty}^{T} (r - T)^2 f(r)dr \tag{9.14a}$$

A simple transformation yields a related measure called *below target risk* (BTR) calculated as:

$$BTR = \sqrt{BTV} \qquad (9.14b)$$

REVIEW OF THE CAPITAL ASSET PRICING MODEL

Investors can reduce the risk in a portfolio through diversification. To demonstrate this effect, the standard deviation was calculated on monthly returns on Intel, General Motors, Fannie Mae, and Merck from 1990 through March 2001. The standard deviation of returns on the four stocks was 42 percent, 31 percent, 25 percent, and 27 percent, respectively. The simple average of these measures was 32 percent. But when the returns were combined into portfolios, the standard deviation of return declined to 21 percent.

Investors can continue this diversification by adding additional issues and weighting the portfolio differently. Because this method of risk reduction is so readily available, investment theorists argue that the market does not compensate for this type of risk.

Risk that cannot be diversified is called *systematic risk*. A portfolio can invest in a riskless asset (U.S. Treasury bills) and assets that contain some amounts of this systematic risk. The more of this risk assumed, the higher the expected return on the portfolio.

The relationship is expressed mathematically as:

$$R_{\text{Portfolio}} = R_{\text{Risk-free}} + \beta * \left[E\left(R_{\text{Market}} - R_{\text{Risk-free}} \right) \right] \qquad (9.15)$$

$$\text{where } \beta = \frac{\text{Cov}_{R_{\text{Market}}, R_{\text{Portfolio}}}}{\text{Var}_{R_{\text{Market}}}}$$

The expected return on a portfolio is the return on a risk-free portfolio plus an incremental amount proportional to the risk. This simplifies to:

$$Y = a + bX \qquad (9.16)$$

This market line defines the parameter called *beta*.[13] Beta measures the risk of a hedge fund relative to the benchmark. To measure beta properly, the regression compares the amount the hedge fund exceeds the risk-free rate versus how much the market portfolio (i.e., the benchmark) exceeds the risk-free rate. For our use with hedge funds, the beta measures how fast the return on the hedge fund goes up or down together with returns in the market.

MEASURES OF RISK-ADJUSTED RETURN

Hedge fund investors prefer a fund with a higher return to a fund with a lower return, if everything else is equal between the two funds. Similarly, nearly all hedge fund investors[14] would prefer a fund with lower risk (however defined) to a fund with higher risk if everything else about the funds (including the level of returns) is equal.

The Sharpe ratio is named for William F. Sharpe, who developed the Capital Asset Pricing Model (CAPM). The index reduces the returns by the risk-free rate, then divides this excess return by the standard deviation of return:

$$\text{Sharpe Ratio} = \frac{\text{Return}_{\text{Actual}} - \text{Return}_{\text{Risk-free}}}{\text{Standard Deviation}_{\text{Return}}} \qquad (9.17)$$

The Sharpe ratio is a measure of the trade-off between return *(ex post)* and the risk the investor was exposed to in order to earn that return.

The Sortino ratio, named after Frank A. Sortino, modifies the Sharpe ratio by substituting downside deviation for the standard deviation:

$$\text{Sortino Ratio} = \frac{\text{Return}_{\text{Actual}} - \text{Return}_{\text{Risk-free}}}{\text{Downside Deviation}_{\text{Return}}} \qquad (9.18)$$

Practitioners sometimes call the downside deviation "bad risk" to distinguish volatility caused by losses from volatility caused by positive returns. The Sortino ratio is, then, a Sharpe ratio that substitutes bad risk for total risk in the denominator.

The Treynor ratio, named after Jack Treynor, also resembles the Sharpe ratio. However, instead of the standard deviation as a measure of risk in the denominator, this indicator uses the portfolio beta:

$$\text{Treynor Ratio} = T = \frac{\text{Return}_{\text{Actual}} - \text{Return}_{\text{Risk-free}}}{\text{Beta}} \quad (9.19)$$

$$\text{Absolute Risk-Adjusted Return} = T + \text{Return}_{\text{Risk-free}}$$

The beta only accounts for the systematic risk in the portfolio (although the unsystematic risk may not be completely diversified away). Differences between the Treynor ratio and the Sharpe ratio reflect the presence of unsystematic or diversifiable risk in the portfolio (often considered desirable in a hedge fund portfolio).

Jensen's alpha is named for Michael C. Jensen and measures the extent that performance exceeds the return expected for the amount of risk assumed:

$$\text{Jensen's Alpha} = \text{Return}_{\text{Portfolio}} - \text{Expected Return} \quad (9.20)$$

$$\text{Expected Return} = \text{Return}_{\text{Risk-free}} + \text{Beta}_{\text{Portfolio}} \times$$
$$(\text{Return}_{\text{Market}} - \text{Return}_{\text{Risk-free}})$$

Although frequently used in hedge fund due diligence reports, the alpha is only relevant if there is a benchmark that the fund should be expected to track. If the fund being measured seeks to generate absolute returns, standard benchmarks (stock indices or interest rates) are not appropriate. If, however, there are many hedge funds following the same style, the market portfolio could be viewed as a composite of their returns (perhaps as published in one of the hedge fund databases, such as HFR, Hennessey, CSFB/Tremont, or Zurich/MAR).

R² VERSUS A BENCHMARK

It is often important to measure how closely a fund tracks a benchmark. Most funds seek to not track a benchmark. Diversification to reduce risk is most effective when the returns on the assets do not track each other. For these funds, a low R^2 is desirable. For others, it might be desirable for a particular fund to track a hedge fund performance series. In this case, a high R^2 is desirable.

To calculate this parameter, the regression from the capital market line can be used. It is also possible to regress the fund return against the market return without netting out the risk-free rate. The regression coefficients will not match the capital market line but the R^2 should be the same. For that matter, with a 2 variable regression (1 dependent and 1 independent), the R^2 is equivalent to the correlation (although it is necessary to square the correlation to match R^2).

OTHER STATISTICS

There are many other ways to describe hedge fund returns. The average return, standard deviation, and variations on these statistics assume returns are normally distributed. If that were true, then the moments of the return distribution (mean, standard deviation, skewness, etc.) should describe the pattern completely. To the extent that returns do not accurately match model distributions, other statistics help in comparing hedge fund returns.

Measuring Drawdown

Drawdown measures the maximum loss (in percent) from any possible starting point and any subsequent NAV. In practice, the maximum loss always occurs from a local high-water mark. To calculate the maximum drawdown, first calculate the high-water mark for the period using month-end values. This high-water mark should be cumulative over the range of performance studied. A high-water mark in previous years is often replaced with a new, higher high point over time (but the previous points are not discarded). The drawdown for each month is the change from the high-water mark. Finally, each monthly drawdown is reviewed and the maximum loss is recorded.

The purpose of the drawdown calculation is to study characteristics of a hedge fund return not described by the average and standard deviation. If the return of all hedge funds were drawn from a normal distribution, this statistic would be irrelevant. Any difference in drawdown not explained by the mean and standard deviation (and perhaps higher moments such as kurtosis) would be due to sample bias.

It is widely believed that returns are not normally distributed. Measures such as the drawdown percent study differences between hedge fund returns that may not be measured with standard statistical and financial methods.

Several related calculations are often presented along with the drawdown percent. The first is the number of months in drawdown. This calculation seeks to give an idea of how much of the time the fund NAV is below the rolling high-water mark. The second related calculation estimates the number of months required to recover from a drawdown. This measure captures how swiftly a fund recovers from a drawdown. The advantage of these two statistics over the drawdown calculation is that these numbers are based on multiple drawdowns, not just the worst drawdown.

Percent Winning Months

The frequency of gain provides an alternative measure of risk. The percent winning months statistic measures the number of months the fund provides a positive return as a percent of all months in the historical series. This measure ignores the magnitude of individual monthly returns and focuses only on the frequency of positive and negative returns. This statistic can be used to derive other statistics, such as the probability of a loss.

Largest Monthly Gain/Loss

Measures of the largest monthly gain and largest monthly loss capture whether the tail of the probability distribution differs from the normal distribution. In comparing two funds with similar returns, investors should prefer the fund with smaller extreme losses. Investors may prefer a fund that has produced spectacularly high returns in the past, perhaps attaching optionlike value to the pattern of return. Conversely, some investors may choose to discount average returns that include extremely positive data points on the basis that these extreme outcomes are not likely repeatable.

Risk of Loss

Risk of loss can be calculated in simple or sophisticated ways. It may be just another name for the statistic measuring the frequency of winning months, but risk of loss can incorporate substantially more information.

One way to generate a more interesting forecast for the risk of loss involves Monte Carlo simulation. A Monte Carlo simulation is a computer model designed to estimate probabilities of events that cannot be estimated directly.

A simple form of Monte Carlo is called *resampling*. Random draws of future returns are drawn from past returns. One notable advantage of this method is that the model makes no assumption about what distribution the returns follow.

If adequate data are not available, the Monte Carlo can add very little information about the frequency of loss. The Monte Carlo can offer insights on the chance of losses of a particular size. It is likely that this information could be discerned from the input data without a Monte Carlo.

When the Monte Carlo has access to significant data, the resampling can yield much more complete information about the frequency of losses and the distribution of returns of various magnitudes. For example, if daily returns are available, the technique can generate robust probabilities for a complete range of returns. Alternatively, monthly returns can be used to predict the probability of loss over 3 months or a year.

A substantially different method of estimating probabilities is related to the Value at Risk™ method of risk management. This method is explored in Chapter 13.

MEASURE WITH CARE

Performance measurement, including risk measurement, is one of the most important issues for investors. Many hedge funds have attractive returns and desirable risk characteristics. Investors are understandably hoping to identify the best funds for their specific investment situation.

Hedge fund investors use a variety of statistics to measure risk and return. Many of these indicators were first used in traditional asset management. Sometimes the traditional measures yield meaningless or misleading results. So, measure with care and use a combination of the traditional and new measures described in this chapter to evaluate and monitor performance.

NOTES

1. In addition, for each of the return methods described, the return relative can be calculated for that method.
2. In fact, the future values would be the same at every year along the way, too.
3. The symbol e is the mathematical constant equal to 2.718282.
4. It does not matter in what order the returns occur because of the associative law of multiplication: $(1.05) \times (1.10) = (1.10) \times (1.05)$, and so on.
5. Data from TASS.
6. The transformed NAV is the independent (Y) variable. It is convenient to use an integer count of months for the X value.
7. To extract the fitted growth rate, reverse the log function and subtract 1: $g = \exp(b) - 1$.
8. *AIMR Performance Presentation Standards™ Handbook,* Second Edition, 1997.
9. Disclosure Documents: A Guide for CPOs and CTAs, National Futures Association, pp. 12–13.
10. Disclosure Documents: A Guide for CPOs and CTAs, National Futures Association, pp. 13–14.
11. For option pricing and as inputs to many risk management models, for example.
12. See Christopher L. Culp, *The Risk Management Process,* Wiley, 2001, page 358.

13. Note that when an investment has an expected return that exceeds the amount predicted by the market line, this is often called alpha. This excess return is neither the *a* coefficient nor the deviation in the numerator of the market line.
14. It is conceivable that some investors would prefer that higher risk in the same way that buyers of lottery tickets accept a chance with negative expected value in return for a possibility of an extreme positive outcome.

CHAPTER 10

Legislation and Regulations Affecting Hedge Funds

The investment industry is highly regulated. Much of the regulation involves disclosure to the investor and to government agencies. Primarily designed to prevent securities fraud, hedge funds avoid much of the regulation by taking advantage of exemptions drafted in the same legislation that created the regulatory environment. The exemptions are based on the premise that sophisticated high net worth investors do not need protection.

This chapter reviews many of the laws and regulations affecting the investment industry and the extent to which each rule applies to hedge funds and, where possible, describes how hedge funds can gain exemption from the rules.

PARTNERSHIP CREATED AS A REGISTERED INVESTMENT

Before beginning a discussion about how to avoid key regulations, it is worth noting that it is possible to create a hedge fund as a registered investment company. The investment pool would file a prospectus with the Securities Exchange Commission (SEC) and provide a copy to each investor. The registration would require considerable disclosure to the investor and to regulators.

The investment manager could register as an investment advisor. The manager would file a Form ADV and periodic updates with the

SEC and would need to satisfy many disclosure requirements to investors.

The manager could also register with the Commodities Futures Trading Commission (CFTC) through the National Futures Association (NFA). The NFA would place specific disclosure requirements on the risk disclosure documents provided to investors. The registration would require the manager to deliver detailed reports to investors on a timely basis and file audited statements annually with the NFA and the CFTC.

These registrations would not prohibit most activities of the hedge fund. In many cases, the disclosure requirements are not substantially greater than disclosure demanded by investors.[1] Fees typical for a hedge fund would appear to be out of line with other registered investment products, however.

While there have been few registered limited partnerships, there is reason to believe this type of business will be more common in the future. Hybrid funds that combine the investment strategies of hedge funds but satisfy registration requirements of mutual funds may offer hedge-fund-like returns to investors who do not qualify as hedge fund investors. For some types of hedge fund strategies, there is no reason to deny access to investors with modest portfolios or less investment expertise.

SECURITIES ACT OF 1933

The Securities Act of 1933 (the 1933 Act) created a registration requirement under Section 5. Securities that do not qualify for exemption from the registration requirement must be registered with the Securities Exchange Commission. An elaborate risk disclosure document called a *prospectus* is filed with the SEC and given to all investors before they invest in the securities. Details of the registered security are in the permanent public record.

Securities that are not registered under the 1933 Act are called *private placements*. The label "private placement" is usually reserved for unregistered stock and bond investments, but hedge funds use the same exemption to avoid registration requirements. Exemption from registration is granted through Rule 506 Regulation D. The exemption allows investment products that will be sold to no more than 35 nonaccredited[2] investors to avoid the registration requirements of Section 5 of the 1933 Act.

The exemption also relieves the issuer from substantially all disclosure requirements if all investors are accredited investors. However, if the list of investors includes one or more nonaccredited investors, the disclosure requirements are the same as for registered securities.

The exemption from Section 5 registration requires that the issuer or underwriter may not advertise the offering. This requirement is generally held to apply to telephone marketing by the hedge fund sponsor. This is a gray area, but many fund managers will market only to potential investors that have independently requested information about the fund(s).

The 1933 Act does not limit the number of investors to 99 or fewer. This requirement has generally been applied to private placements. Until recently, hedge funds limited their distribution to no more than 99 investors. This second limit, however, comes from language in the Investment Company Act of 1940 (the 1940 Act).

INVESTMENT COMPANY ACT OF 1940

Section 3(c)1 of the 1940 Act allows for exemptions from registration required elsewhere in the Act. The investment must be sold to no more than 99 investors, which are counted according to rules established by the SEC. Naturally, individuals count as beneficial owners. However, an individual who invests directly and as beneficiary of a trust would count only once.

An institution may count as one investor or multiple investors. Integration rules monitor whether the investor in the fund holds more than 10 percent of its investments in the hedge fund and whether the investor holds more than 10 percent of the capital of the hedge fund. If both situations exist, the hedge fund must count each of the investors in the investing entity as separate investors in the hedge fund. Where multiple partnerships have been created to invest in nearly identical assets, the SEC may argue that investors in the multiple partnerships be accumulated to qualify for the Section 3(c)1 exemption.

To qualify for the exemption, the investment must not be offered to the general public. This means that details of the offering should not be disseminated broadly. To substantiate compliance, documents describing the investment are usually numbered and a record is kept of where each copy is delivered. The exemption requires also that the investment be sold to accredited investors. In practice, up to 65 percent of the investors (100 percent minus 35 percent) must qualify with adequate wealth or income.

The National Securities Market Improvement Act of 1996 created an additional exemption to the 1940 Act. The Act created a new Section 3(c)7 to supplement the provisions of 3(c)1. With the new exemption, a private placement can have up to 500 investors. However, each of the investors must be "qualified purchasers." These investors must be individuals or families having investments totaling $5 million, plus certain investment advisors, trusts, and companies with $25 million that are composed entirely of qualified purchasers.

The legislation made provisions for partnerships exempt under 3(c)1 to convert their exemption to the 3(c)7 standard. For many funds that rely on the 3(c)7 exemptions, the minimum size for investment does not affect the fund's ability to raise money. Instead, administrative issues dictate the minimum investment.

TAXPAYER RELIEF ACT OF 1997

The Taxpayer Relief Act of 1997 (TRA 97) included many provisions that do not affect hedge funds. In addition, TRA 97 made it easier for managers to run an offshore fund.

Domestic hedge fund managers need to be fairly certain that a fund established outside the United States will not be taxed as a U.S. business. If nearly all the administration of the business occurs within the United States, it is possible that the IRS would claim that the offshore fund was really a domestic organization. If that were to occur, foreign investors could be subject to backup withholding (up to 30 percent at present). Depending on local tax laws and treaties, this levy could amount to additional taxation. It is also possible that the entire business, which is generally a corporation, could be subject to corporate income taxes, creating an additional layer of taxation.

To clarify the requirements for tax treatment as an offshore fund, the IRS created a list of 10 Commandments that, if observed, allowed the offshore fund to confidently avoid being treated as a U.S. organization for tax purposes. The rules were included in Internal Revenue Code (IRC) 864.

TRA 97 repealed the 10 Commandments. While the act did not completely eliminate the need for offshore administrative support, it did simplify the requirements and eliminate some of the need to create organizations to satisfy the letter of the IRC requirements.

INVESTMENT ADVISORS ACT OF 1940

The Investment Advisors Act of 1940 created the regulation mechanism to monitor and oversee money managers. The Act contains provisions for record keeping, reporting, advertising, registration, and administration, and prohibits certain types of transactions.

The record-keeping requirements control the custody of client securities. The manager must segregate client positions so that creditors of the investment manager do not have legal claim to the securities in the event of default by the manager.

The record-keeping requirements also establish compliance procedures. These compliance procedures are a series of internal procedures designed to ensure that the manager and its employees comply with securities laws both when operating as an employee of the manager and when trading securities in their personal accounts.

The Act requires the manager to report to investors. The Act, together with the SEC, which enforces the Act, defines specific reporting requirements, including the content and frequency of reports to investors.

Managers must also report to the SEC. In addition to investment performance, the information provided to the SEC documents details of the staff, investment procedures, and operations.

The SEC has deferred to industry to establish detailed performance reporting requirements. The agency has made it clear that the independent Association for Investment Management and Research (AIMR) standards are acceptable as a minimum standard for performance measurement.

The Act established a list of prohibited transactions. A manager is not allowed to front run an order for an investment client. Front running involves buying or selling a security in a personal account or another client's account in advance of a known order in the firm. Instead, the manager needs to create an allocation procedure to distribute the transactions fairly. The Act also defines limits on soft dollar transactions. These arrangements provide for a broker to buy or pay for products and services used by the investment manager and to be reimbursed by commissions collected from the clients of the manager. Such transactions are limited to products or services that directly benefit the investment clients. Because the agreements shift some of the costs of providing investment management onto the clients (in addition to explicit fees), the agreements must be disclosed to the clients.

Registered investment advisors must file Form ADV to comply with the Advisors Act. The current form on the SEC website is more than 80 pages (including instructions), but much of the information is very basic. Online reporting has recently simplified the filing procedure somewhat.

The Form ADV requires advisors to describe details of their advisory service, disclose fees of all types, describe their clients, and describe the types of investments and strategies employed, and it must include an audited balance sheet.

The SEC will audit each registered manager. The audit reviews record-keeping procedures, compliance, and other requirements.

Exemption to the Investment Advisors Act is provided in Section 203(b)(3) of the Act. Registration is not required for managers with fewer than 15 clients. The typical hedge fund counts as one client for a manager, so most hedge fund managers are not required to register under the Act.

In return for the exemption, managers cannot advertise their services as investment managers. There is no clear definition of what constitutes advertising, although some believe that merely providing data to hedge fund databases constitutes advertising because the information is readily made available to potential investors. A no-action letter from the SEC to one data provider suggests that the SEC does not intend to restrict this type of disclosure. Many believe that unsolicited telephone calls made by a manager or one of its agents does constitute advertising. Managers may respond freely to clients that request information, providing printed marketing material and promotional presentations.

The Act established documentation and record-keeping requirements and requires annual surprise audits of securities positions by an independent certified public accountant.

Despite the exemption from registration, the general partner of a hedge fund is deemed to have custody and physical possession of client securities. The general partner is responsible for the securities even if a third-party custodian holds the securities. Therefore, the manager must provide for segregation of fund positions, maintain adequate records, and is subject to verification.

EMPLOYEE RETIREMENT INCOME SECURITY ACT OF 1974

The Employee Retirement Income Security Act of 1974 (ERISA) applies when 25 percent of the fund capital is derived from employee benefit plans. Most hedge funds are not affected by ERISA. In fact, fund documents often grant general partners power to return investments to investors if there is danger that ERISA provisions will apply to the fund.

If the fund does maintain ERISA assets above 25 percent of capital, the assets in the fund are considered plan assets, which means that the fund must comply with the provisions of ERISA. It establishes the fund manager as a fiduciary and imposes higher standards of care. In addition, certain transactions and certain fee structures are not allowed.

COMMODITIES EXCHANGE ACT OF 1936 (AMENDED IN 1974)

The Commodities Exchange Act required an industry self-regulating body be created to implement provisions of the Act and to regulate many types of commodity activities.

The NFA was created to act as the industry self-regulating organization. Although nominally independent of the CFTC, in practice, the two groups work closely together. Hedge funds primarily have contact with and disclosure requirements to the NFA.

The NFA imposes performance disclosure requirements, requires audited financial statements annually, and requires additional disclosure on NFA forms. In addition, the NFA controls the content of many documents provided to investors, including risk disclosure documents and marketing literature. The NFA also conducts periodic audits of fund documents.

Hedge fund managers must register as a commodity pool operator (CPO) if the fund trades futures, futures options or cash, and forward commodity contracts. While exemptions do exist, the thresholds (size of pool, number of investors in the pool, and the percentage of business conducted in futures) are very small. Very few hedge funds are exempt if they use futures at all.

Some commodity pools are not hedge funds. These funds invest almost exclusively in futures products (including options on futures). There are also hedge funds that are not commodity pools. For example, an equity hedge fund that makes no use of futures would not be considered a commodity pool and would not need to register with the NFA. To complicate matters, many hedge funds are considered commodity pools by the CFTC and the NFA but are viewed as hedge funds by fund managers, investors, and outside observers.

UNRELATED BUSINESS TAXABLE INCOME

Not-for-profit entities may invest in hedge funds. Pension plans and university endowments are two common tax-exempt organizations that invest in hedge funds. Typical investment strategies often create unrelated business taxable income (UBTI).

Investment income is generally not taxable for an exempt organization. However, if the tax-exempt organization tries to shelter otherwise taxable business income unrelated to the purposes of the tax-exempt organization, the IRS does tax the unrelated income. Although hedge fund returns closely resemble other types of investment returns, leverage used by the hedge fund frequently triggers UBTI.

Taxes on hedge fund income reduce the attractiveness of hedge funds for tax-exempt organizations. Hedge funds that use little or no leverage are more attractive for pension funds and endowments.

BLUE SKY LAWS

Designed to protect investors, state laws that regulate investments and investment companies are often called *blue sky laws*. Strong federal regulation is designed to replace a patchwork of different rules across the United States. There has been considerable reform in state regulations and there is considerable uniformity between states. In particular for hedge funds, most states recognize the exemptions to registration under the 1933 and 1940 Acts. In addition, most states do not require an investment company to register in the state if there are six or fewer investors from that state in the fund.

Hedge funds should file Form U-2 Uniform Consent to Service of Process in the state of each investor in the fund. The form is a commitment to comply with state laws concerning the registration and sale of securities. In addition, the manager grants jurisdiction to state authorities as if the fund had operations in the state. The same U-2 form is accepted in 53 regions including most states, the District of Columbia, and several U.S. protectorates.

RISK DISCLOSURE

Several regulatory bodies require managers to provide specific risk disclosure to potential investors. The SEC, the CFTC, the NFA, the Financial Accounting Standards Board (FASB), the Association of Independent Certified Public Accountants (AICPA), and the Association of Investment Management and Research (AIMR) all stipulate content of risk disclosure documents. The FASB is considered the most authoritative source for standards. The AICPA guidelines apply mostly to accounting documents and to accounting content in legal documents.

AIMR requirements pertain primarily to the performance information contained in risk disclosure documents. For many organizations, performance of multiple accounts must be combined to calculate representative performance. The guidelines document how performance on individual accounts should be combined to form a benchmark. The AIMR requires that the manager disclose the type and size of fees whether or not performance is reported net of fees. It requires the manager to disclose the extent of leverage and the use of derivatives. It also requires that the manager disclose any material change in personnel that has occurred during or since the performance period.

In addition to specific disclosure requirements, common legal standards demand substantial risk disclosure. In particular, the content of legal risk disclosure documents must comply with antifraud provisions. Extensive risk disclosure can also minimize the damage from civil litigation. Much of the required content would be included in risk disclosure documents even if the statutory requirements were eased.

REPORTING REQUIREMENTS

The ongoing reporting requirements (to investors and others) are extensive even for funds granted exemptions from the main securities acts. Most hedge funds must publish a condensed schedule of investments that should show both geographical and industry concentrations. It need not show actual positions. However, if a position is greater than 5 percent of assets, the fund should disclose the issuer. Hedge funds sometimes find this requirement unacceptable. Information about large positions is generally a closely guarded secret. When funds refuse to comply, auditors may issue a qualified audit opinion.

The fund should publish a statement of assets and liabilities, a statement of operations, a statement of change in partnership capital, and a statement of cash flows. Typical disclosure includes descriptive footnotes that should describe the structure of the business organization, disclose significant accounting policies and allocation methodologies, list related parties, describe the risk of off-balance-sheet items, describe the methods used to determine fair value, and disclose derivatives positions.

Additional supplemental material is generally provided. The manager of the fund writes a letter to investors monthly or quarterly. The manager usually discloses a capital statement to investors. The CFTC requires that funds it oversees must maintain a schedule of capital. Usually, the partnership agreements require a similar schedule even for unregulated funds.

The CFTC has additional record-keeping requirements for hedge funds that must register as a CPO. The managers must maintain a detailed trade blotter. They should maintain a ledger of all cash movements. They should provide results to investors within 30 days of each reporting period, including gains and losses, fees, commissions, other expenses, net income, capital transactions, and net asset value (NAV).

These disclosure rules are included in Sections 4.21, 4.22(a)–(d), 4.23, 4.24, 4.25, and 4.26 of the CFTC Act. Partial relief is available in Section 4.7 of the Act. Section 4.7 does not eliminate disclosure requirements. However, disclosure can be quarterly rather than monthly.

To take the Section 4.7 election, all investors in the fund must be qualified eligible participants (QEPs). A QEP may be an individual with $2 million in investments or $200,000 in margin (or a combination), certain organizations with $5 million in assets, accredited individuals or organizations (under SEC Regulation D, Rule 501), or offshore individuals or organizations.

Under certain conditions, the CFTC may deem the general partner to have both custody and possession of investment assets. Under these circumstances, the CFTC imposes more stringent record keeping. In addition, the manager/fund is subject to a periodic securities count.

The AIMR standards for performance are the de facto minimum standards for calculating and disclosing performance. Although the SEC has not officially adopted the standards, through a series of no-action letters, it has communicated that it is content with the standards.

The AIMR standards are detailed and lengthy. They require that fees should be included in performance calculations. Returns should include realized gains and losses. Returns over multiple periods should be time-weighted averages. Support for return calculations must be retained and available for display. The AIMR has rules for combining multiple accounts into a fair index. Finally, the AIMR requires funds to show a minimum of 10 years of performance data. For funds having less than 10 years of returns, all returns available must be published.

Two source documents from the AICPA impose reporting requirements on hedge funds. The AICPA Investment Company Audit Guide applies to all audited hedge funds. The AICPA Audit Guide for Commodity Pools applies to audited hedge funds that have registered with the NFA and the CFTC.

ESTABLISHING FAIR VALUE

Many different methods are used to establish value for published reports. Some instruments are listed and trade on an exchange, including common stocks that trade on the New York Stock Exchange or American Stock Exchange, most futures contracts, and exchange-traded puts and calls.

The fund may value these assets in a number of different ways; however, it must use the method consistently. It may use the daily last price or closing price; it may price long positions at the bid price at the time of close and short positions at the ask price at the time of close; it may average the bid and ask to create a midprice. Other methods to determine price to reflect large blocks, illiquidity, and other factors may also be used.

A second group of securities trades actively over the counter. Thus, although there is no organized exchange, an active group of market makers creates a market. Examples include Nasdaq stocks and U.S. Treasury securities. A fund can use price quotes from Nasdaq data feeds and quotes from market makers. Although there may be no single settlement price, a fund can use bid and offer prices or midmarket prices. Many government securities dealers price all U.S. Treasury notes, bonds, and bills at a consistent time daily. It is important that the fund apply a consistent methodology for pricing over-the-counter assets.

Some assets must be valued in good faith by the manager. There may be no available price for private equity issues, derivative securities, and real estate. In such cases, the directors of the fund must establish a method. Some derivatives dealers provide routine mark to market values for trades they originate. In other cases, reasonable methods must be created that approximate the same standard of fairness as for exchange-traded assets.

There is some relief for valuing short-term assets. The fund is not a money market mutual fund with a fixed net asset value equal to $1, however, so the shortcut applies only to instruments less than 60 days to maturity. For such assets, it is generally acceptable to approximate the value from cost information. Using yield mathematics appropriate for the instrument, the security can be repriced using the purchase yield.[3]

Most fixed-income securities other than U.S. Treasury securities (primarily corporate and municipal bonds) create a different problem. Although the bonds trade over the counter like Nasdaq stocks and government bonds, there are countless issues. Many issues are not regularly traded. Dealers can nevertheless provide actual bids or fair valuation of individual issues. Commercial services price individual issues on demand using specific details (coupon, maturity, call features) and general information (yield spread over Treasury issues, liquidity premium, etc). These methods can be reasonably accurate if the pricing factors are kept up-to-date.

STATUS AS INVESTOR OR TRADER

An investment fund can either be considered an investor or a trader. Regardless of any connotations about holding period, investment objective, or even investment style, the classification can have significant consequences to fund investors.

Suppose that the Internal Revenue Service (IRS) considers the fund to be only an investor instead of a business actively engaged in a trade. In this situation, many expenses for the fund are not included in the income statement of the fund. For a fund with leverage, interest expense would be included on the fund return. Other expenses (notably fees) would not be deducted. The income allocated to investors could be described as gross income.

The expenses not allowed on the partnership (or limited liability corporation) tax return get allocated separately to the investors. These expenses would appear on individual 1040 returns as miscellaneous itemized deductions. These deductions are only allowed to the extent that they exceed 2 percent of adjusted gross income. Further, itemized deductions are reduced for individuals with high incomes. As a result, they are not fully deductible for most investors.

The deductions are disallowed or reduced by some states. For example, in New York State, deductions can be reduced by up to 50 percent. Illinois income tax is a flat tax that would tax the gross return without reduction for the expenses.

Net losses in the hedge fund would probably be considered passive. The limitations on passive losses were designed to prevent abusive tax shelters. The hedge fund investor without sufficient passive income (other hedge fund returns or passive real estate returns) may discover that a real loss cannot be used to offset other taxable gains.

If the fund is considered a business (i.e., a trader), then all expenses are allowed on the partnership return. The return allocated to investors is truly a net return. In most cases, this means that investors will not be allocated expenses to be reported as itemized deductions. In addition, hedge fund returns should be considered active, that is, not limited by the passive loss rules.

There are limitations on interest expenses that exceed investment income, whether the fund is treated as an investor or a trader. If the fund is treated as a trader, the excess interest expense is allocated to individual investors. The expense, however, can be reported as a business or trade expense and remains deductible.

Quite a few court cases have reviewed the question of whether a partnership was an investor or a trader. The facts of the cases and issues do not provide a clear answer. A fund that has a business purpose and made money (or at least expected to make money) distances itself from tax shelters organized specifically for tax avoidance. The courts have looked at the turnover rate and the number of trades. It would be constructive if the fund manager actively made trading decisions that did not resemble prearranged trades with convenient tax consequences. It would be damaging if the fund did not have substantial economic risk. In some cases, it may be relevant whether income came primarily from gains and losses or interest and dividends.

FOREIGN PARTNERS IN A PARTNERSHIP

Foreign partners in a U.S. partnership do not want to be taxed as a U.S. investor. If the fund is considered a dealer (not a very typical situation), it is likely that the fund would be considered actively engaged in a trade. As such, the foreign partner's participation would be taxable as if the investor were a U.S. investor, because that participation would carry with it a proportional share of the active engagement. In this situation, the foreign partner would be subject to both withholding (up to 30 percent) and taxation.

More typically, a hedge fund is not considered actively engaged in a business or trade. In this case, the offshore investor is still subject to withholding. The foreigner's home tax policy and tax treaties between the two nations determine the actual tax paid. In practice, most offshore investors do not invest in U.S. domiciled funds.

HOT ISSUES ALLOCATIONS

Hedge funds can purchase initial public offerings (IPOs) of common stock. When the initial offering is fully subscribed and is expected to open above the offering price, the issue is called a *hot issue*. National Association of Securities Dealers (NASD) dealers are not allowed to sell hot issues to NASD members or to parties related to the transaction. This limitation was created with Article III of the NASD Rules of Fair Practices.

Partners who are ineligible to participate in the IPO are called *restricted partners*. They may not participate in a deal. The fund, however, may participate if it allocates the returns of the hot allocation using special rules. These special allocations ensure that restricted partners do not participate in the offering.

To accomplish the special allocation, the hot issues may be placed in a special account. The position may not affect the net asset value of the fund. The fund must develop special fee provisions to account for the different treatment of partners.

SIDE-POCKET ALLOCATIONS

Side-pocket allocations work much like hot issue allocations, albeit for different reasons. Side-pocket allocations are holdings of illiquid or hard-to-value investments that are held in separate accounts. The ownership allocation is not adjusted as investors enter or exit the fund. An exiting investor usually may not liquidate the side-pocket allocation until the assets are sold and the proceeds disbursed. Similarly, a new investor acquires no ownership in the established allocation for this group of assets.

Typically, there is no interim mark to market on side-pocket allocations. When valuation is difficult to establish, this may be the only realistic alternative. However, if some portion of assets is not marked to market, investors have less information about the value of their investment. Also, when part of the portfolio is not revalued, it is impossible to fairly calculate measures of risk such as volatility and Sharpe ratios.

OFFSHORE ISSUES

United Kingdom

If a fund has a substantial investment made by investors from the United Kingdom, tax issues of those investors may become relevant to the fund. For a foreign fund, investors are not taxed on undistributed income or gains. The UK investors have a capital gain exemption of £6,800 per year. In addition, so-called taper relief provides for lower rates for investments held for at least 3 years.

Funds that distribute 85 percent or more of their income are considered distributing funds. These funds share the favorable treatment of gains. For funds that do not qualify as distributing funds, such gains are taxed as ordinary income and do not qualify for either benefit.

Germany

There are three classifications of offshore funds in Germany. The category known as high-level funds or white funds are either registered in Germany or are listed on a German exchange and have a German fiscal agent. These funds are, in general, not treated differently from German domestic funds. In particular, they are taxed the same way as local funds. Most income and gains are not taxed until the returns are distributed to investors.

The second category of German hedge funds is called medium level. This type of fund has a German fiscal agent and complies with the German reporting requirements. Investors in medium-level funds pay taxes on distributions as well as "deemed" distributions, which include fund income and recognized capital gains.

The third category is called low level, a group that includes all funds not classified as high level or medium level. Investors are taxed on actual distributions and 90 percent of gains in NAV, which include unrecognized gains and losses.

Australia

Investors in hedge funds domiciled in Australia are taxed up to 47 percent on income and gains that are distributed but are not taxed on undistributed recognized income. When the investors redeem their investment, they receive favorable tax treatment on the appreciation.

Investors in offshore funds are taxed on the distributions up to 47 percent. Investors can receive credit for foreign taxes paid. Investors are also taxed on undistributed income and capital gains. When investors redeem their offshore investment, they also receive favorable tax treatment on the appreciation.

BEST PRACTICES

A hedge fund should employ adequate legal support either within or outside the fund to ensure that the fund operates in compliance with laws and regulations. As obvious as this sounds, the task of complying is significant and many funds start up with minimal support.

In light of lawsuits following the 1998 default on Russian securities and complications caused by termination provisions and margin rules, an industry committee recommended[4] that legal staff closely review terms of contracts, looking for consistency and seeking to avoid nonstandard or ambiguous provisions.

The committee recommended[5] that fund managers should review the filing requirements for compliance with securities laws and regulations. Tasks should explicitly be assigned to employees with accountability to ensure timely compliance.

The committee also recommended[6] that funds should adopt employee compliance procedures to assure conformity with a fund's employee compliance rules. The fund's compliance rules should document confidentiality rules, trading rules, and rules limiting the flow of information within the fund and should require employees to comply with securities laws.

NOTES

1. Some hedge funds provide much less detail than would be required by a mutual fund; for example, funds that use futures must make all the disclosures required by the CFTC. Also, investors typically demand audited financial statements even when regulators do not.
2. An accredited investor is an individual with $1 million net worth or income exceeding $200,000 per year for 2 years or certain business entities with at least $5 million in assets.
3. See SEC Rule 2 A-7.
4. *Sound Practices for Hedge Fund Managers,* February 2000, paragraph 28; available at http://planethedgefund.com/articles/Sound_Practices. doc.
5. Ibid., paragraph 33.
6. Ibid., paragraph 34.

CHAPTER 11

Accounting for Hedge Funds

Accounting has been called the language of business. Because hedge fund performance is relatively easy to measure and because both investors and managers are intensely interested in the return, accounting is a very important function provided by the hedge fund manager.

Hedge fund managers follow the same accounting rules and conventions as manufacturers and retailers. Hedge funds have (like most businesses) several unique transactions and somewhat unique reporting requirements that necessitate some specialized accounting methods. This chapter reviews how standard accounting methods are adapted to measure hedge fund performance.

This text does not attempt to teach accounting to readers who have not previously been exposed to the material. Neither does it prepare the reader to discuss critically topics of accounting theory, Financial Accounting Standards (FAS) rulings, or audit techniques. Rather, the chapter offers a general review of accounting and shows how basic accounting entries can be used to accomplish recurring specialized reporting for hedge funds. Chapter 12 discusses basic allocation schemes for reporting results to investors.

REVIEW OF DOUBLE ENTRY BOOKKEEPING

Double entry bookkeeping requires all entries to be made with matching debits and credits. By convention, debits are displayed in a column offset to the left of credits. All entries are posted as positive

TABLE 11.1   T-Account Entries for Stock Purchase

1000 Cash		1500 XYZ Common	
3/17/01		3/17/01	$50,125.45

numbers. Applying conventional mathematical standards, credits would be positive numbers and debits would be negative (or vice versa). In practice, accounting programs frequently maintain separate fields for debits and credits so that it is possible to display negative debits (an overdrawn checking account, for example) or credits (such as negative net worth).

Debits and credits may be demonstrated in two ways. Textbooks show T-accounts, which emphasize the debit/credit system. Table 11.1 shows T-accounts of a purchase of 2,000 shares of XYZ common stock on 3/17/01. A shorter way to represent the same transaction is shown in Table 11.2. An even shorter form that emphasizes the pairing of debits and credits is shown as Table 11.3. This form has the disadvantage of not handling postings with multiple debits or credits.

As can be seen in the tables, one or more debit entries are associated with one or more credit entries. This collection of debit(s) and credit(s) is called a *posting*. Basic accounting rules demand that the sum of all debits equals the sum of all credits in that posting. Because each posting requires debits to equal credits, the sum of all debits posted also must equal the sum of all credits. If they do not, the books are out of balance or "out."

TABLE 11.2   Journal Entries for Stock Purchase

Date	Account	Debit Amount	Credit Amount
3/17/01	1000	$50,125.45	
3/17/01	1500		$50,125.45

TABLE 11.3 Compact Journal Entries for Stock Purchase

Date	Debit Account	Debit Amount	Credit Account	Credit Amount
3/17/01	1000	$50,125.45	1500	$50,125.45

The debits or credits are accumulated in accounts such as Cash, Travel Expenses, and Paid-in Capital. These accounts are classified as (1) income, (2) expense, (3) asset, (4) liability, or (5) equity.

In the foregoing example, the number 1000 was associated with the cash account and 1500 was assigned to the stock position. In the that scheme, accounts 1000–1999 might be reserved for assets, 2000–2999 for liabilities, 3000–3999 for expenses, 4000–4999 for income, and 5000–5999 for equity accounts. It is useful to subdivide the categories further so that similar types of expenses have neighboring numbers. This simplifies the effort to organize the data into neat reports. Also, repo interest expense may be 3525 and reverse repo interest income could be 4525 (or any other pattern) to make the scheme easier to recall.

In the foregoing example, it also might be useful to use multiple account numbers to carry details otherwise not available with double entry bookkeeping. For example, if a single account, 1500, is used for all issues of common stock, the books will fairly represent the position. However, if 1500 is assigned to one issue, 1510 to a second, and so forth, the general ledger program will keep track of historical cost for each position. However, this detail may still not be sufficient if the fund acquires multiple positions in issues and needs to preserve the cost of individual lots. In this case, extra ledgers (often just Excel worksheets) called subledgers can carry this additional information. The advantage of special purpose software designed for hedge funds is that much of that subledger detail and extensive reporting is integrated into the general ledger software and works from a single data source.

Income accounts and expense accounts are subtotaled on a report called an *income statement*. Despite the discipline of double entry bookkeeping, income and expenses are generally not equal. Net income is calculated to force the debits (generally the expenses) to equal the credits (mostly income accounts). To keep the system in balance, the net income (loss) is treated like a debit (credit) and the offsetting entry is an increase (decrease) in net worth.

Asset, liability, and equity accounts are subtotaled on a report called a *statement of position* or *balance sheet*. The sum of the debits should match the sum of the credits (when a credit offsetting the net income is included).

An income statement accumulates income and expense entries during a range of time. It measures flows through the ledger system over time. In contrast, a balance sheet measures the assets, liabilities, and equity (cumulatively since inception) at a particular point in time.

Certain entries do not correspond with a specific transaction. For example, a bond earns interest every day. Generally, the amount is not posted until the payment date (monthly for mortgage-based issues and semiannually for most other U.S. fixed-income assets). When income and balance sheets are produced, it is important to accrue part of that income. In this case, a credit for a portion of the income is posted as an accrued asset. This accrual account resembles a receivable, except that the accrual is not legally payable at the time the statements are produced.

Accruals can (and should) be used to allocate lumpy costs more evenly over the year. For example, large expenses such as annual audit fees can be accrued monthly (or even daily).[1] A debit for the expense is posted with a credit to a balance sheet account called an *accrued expense*. Despite the name, it is really a liability used to store the expense until it is actually paid. When the fee for the service is received, the credit to cash is paired with a debit to the accumulated expense balance sheet account (not an income sheet account).

Examples of common income accruals include bond interest, common stock dividends,[2] and management fees. Examples of common expense accruals include management fees, investment income, rents, taxes, and salaries.

Depreciation can be used to spread the decline in asset value over time. Generally, the original value of the assets is not reduced. Rather, an expense (debit) is paired with an accumulation account.

Accumulated depreciation is a special kind of asset account called a *contra-asset* that takes on a negative value (although, like most accounting reporting, the negative sign (–) is not displayed). Eventually when the asset is taken out of service, it is moved from the balance sheet with a credit for the original (zeroing out the asset amount) and a debit to the accumulated depreciation account (zeroing out the contra-asset) and possibly an expense, if the accumulated depreciation is less than the carrying value of the asset.

ACCOMPLISHING FUND MANAGEMENT TASKS IN DOUBLE ENTRY ACCOUNTING

Hedge funds must base their income sheet and balance sheet on updated market values of their positions. It is possible to mark a position to market using the general ledger program, but it may be more intuitive to use a separate program to calculate mark to market (a spreadsheet, for example). The mark to market is the sum of the change in value from cost to current market for each position. However, this calculation requires maintaining duplicate data and is prone to errors. The entries in Table 11.4 accomplish the same result, do not require duplicate entries, and do not affect the general ledger figures.

The posting on 3/31/01 removes the asset (Account 1500) from the books at cost and replaces the amount with the current value. A gain account (for example, 3750—Unrecognized Short-Term Gain) is

TABLE 11.4 Mark to Market and Reversal

Date	Account	Debit Amount	Credit Amount
3/31/01	1500		$50,125.45
3/31/01	1500	$54,000.00	
3/31/01	3750		$3,874.55
4/01/01	1500	$50,125.45	
4/01/01	1500		$54,000.00
4/01/01	3750	$3,874.55	

used both to make sure the debits match the credits and to calculate the individual mark to market. This technique forces the accounting software to sum each gain and easily feeds the results into the accounting reports. Then the transactions on 4/1/01 reverse all the effects of the mark to market and reestablish the cost basis. This greatly simplifies the task of validating the accounting records against actual trading tickets because the assets are all carried at historic cost at all times except when statements are prepared (monthly or quarterly).

When a closing transaction is made (a sale following a purchase or a purchase following a short sale), the asset must be removed from the books and a gain or loss must be calculated. In the example shown as Table 11.1, we bought a position in XYZ stock, called an *opening buy*.[3] For opening transactions, these simple entries are enough.

However, if we sell the position in XYZ on 4/12/01, we cannot use the entries in Table 11.5. Those entries do not recognize the $10,000 gain on the position and would also create a short position in account 1500 (XYZ Common). The correct entries use the historical cost basis and the current sale proceeds to calculate an entry to balance the posting as in Table 11.6. In that transaction, a new account (3750—Short-Term Gain) balances the entries and picks up the gain on the sale.

If the fund holds other shares in addition to those purchased on 3/17/01, the amount to remove as a gain (as in Table 11.6) would be based on the cost basis that the fund wants to recognize. The credit amount might reflect some shares from the 3/17/01 trade and additional shares from another cost.

The sale may move the fund from long to short. In this case, a portion of the sale is considered a closing trade and the balance is an

TABLE 11.5 Closing a Position Incorrectly

Date	Account	Debit Amount	Credit Amount
4/12/01	1500		$60,125.45
4/12/01	1000	$60,125.45	

TABLE 11.6 Closing Entries for Trade Liquidation with Gain

Date	Account	Debit Amount	Credit Amount
4/12/01	1500		$50,125.45
4/12/01	1000	$60,125.45	
4/12/01	3750		$10,000.00

opening sale. For example, suppose the fund sells 4,000 shares for $120,250.90. The required entries are shown in Table 11.7, where the posting merges the entries from the prior two examples (2,000 shares closing and 2,000 shares opening). In practice, the debit to account 1000 could be made for the sum of the individual amounts. The account shown as 2500 reflects a liability used to store short positions in XYZ common. A liability is used instead of a negative asset value.

Generally, the data are stored and the reports are created each time they are accessed. This is important because the date transactions are posted does not need to match the date of the entries. It is generally best to enter transactions when they are known, even if they occur in the future. For example, suppose you bought $10,000,000 face amount of commercial paper on 7/15 for $9,850,000 (maturing in 90 days at a discount interest rate of 6 percent). If the maturing entries are posted at the time of the trade, the details of the transaction do not need to be researched at maturity. Refer to Table 11.8. This method of posting transactions in the future can also be used for for-

TABLE 11.7 Posting a Sale Moving the Fund from Long to Short

Date	Account	Debit Amount	Credit Amount
4/12/01	1500		$50,125.45
4/12/01	1000	$60,125.45	
4/12/01	3350		$10,000.00
4/12/01	2500		$60,125.45
4/12/01	1000	$60,125.45	

TABLE 11.8 Maturing Discount Instruments and Recognizing Income

Date	Account	Debit Amount	Credit Amount
1/15/01	1000-Cash		$9,850,000
1/15/01	1200-ST Investment	$9,850,000	
4/15/01	1000-Cash	$10,000,000	
4/15/01	1200-ST Investment		$9,850,000
4/15/01	3000-Interest Income		$150,000

Note: ST stands for short-term.

TABLE 11.9 Simple Posting of Unsettled Trade

Date	Account	Amount	Amount
4/2/01	1000-Cash		$1,000,000
4/2/01	1500-XYZ Common	$1,000,000	

ward-settled trades. For example, a stock purchased on 3/29/01 and settling 4/2/01 (after a weekend and over a quarter end) might be posted as in Table 11.9. In this case, it is not only convenient to post the transaction in advance of the settlement date, but it is necessary to enter the trade so that gains or losses at the end of the quarter (later the same day) can be included in financial reports.

Unfortunately, if financial statements are produced at month end, this trade will not be included on the balance sheet and in the leverage calculations, even if this effort is made to include the trade in performance calculations. Tables 11.10 and 11.11 show two alternatives, which might be journaled at the time of the trade, allow the positions to be marked to market (not shown here), and will disappear from the statements without further effort or entries.

TABLE 11.10 Posting Unsettled Trades on Trade Date (specific)

Date	Account	Amount	Amount
3/29/01	2000-Payable		$1,000,000
3/29/01	1500-XYZ Common	$1,000,000	
4/02/01	2000-Payable	$1,000,000	
4/02/01	1000-Cash		$1,000,000

TABLE 11.11 Posting Unsettled Trades on Trade Date (aggregate)

Date	Account	Amount	Amount
3/29/01	2000-Payable		$1,000,000
3/29/01	1800-Unsettled Securities	$1,000,000	
4/02/01	2000-Payable	$1,000,000	
4/02/01	1000-Cash		$1,000,000
4/02/01	1500-XYZ Common	$1,000,000	
4/02/01	1800-Unsettled Securities		$1,000,000

When a fund manager runs mirrored funds (domestic and international), there is frequently a need to rebalance at month end. For example, suppose a manager had two funds that each contained $50 million in capital. At month end, the domestic fund experiences $2 million in withdrawals and the international fund receives an addition of the same amount (by coincidence). Suppose also that the manager holds 50,000 shares of XYZ common, divided equally before the monthly flows. After the month end, the domestic fund should own 24,000 shares (48 / (48 + 52) × 50,000) and the offshore fund should own 26,000 shares (52 / (48 + 52) × 50,000). To rebalance, the domestic fund could sell 1,000 shares to the offshore fund at the month-end valuation price.

This rebalancing works well with the mark to market methods discussed earlier. In this case, the domestic fund would mark its 25,000 shares to the month-end value, reverse the recognition, then journal the sale, and the recognized gain would be calculated from the historical cost and would replace the original cost basis. It is important, though, to make sure that the entries are posted so that the fund does not receive credit for both a mark to market unrecognized gain (loss) and a recognized gain (loss).

JOURNALING LEVERED TRANSACTIONS

Hedge funds typically borrow money to establish levered long positions or sell short securities they do not own. Although these transactions may not look familiar, they are not difficult.

TABLE 11.12   Journaling Fixed-Income Securities

Date	Account	Amount	Amount
5/15/01	1400-Tsy 5½	$25,250,000	
5/15/01	1900-Accrued Interest	$328,125	
5/15/01	1000-Cash		$25,578,125

Note: Tsy stands for U.S. Treasury Notes.

Suppose a fund buys $25,000,000 face amount of government bonds on 5/14/01 at 101. If the bond pays a semiannual coupon of 5½ percent on 2/15 and 8/15, there is accrued interest roughly equal to one-quarter of the annual coupon income. The purchase (shown on the 5/15 settlement date) would be journaled as in Table 11.12.

The fund might arrange to borrow $25 million on a secured basis in the repo (repurchase agreement) market. Suppose the fund borrows the money for 1 week at 4.5 percent. The financing trade, the liquidation of the financing trade, and the interest would resemble the entries in Table 11.13. Note that this transaction reflects the leverage of nearly 100:1, routinely possible in the bond market. Also, the repo balance is booked as a liability because the cash amount must be repaid to the lender after a week.

Short position would be posted in nearly the same way (except that liabilities replace assets and assets replace liabilities in the journal entries in Tables 11.12 and 11.13). In Table 11.14, the short position in common stock is booked as a liability and generates $25 million in cash.[4] The cash (plus $3 million additional funds) is used to collateralize a loan of shares, which are used to make the delivery

TABLE 11.13   Journaling Financing Trade and Liquidation of Financing Trade

Date	Account	Amount	Amount
5/15/01	1000-Cash	$25,000,000	
5/15/01	2400-Repo Loans		$25,000,000
5/22/01	3400-Repo Interest	$21,875	
5/22/01	2400-Repo Loans	$25,000,000	
5/22/01	1000-Cash		$25,021,875

TABLE 11.14 Short Sale of Stock with Financing Entries

Date	Account	Amount	Amount
5/15/01	2400-XYZ Common		$25,000,000
5/15/01	1000-Cash	$25,000,000	
5/15/01	1000-Cash		$28,000,000
5/15/01	1200-Stock Loan	$28,000,000	
5/22/01	4400-Rebate Interest		$21,875
5/22/01	1400-Stock Loan		$28,000,000
5/22/01	1000-Cash	$28,021,875	

on the outright short. The cash collateral is treated as a short-term loan that is paid a rebate (a below-market rate of interest). Whereas the repo interest in the previous example is an expense, this rebate interest is income.

When a bond pays a coupon or a stock pays a dividend, a substitute payment must be made to the actual owner because the issuer makes the payment to the party holding the security. For long positions, the financing counterparty sends the fund the payment by bank wire. For short positions, the fund must wire the payment to the party who lent securities.

For bonds, some part of the coupon income may have already been accrued. As seen previously, accrued interest may have been journaled at the time of purchase/sale or at month end to accrue income between payment dates. Table 11.15 shows an example of entries to pick up coupon income where additional income was accrued up to the previous month end.

In the previous example, accrued interest was equal to $5\frac{1}{2}$ months income at $5\frac{1}{2}$ percent on $25 million face amount at month end.

TABLE 11.15 Typical Entries for Coupon Payment

Date	Account	Amount	Amount
5/15/01	1900-Accrued Interest		$630,208.33
5/15/01	4200-U.S. Interest		$57,291.67
5/15/01	1000-Cash	$687,500	

A semiannual coupon was received as cash. The residual portion of income is the part of the coupon not previously accrued as income.

Because stock dividends are not accrued, the entry contains only a credit (debit) to cash and income (expense) for long (short) positions.

When a dividend payment or bond coupon is paid, the value of the security declines. Typically, the positive income received is used to reduce the value of financing debt. Similarly for short positions, the fund reduces the required collateral at the time of a coupon or dividend and uses the cash to make payments made to others.

JOURNALING FUTURES, SWAPS, AND OTHER DERIVATIVES

The notional amount of futures and over-the-counter derivatives do not appear on financial statements. This information is carried on the footnotes to the financial statements. Generally, the footnotes report only aggregated information for the firm.

When a fund opens a futures account, the cash transferred is entered into the accounting ledger as shown in Table 11.16. This amount appears on the balance sheet regardless of whether futures positions are subsequently created. However, when statements are produced (at month end, for example), the positions are marked to market. A gain would appear as an increase in the amount due from the broker. For example, if futures positions made $10,000, the entries would read as in Table 11.17.

Like the cash market example, if the foregoing entry is reversed and the cost of the futures position is re-created, it probably reduces information needs and improves the reliability of statements.

A loss would appear similarly. A debit for the loss would match a credit to the account Due from Broker, reducing it by the amount

TABLE 11.16 Funding the Futures Brokerage Account

Date	Account	Amount	Amount
6/12/01	1000-Cash		$25,000
6/12/01	1600-Due from Broker	$25,000	

TABLE 11.17 Recognizing Unrealized Gains on Futures Positions

Date	Account	Amount	Amount
6/30/01	1000-Trading Gains		$10,000
6/30/01	1600-Due from Broker	$10,000	

of the loss. Under FAS 133 (see following section), accountants might want to create a liability to carry the mark to market loss instead of crediting the Due from Broker account.

For over-the-counter derivatives, generally no cash is exchanged at the onset of the transaction and no entries are journaled. Like the futures situation, gains and losses are recognized each statement period. However, offsetting these income items would be an asset or liability. See the example in Table 11.18.

Losses would be journaled against a liability with a similar name. The general ledger program could contain accumulations for gains and accumulations for losses as liabilities. However, for financial reporting, only the net gain or net loss accumulation is displayed.

FAS 133

The Financial Accounting Standards Board (FASB) issued Statement 133 (FAS 133), *Accounting for Derivative Instruments and Hedging Activities,* in June of 1998. The statement replaces provisions from FAS 52, 80, 105, 107, and 119.

FAS 133 defines derivative securities somewhat more broadly than earlier statements. For FAS 133, a derivative must gain or lose value or determine cash flows based on one or more exogenous factors. It must have a clear notional amount, even if there is no change of title on the notional amount. It should require little or no initial in-

TABLE 11.18 Recognizing Gain on Derivative Transactions

Date	Account	Amount	Amount
6/30/01	1000-Trading Gains		$10,000
6/30/01	1350-Swap	$10,000	

vestment. Finally, it should be relatively easy to close out or resell the position by making a net cash payment.

FAS 133 requires that hedges be carried at fair value; however, it controls the timing of the reporting. The FASB sought to allow hedgers to match the timing of gains and losses on hedged assets with gains and losses of effective hedges. Although the FASB did not create a measure or standard of effectiveness, by custom and practice, hedgers use statistical correlation.

For hedges that are somewhat effective, part of the gain or loss on the derivative may apply the provisions of FAS 133. The remaining portion of the gain or loss must be recognized in the income statement at least quarterly. For example, if a hedge correlates 70 percent with the underlying position being hedged, 70 percent of the gain or loss will qualify for hedge treatment. The remaining 30 percent of the gain or loss on the derivative must be reported on the income statement with no offset from the unrealized amount from the hedged asset.

FAS 133 identifies three types of hedges. Fair value hedging seeks to match the gains/losses on an asset or liability to gains/losses on the hedge position. For this type of hedge, FAS requires both the gain/loss on the hedge and the gain/loss on the hedged asset to be reported on the income statement.

The second type of hedge is called a cash flow hedge. The cash flows are uncertain (and perhaps cannot be forecasted accurately). To qualify, the derivate must reduce the uncertainty of the net cash flows. Gains and losses from cash flow hedges affect equity, but the effect on earnings is deferred.

The third category of hedges identified by FAS 133 pertains to net investments in foreign operations. Derivative gains or losses hedging offshore risks are recognized as translations gains or losses.

ACCOUNTING FOR INVESTMENT PORTFOLIOS

Investment managers need large amounts of information to run portfolios, monitor risk, and report results to investors. Much of the information is already in the general ledger system. It is possible to take advantage of that information and still preserve the accounting record for financial reporting.

Sometimes the portfolio needs require subaccount details not readily preserved in a general ledger system. In this situation, some of the techniques described in this chapter can be created with multi-company accounting models. This software is designed to allow the user to establish unique general ledger systems for two or more "subsidiaries," then merge them into a parent.

Portfolio reporting and tax reporting both create needs for information not easily recorded in a general ledger program. For example, trade dates are not needed for a complete accounting record. This information may be recovered from journaled transactions, especially if supplemental documentation fields are used. However, the general ledger program does not have the ability to use this information intelligently later. Similarly, where detailed cost information is needed to calculate gains and losses, it may be difficult or impossible to preserve it all.

Internal Controls

Many disasters reported by the press occurred because of a lack of internal controls. Merrill Lynch discovered a loss on its Mortgage Trading Desk that it claimed stemmed from trades a trader had executed but had not entered into the firm's accounting records (a charge denied by the trader, Howard Rubin). The forced sale of Barings Bank was the result of oversized positions in futures traded by Nick Leeson unknown to top management. Supervisors at Sumitomo Bank and Daiwa Bank, and investors in Orange County, California, had little or no understanding of risks they faced or whether the positions complied with internal guidelines.

Internal controls cannot eliminate all losses. Results from investment products are uncertain and it is not reasonable to expect decision makers to anticipate all outcomes. It is more unreasonable to expect those traders to overweight the outcome that actually occurred as if the trader had the benefit of hindsight.

Internal controls can ensure compliance with established trading guidelines. Many of the worst-case scenarios cannot occur if the positions comply with guidelines.

NOTES

1. If the amount of the accrued expense is material, the accrual can be approximated outside the general ledger system in calculating NAV between accounting periods.
2. Unlike bonds, which legally accrue interest every day, stock dividends are accrued only on the ex-dividend date until the payment date.
3. A sale to create a new short position is called an *opening sale;* a sale that reduces a long position is called a *closing sale;* and a purchase that reduces an existing short position is a *closing buy.*
4. In practice, the stock would settle 3 business days after the trade date, so an extra step recording the position as an unsettled trade (liability in this case) would probably be used, especially if the settlement occurred over a period when partners could enter or exit the fund.

CHAPTER 12

Tax Reporting for Hedge Funds

As described in Chapter 6, hedge funds in the United States are usually organized as a partnership or limited liability corporation. Unlike individuals and standard (C) corporations, these businesses do not pay taxes. Instead, they allocate all results to the investors. These allocations may directly affect an investor, resulting in more or less cash for the investor at some time. Some allocations may only affect the tax liabilities of the investors. The rules for allocating performance are guided by the partnership agreement. Tax law, however, limits how these allocations can be made.

Tax law pertaining to partnerships is very complicated. There is a long history of partnerships legally exploiting tax code to create tax shelters. There is nearly as long a history of legislation designed to prevent partnerships from manipulating tax rules to avoid paying taxes. The resulting body of rules applies to hedge funds, even though they are not set up as tax shelters.

This chapter describes how results are allocated to investors. A variety of methods are allowed. Several variations are presented. Each hedge fund manager should decide which method is best, taking into account the types of investments, holding period, and tax status of its investors.

FLOW-THROUGH ALLOCATION METHODOLOGIES

Figure 12.1 shows a time line that represents the timing of events in a typical purchase and sale and the chronologies of the financial accounting and tax reporting entries. The time line shows the purchase

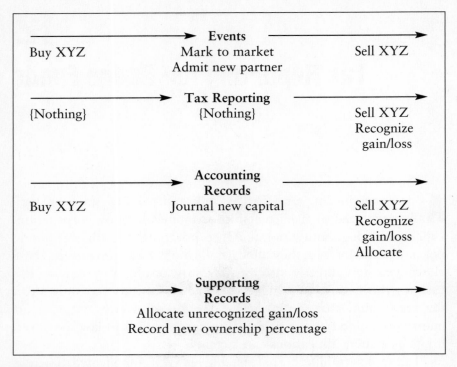

FIGURE 12.1   Time Line of Accounting Entries
(For hedge funds that make a mixed straddle election, it is not true that "nothing" is reported. Unrealized gains/losses are recognized and allocated throughout the holding period, simplifying the allocation.)

of XYZ common stock. A new partner is admitted. Finally, the partnership sells the shares of XYZ common. The financial records show the purchase, the addition of capital and the sale, and the recognized (unrealized or mark to market) gain or loss at the time the new partner is admitted.

Most partnership agreements and generally accepted accounting principles (GAAP) require that the position in XYZ common be marked to market, that the unrealized gain be included in the net asset value of the fund, and that the fund pay incentive fees based on the interim value of XYZ. However, the tax reports do not include the gain or loss until the gain or loss is realized (by closing out the position). It would appear that the firm *must* run two sets of accounting books. The first set would follow GAAP procedures; the second set would follow the requirements of the tax code.

Although it is possible to maintain nearly duplicate books, it is much more common to maintain only the GAAP records, make certain adjustments, and preserve additional information in nonledger accounts to create the tax reporting. It is necessary to maintain additional detailed records so that the equivalent to a second general ledger can be constructed. With this detailed nonledger information, tax accountants can allocate taxable income to partners as if duplicate books were being maintained.

This nonledger solution has many advantages over running duplicate accounting records. First, it is very difficult to keep the parallel ledgers in agreement. Second, running duplicate books requires wasteful duplication of efforts. Third, the method described in the following text provides additional information that makes tax reporting easier.

The information required for partner allocation is preserved in memorandum files for each partner. For example, the cost of XYZ, the interim value for the position, each partner's ownership percentage, and the portion of each gain/loss attributed to a partner are recorded in files (often just computerized worksheets). The information is recorded for each partner for each subperiod where ownership percentages changed and mark to market value was recorded. Similar information is also recorded for each position in the fund. Finally, the information is added to the memorandum files each time any partner enters or exits the fund and every regular accounting cycle. Some accounting methods (see following text) require the individual details be preserved. Other techniques require only running totals of this information.

Tax allocation reconciles the gain/loss eventually *realized* in the GAAP accounting records with the gains and losses already *recognized* on the partnership books.

The Internal Revenue Service, Department of Treasury regulations, and a long line of court cases control tax allocation. The primary requirements for tax allocation appear in Treasury Regulation 1.704, commonly called Regulation 704, which has evolved to prohibit taxpayers from using allocation schemes to reduce or eliminate tax liability.

A hedge fund is typically set up as a limited partnership or limited liability corporation. These two types of businesses pay no federal income taxes. Instead, the income, expenses, and gains and losses are allocated to the investors and taxed on the investors' tax forms.

Income and expense items must be allocated to investors at each break period. A break period occurs when one or more partners enters or withdraws from the fund (in whole or in part). When this occurs, ownership percentages usually change. A break period also occurs when revenues and expenses are allocated to investors (usually at least quarterly) even if the partnership percentages do not change.

The allocation procedures of the fund have substantial economic effect. This means that the rules for allocating both benefits and burdens to partners for tax reporting must correspond with how the benefits and burdens (the real gains and losses . . . the money) are actually distributed. The firm must maintain capital accounts consistent with this economic substance and liquidations must also respect this economic substance. In particular, all partners must be required to restore a negative capital balance within 90 days. The economic effect of the allocation must also be substantial, that is, the effect of the allocation may not be solely to distribute or redistribute the tax burden.

The allocations are subject to a so-called ceiling rule, which limits the deductions for partners to the deduction for the fund. When a fund disposes of a security, some partners may have been allocated gains and others losses because they entered the partnership at different times. However, if the fund made money on the position, it is not possible to allocate losses to any partner. Unfortunately, even well-designed, well-intended allocation schemes are sometimes tripped up by rules designed to limit tax abuse.

To clarify the meaning of the ceiling rule, suppose that two partners contributed $100 each to a partnership. The partnership made a $200 investment. Later, the investment had risen to $300 and a third investor was admitted as an equal partner in return for a capital investment of $150. If the investment is sold for less than $300, the new investor experiences a loss on that investment. However, if the partnership sells the investment for more than $200, the partnership experiences a gain. The ceiling rule prohibits allocating a loss to any investor when the partnership shows a gain.

Regulation 704 allows transactions to be allocated on a transaction-by-transaction basis or in aggregate. The rules are complicated but reasonable. The rules give rise to several different methods for allocating the results of the partnership to its partners. These methods are the main topic of this chapter.

ALLOCATING REVENUES AND EXPENSES

Two methods exist for allocating routine revenues and expenses.[1] The first method is called interim closing of the books, a method that allocates these amounts by the economic ownership percentage. In fact, the interim statements are not needed to implement this method. Instead, the economic ownership percent is applied to each expense. The results are the same as if the books were closed more frequently and the interim results were allocated explicitly. The second method is to prorate the allocation of revenues or expenses. The items are usually prorated based on time, but other methods are allowed if they are reasonable and consistent.

Suppose Jack and Jill become equal partners on January 1. The partnership incurs a $9,000 cost for auditing in March. Joe joins the partnership July 1, getting a one-third interest in the firm. Table 12.1

TABLE 12.1 Interim Allocation of Expense Item(s)

Partner	Allocation of Item Prior to Joe Joining	Allocation of Item with Joe	Total
Jack	$4,500	$0	$4,500
Jill	4,500	0	4,500
Joe	0	0	0
Total	$9,000	$0	$9,000

TABLE 12.2   Prorated Allocation of Expense Item(s)

Partner	Allocation of Item Prior to Joe Joining	Allocation of Item with Joe	Total
Jack	$1,800	$1,800	$3,600
Jill	1,800	1,800	3,600
Joe	0	1,800	1,800
Total	$3,600	$5,400	$9,000

shows the allocation of this expense, assuming the interim closing of the books method. This method allocates all the $9,000 to Jack and Jill (50 percent each) because they were equal partners before Joe entered. Whether or not the books were actually closed before Joe entered the fund, the allocation assumes that the books were closed for the purpose of allocation. As a result, no audit expenses are left to allocate to Joe in the second half of the year.

The prorated allocation of this expense (see Table 12.2) uses a simple method to redistribute the expense. For this example, 20 percent is allocated to Jack and 20 percent is allocated to Jill for the first half of the year. Each of the three partners is allocated 20 percent of the expense for the second half of the year. As a result, 100 percent of the expense is allocated to the investors. Alternatively (not shown here), half of the total expense could have been allocated to the first half of the year (split two ways) and the remaining half allocated to the second half (split three ways).

For this particular expense and this year, the interim closing method seems fairer because the audit fee probably applies to services rendered early in the year before Joe joined the partnership. In fact, the work relates to transactions in the prior year and we do not have enough information to know about other flows that may affect our view of fairness. All these facts can be considered when making a decision on how to allocate.

The fund also does not need to wait until an expense is journaled to begin the allocation. In Chapter 11, we show how anticipated expenses could be accrued in advance in the GAAP financial accounting records. This accrual is an example of an allocation method and can be used for tax allocation if it can be defended as reasonable.

ALLOCATING GAINS AND LOSSES

Allocations of gains and losses may be made using the layered method or the aggregate method.

Layered Allocation

The layered method of allocation tracks the value of each security during each break period. Details are recorded so that eventual realized gains or losses can be allocated to each partner as if they held a portion (often a changing portion) of the position directly. The method applies to specific lots of all positions. A new "layer" of information is recorded for each partner, each lot, each break period.

The data required to preserve this level of detail can be quite large. Table 12.3 shows the number of layers that must be preserved under various assumptions and shows the number of layers for funds having between 50 and 400 tax lots. The number of lots is almost always higher than the number of issues in the fund because the fund can have two or more lots for one issue whenever the positions were acquired at different times and prices.[2] Lots become layers at each

TABLE 12.3 The Burgeoning Problem of Tax Lots

| Lots | Layers | Number of Partners | | | |
		25	50	75	100
50	300	7,500	15,000	22,500	30,000
100	600	15,000	30,000	45,000	60,000
150	900	22,500	45,000	67,500	90,000
200	1200	30,000	60,000	90,000	120,000
250	1500	37,500	75,000	112,500	150,000
300	1800	45,000	90,000	135,000	180,000
350	2100	52,500	105,000	157,500	210,000
400	2400	60,000	120,000	180,000	240,000

break period. Table 12.3 assumes that the average lot is held for six break periods and that each investor is allocated six layers for every lot.

Six layers per lot may be realistic for funds that allow investors to enter monthly. Funds with quarterly break points and rapid turnover of positions may have considerably fewer layers per lot but many more lots. Funds with more investors have a larger data requirement. Because the number of layers is the product of these factors, the number of lots can become very large.

Consider a simple example. On May 1, Jack and Jill are equal (50 percent) partners. The fund buys 1,000 shares of XYZ for $10 per share on May 15. On May 31, the fund marks XYZ at $12. On June 1, the fund admits Joe as a one-third partner. On June 30, the fund marks XYZ at $15. Finally, on July 15, the fund sells XYZ at $16. Figure 12.2 shows memorandum accounts for each partner.

The fund realizes a gain of $6,000 ($16 − 10) × 1,000 shares. If the fund allocated like a mutual fund, the gain would be allocated according to the current economic interest (one-third interest for each partner). That would allocate $2,000 to each partner. However, Regulation 704 does not allow this method. Instead, the gain is allocated according to the layers of unrealized gains attributed to each partner since XYZ was purchased (see Table 12.4).

Both Jack and Jill are allocated 50 percent of the gain from $10 to $12. Joe gets none of that gain because he had not invested when that gain occurred. After Joe joined the partnership, all three were allocated one-third of the gain from $12 to $15 at month end. The gain from $15 to $16 is also allocated equally because the partnership percentages did not change but is shown separately because the allocation occurred midmonth. The allocation at the time the trade was closed out allocated only the gain from the month-end price of $15 to the sale price of $16.

Most people believe that layered allocation produces the fairest results. Investors are allocated gains and losses for tax purposes that exactly match the economic gain or loss they experienced. The timing of the tax consequences agrees exactly with the timing each investor would expect if each partner held the position privately.

Jack's Memorandum Account

Date	Unrecognized Gain	
31 May	$1,000	= 1,000 × (12 − 10) × 50%
30 Jun	$1,000	= 1,000 × (15 − 12) × 33.3%
15 Jul	$ 333	= 1,000 × (16 − 15) × 33.3%
	$2,333	

Jill's Memorandum Account

Date	Unrecognized Gain	
31 May	$1,000	= 1,000 × (12 − 10) × 50%
30 Jun	$1,000	= 1,000 × (15 − 12) × 33.3%
15 Jul	$ 333	= 1,000 × (16 − 15) × 33.3%
	$2,333	

Joe's Memorandum Account

Date	Unrecognized Gain	
31 May	n.a.	Not a partner yet
30 Jun	$1,000	= 1,000 × (15 − 12) × 33.3%
15 Jul	$ 333	= 1,000 × (16 − 15) × 33.3%
	$1,333	

FIGURE 12.2 Sample Memorandum Accounts (n.a. stands for not applicable.)

Layered allocation often produces tax allocations that violate the ceiling rule. For example, if the fund realizes a profit on an issue, it may not allocate losses to any individual investor. This limitation makes it harder for abusive tax shelters to allocate income simply to minimize tax burdens.[3] However, investors that joined the partnership after the lot was established may have experienced *real* losses. In-

TABLE 12.4   Layered Allocation of Gain

Partner	Sum of Layered Amount	Allocation
Jack	$2,333	$2,333
Jill	2,333	2,333
Joe	1,333	1,333
Total	$6,000	$6,000

stead of receiving a loss allocation (which would reduce the partner's tax liability), other partners are distributed a gain smaller than their economic gain.

When some partners experience gains and other partners experience losses on a particular lot, the ceiling rule limits the partnership's ability to allocate the results. Consider the previous example but with a final sale price of $11. The memoranda accounts are shown in Figure 12.3.

The fund realizes a gain of $1,000 ($11 − 10) × 1,000 shares. The gain cannot be allocated according to the layers of unrealized gains attributed to each partner since XYZ was purchased. Instead, the gain must be allocated to the partners showing gains on their memorandum account. In this case, Jack and Jill are allocated a smaller gain because Joe was not allocated a loss for tax purposes (see Table 12.5).

The fund can do several things to reduce the impact of the ceiling rule. It can apply curative allocations so that the discrepancy between the tax books and the partnership books is eliminated. It is possible to assert that the ceiling rule need only apply to annual allocations. In this case, most of the ceiling violations with individual lots would disappear.

Aggregate Allocation

The IRS approved aggregate allocation in 1994. The method collects similar unrecognized gains attributed to each partner into a memorandum account. Unlike the layered method, it is not necessary to preserve any of the details on individual lots or different break peri-

Jack's Memorandum Account

Date	Unrecognized Gain	
31 May	$ 1,000	= 1,000 × (12 − 10) × 50%
30 Jun	$ 1,000	= 1,000 × (15 − 12) × 33.3%
15 Jul	$(1,333)	= 1,000 × (11 − 15) × 33.3%
	$ 667	

Jill's Memorandum Account

Date	Unrecognized Gain	
31 May	$ 1,000	= 1,000 × (12 − 10) × 50%
30 Jun	$ 1,000	= 1,000 × (15 − 12) × 33.3%
15 Jul	$(1,333)	= 1,000 × (11 − 15) × 33.3%
	$ 667	

Joe's Memorandum Account

Date	Unrecognized Gain	
31 May	n.a.	Not a partner yet
30 Jun	$ 1,000	= 1,000 × (15 − 12) × 33.3%
15 Jul	$(1,333)	= 1,000 × (11 − 15) × 33.3%
	$ (333)	

FIGURE 12.3 Memorandum Accounts When Some Investors Have Gains and Others Have Losses (n.a. stands for not applicable.)

ods. For many hedge funds, the aggregate method is substantially easier to calculate and gives nearly identical results as the layered allocation.[4] This is especially likely when the fund holds securities for short periods. During this short time, there is little change in the partnership percentages, and gains and losses are realized on the tax

TABLE 12.5   Layers Allocation Under Ceiling Rule

Partner	Sum of Layered Amount	Desired Allocation	Allowed Allocation
Jack	$ 667	$ 667	$ 500
Jill	667	667	500
Joe	(333)	(333)	0
Total	$1,000	$1,000	$1,000

books in the same tax period as they are recognized on the partner's books.

It is important to point out that investors will eventually be allocated taxable income exactly equal to the economic gain or loss they experienced. Differences between the two methods affect the timing to the allocated tax amounts, not the magnitude. There can be differences in the characterization of the income, however. Unless special effort is made to allocate long-term and short-term income fairly, partners could experience an economic impact. Also, a multitude of complications in the tax code (scaled-out deductions, progressive tax rates, changes in tax rates over time, the $3,000 limit on tax losses) and the time value of deferral may create an economic impact.

There are five aggregate allocation methods allowed by the IRS. Other methods or variations are permitted as long as they are reasonable. Regardless of method, the allocation must preserve the characterization of items (short-term gain, long-term loss, tax-exempt interest, etc.). The allocation method must be applied consistently. In addition, the method should not be designed entirely to minimize tax payments.

Like the layered allocation method, a memorandum account is established for each partner. The purpose of this memorandum account is also to tie together the partnership books that recognize gains and losses at each break period to GAAP statements used as input to tax reporting.

Gains and losses are accumulated into these memoranda accounts for each position. It is not necessary to preserve details about individual lots. It is not necessary to know which securities were responsible for the gain or loss. It is only necessary to accumulate the sum of all this information. This running total of recognized gains is reduced (increased) by the amount of gains (losses) allocated to each partner. This running total is called the *beginning unrealized memorandum account balance*[5] (BUMAB). The same total after allocations have been made at the end of the break period is called the *ending unrealized memorandum account balance* (EUMAB).

Reversal to the Extent of BUMAB

The reversal to the extent of BUMAB method allocates realized gains and losses to partners in proportion to their BUMAB. If realized gains/losses are large enough that all memo balances have been reduced to zero, the remaining gains/losses are allocated according to the economic percentage of each partner.

Different issues arise as described in the following situations. For the simplest case, assume that the amounts as shown in Table 12.6 have been accumulated in each partner's memorandum accounts.

Each of the partners has different positive (or negative) balances reflecting positive profits for the partnership in the current or past periods. For example, Jack has $300 that has been allocated to him, representing one-third of the memorandum totals. During the period just ending, a $200 gain was realized in aggregate on all closed-out positions. Jack is allocated one-third of the realized gain equal to $67 and his memorandum balance is reduced by the $67 allocation. The remaining gain is allocated to Jill ($44) and Joe ($89) in proportion to their contribution to the fund total BUMAB.

TABLE 12.6 Allocating to the Extent of BUMAB When All Investors Have Gains or All Investors Have Losses

Partner	BUMAB	Pro Rata Percentage of BUMAB	Allocation of Net Realized Gain
Jack	$300	33	$ 67
Jill	200	22	44
Joe	400	44	89
Total	$900	100	$200

TABLE 12.7 Allocating Gain in Excess of BUMAB When All Investors Have Gains or All Investors Have Losses

Partner	BUMAB	Current Economic Percent	Pro Rata Percent of BUMAB	Allocated per BUMAB	Allocated per Holding
Jack	$300	30	33	$300	$ 90
Jill	200	20	22	200	60
Joe	400	50	44	400	150
Total	$900	100	100	$900	$300

The situation is slightly more complicated when the gain realized exceeds the fund total BUMAB. In this second case, all partners have positive (or negative) BUMAB amounts (see Table 12.7). However, the $1,200 gain realized exceeds the fund total BUMAB by $300. In this case, the $900 is allocated to the partners to the extent of their BUMAB amounts. The remaining gain is allocated to the partners in proportion to their current economic percent.

The third case resembles the second step of the previous case. In this situation, all partners have positive BUMAB amounts but the fund must allocate a loss (see Table 12.8). In this case, the BUMAB amounts are ignored. The loss is allocated exclusively on the basis of the partners' current percentage ownership of the fund. The memorandum balance for each partner is updated by subtracting the negative allocation. In this case, the EUMAB for Jack, for example, would rise to $390. The EUMAB for the fund would rise to $1,200.

TABLE 12.8 Allocating a Loss When All Partners Have Gains

Partner	BUMAB	Current Economic Percent	Pro Rata Percent of BUMAB	Allocated per BUMAB	Allocated per Holding
Jack	$300	30	33	$0	($90)
Jill	200	20	22	0	(60)
Joe	400	50	44	0	(150)
Total	$900	100	100	$0	($300)

TABLE 12.9 Allocating When Some Partners Have Gains and Others Have Losses

Partner	BUMAB	Current Economic Percent	Pro Rata Percent of BUMAB	Allocated per BUMAB	Allocated per Holding
Jack	$300	30	60	$300	$ 75
Jill	200	20	40	200	50
Joe	(200)	50	0	0	125
Total	$300	100	100	$500	$250

When one or more partners has a positive BUMAB amount and one or more partners has a negative amount, the realized amount is allocated to those partners where the allocation will reduce the disparity between the partnership books and the tax books. In the case shown in Table 12.9, Joe has a negative memo balance and the realized gain exceeds the $500 BUMAB for Jack and Jill. In this case, Joe's memorandum balance is ignored for the allocation of the first $500 of gains. The allocation of the $500 between Jack and Jill is weighted by the amounts of their memorandum balances. The remaining $250 is allocated to all three partners according to their current ownership percentage.

Full Reversal of BUMAB

A second method of aggregate accounting, full reversal of BUMAB, assumes you immediately attempt to eliminate the memorandum balances for all partners by allocating the full amount to each partner. For example, if the fund recognized a gain of $500 but it had a total BUMAB of $900, the fund would start by allocating $900 to the investors so as to eliminate all memo balances (see Table 12.10). The $400 excess allocation would not be allowed on the fund's tax return, however. Therefore, the amounts allocated to partners are reduced by $400. However, the adjustments reflect the current economic percentage of the partnership interests. For example, if Joe were allocated using just his 4/9 weighting (the reversal to the extent of BUMAB method), he would be allocated $222.22 of the $500 gain.

TABLE 12.10 Full Reversal of BUMAB Example

Partner	BUMAB	Current Economic Percent	BUMABs	Difference	Allocated per Holding
Jack	$300	30	$300	($120)	$180
Jill	200	20	200	(80)	120
Joe	400	50	400	(200)	200
Total	$900	100	$900	($400)	$500

Instead, he is allocated only $200. Although his balance remains further out of line relative to the tax records, the other partners are closer. The difference between the partnership records and the tax records is split according to the current ownership percentages.

Beginning Realized in Aggregate

The beginning realized in aggregate method is a FIFO (first in, first out) method of allocation. Memorandum balances are accumulated as with the previous methods; however, the subtotals are preserved for each break period. Realized gains and losses are applied to the earliest memorandum balances.

In Table 12.11 the fund has quarterly break periods. Joe is not a partner until the second quarter. The fund realized a $100 gain and allocated the gain equally to Jack and Jill to reduce the outstanding first-quarter memorandum balance for these partners. Note that this allocation puts Jill's memorandum balance further out of line. Her

TABLE 12.11 Example of Beginning Realized Aggregate Allocation

Partner	Beginning Gain or Loss (Jan1)	Change Q1	Change Q3	Change Q4	Total Unrealized	Current Economic Percentage
Jack	$0	$250	$300	($250)	$ 50	20
Jill	0	250	300	(350)	(50)	30
Joe	0	0	300	(150)	150	50
Total	$0	$500	$900	($750)	$150	100

Jack	$ 50	= $100 × 250/500
Jill	$ 50	= $100 × 250/500
Joe	$ 0	= $0
Total	$100	

FIGURE 12.4   Allocations to Investors Based on Table 12.11

EUMAB rises to –$100 (see Figure 12.4). If the most important objective for the fund is to reduce the size of all the memorandum balances, the allocation should have been made exclusively or primarily to Joe. This method, however, seeks to time the tax reporting to be consistent with the timing of all previously recognized gains and losses.

Annual Aggregate Book-Tax Capital Account Disparity

Unlike the previous methods, the annual aggregate book-tax capital account disparity method does not rely on memorandum balances. Instead, separate books are kept for partnership and tax purposes. Most items (administrative expenses, etc.) are allocated according to the current economic percentage for each partner. Gains and losses are not allocated according to the preliminary financial reports. At the end of the year, the capital amounts of each partner (updated for

TABLE 12.12   Allocation to Minimize Disparity Between Tax Accounts and GAAP Records

Partner	Book Capital	Tax Capital	Disparity ($)	Disparity (%)	Realized Allocation
Jack	$1,000	$ 650	350	71	$214
Jill	400	320	80	16	49
Joe	600	540	60	12	37
Total	$2,000	$1,510	490	100	$300

the current year returns) are compared. Gains and losses are allocated to bring the two sets of books closer together.

In Table 12.12 there is a $490 difference between the two sets of books before $300 of realized gains is allocated. The $300 is allocated by the weights for each partner relative to that $490 difference. Jack has 71 percent of the $490 difference (350/490), so he gets $214 (71 percent of $300) in taxable gains allocated to him.

Break Period Book-Tax Capital Account Disparity

The break period book-tax capital account disparity allocation method is exactly like the annual aggregate book-tax capital account disparity method just described, except that the allocation takes place at each break period.

TAX ALLOCATION UNDER MIXED STRADDLE ELECTION

A fund may make a mixed straddle election if substantially all its trades would be considered identified straddles. Under the mixed straddle election, all positions are valued at each break period and the gains and losses are allocated to partners both on the partnership books and the tax records (see Figure 12.5).

Funds that make a mixed straddle election do not have timing differences between their tax records and their partnership records. As a result, they can use a dramatically simpler method to allocate gains and losses. Rather than maintaining percentage ownership information, the partners can be sold units in the fund.

These units are much like mutual fund shares. At the beginning, a fund may price a unit at $1,000. Each investment is assigned a fractional number of units. At each break period, net asset value equals the net equity of the fund (assets minus liabilities) divided by the number of units outstanding. Partners enter and exit at the net asset value (NAV) amount and the number of units is adjusted.

All taxable amounts are allocated to the total number of units each break period. Lumpy expenses such as annual audit fees are ac-

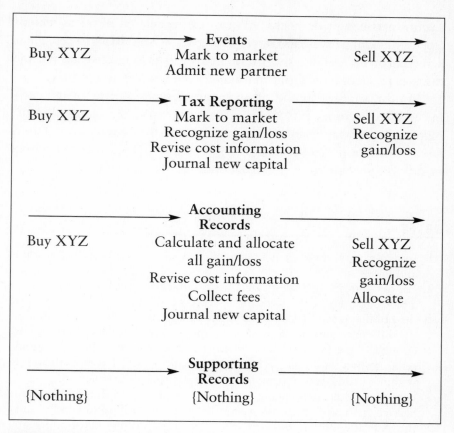

FIGURE 12.5 Mixed Straddle Time Line

crued each break period. The allocation that is made to each individual partner is the sum of the allocations to the appropriate number of units for each break period.

BE PREPARED

Tax reporting is one of the most difficult tasks pertaining to running a hedge fund and probably the subject most people inside or outside the hedge fund community understand least. There are many complications involving side-pocket allocations, unrelated business income (for tax-exempt investors), state tax laws, offshore tax issues, characterization issues (e.g., short-term gains versus long-term gains), and the fact that tax laws differ markedly from country to country.

Fund managers should provide for adequate tax reporting early in the life of a fund. It is much easier to preserve the required information day to day than to re-create it after the year is over. Funds have been shut down because they got behind in their record keeping or did not provide for tax and accounting requirements.

NOTES

1. Just to clarify, these rules in general may not be used to allocate gains and losses.
2. For tax allocation, a layer can consist of the average of several prices for a particular day. Trades on different days cannot be combined, because the holding period for long-term tax treatment is different. In practice, the difference may not be material if the fund never holds positions long enough to get favorable tax treatment. It may be possible to combine separate lots into a single lot after a break period. Layered allocation within spreadsheets may be impossible without this reduction.
3. For an example of a scheme considered abusive by the Internal Revenue Service, assume a partnership acquires an asset, then fraudulently values the asset low and admits a partner that does not pay taxes (a pension fund or endowment, for example). If the asset is subsequently sold at the original cost, a net loss would be allocated to the taxable investors and a gain would be allocated to the nontaxable investors.
4. Under most circumstances, the difference between the methods is limited to the timing of the gains and losses allocated to individual partners. If a partner is allocated (for tax purposes) a gain that exceeds the economic gain, the same partner will later receive an allocation less than the economic gain.
5. The terms for several of the methods employed in tax allocation are described in Will Taggart, Jr., and Gina M. Biondo, *Hedge Funds: A Comprehensive Tax Planning Guide*, Pricewaterhouse Coopers LLP, 1996. Other writers have used slightly different language to describe the same concepts. The *Guide* nomenclature is used in this chapter for consistency.

CHAPTER 13

Risk Management for Hedge Funds

Risk management remains one of the hottest topics in investment management. To learn more, the reader is directed to the many great books that have been written on the subject.[1] To fit into a single chapter, this discussion is limited to a fairly nontechnical description of the major methods. This chapter focuses on the needs for risk measurement and control in a levered investment portfolio.

CONTRASTING INVESTOR AND INTERNAL RISK MEASUREMENTS

Hedge funds can invest in nearly any financial instrument, including stocks, bonds, currencies, commodities, futures, options, derivatives, private equity, and venture capital. Hedge funds can combine risk from one or all of these asset groups. Hedge funds have additional risks associated with the use of leverage, including the direct effect that leverage can have, risks associated with the withdrawal of that leverage, and credit exposures from counterparties.

Risk management is as important for hedge fund managers as it is for hedge fund investors. Chapter 9 defines various measures of risk, including drawdown, the fund's Sharpe ratio, the volatility of returns, probability of loss, Sortino ratio, and many others.

Measures of hedge fund risk available to investors are not adequate to control risk within a hedge fund. First, the net asset value (NAV) and the associated return are aggregated. They provide no information about what types of trades cause gains or losses. In fact, the net nature prevents the investor from observing gains or losses for sections of the fund's portfolio, which may appear less volatile because of diversification. NAV may understate the actual volatility of even this aggregate value when parts of the portfolio are not regularly marked to market (common with private equity and real estate assets). Second, the investors' measures of risk are backward looking. While some investors may be given the chance to monitor some of the risk measures discussed in this chapter, most investors must be satisfied with measures derived from past performance. Managers cannot wait for a gain or loss to occur to gain some measure of risk exposure. For many types of trades, the job of risk measurement (and risk management) begins before an investment is acquired by the hedge fund.

RISK MODELS THAT DO NOT RELY ON PROBABILITY

This chapter begins with techniques that do not rely on probability. These models attempt to provide a precise measure of current risk. Other models build on this position information to develop a range of possible future returns.

Fixed-Income Risk Management

The bond market provides a good starting place to develop risk management methods because much of the risk can be precisely measured. The price of a bond is equal to the present value of the coupon and principal payments minus a small adjustment called *accrued interest*. For a bond that pays income annually, the value is:

$$\text{Present Value} = \sum_{\text{Years to Maturity}}^{t=1} \frac{\text{Cash Flow}_t}{\left(1 + \text{Yield}\right)^t} \tag{13.1}$$

where t is the time in years until a particular cash flow is received.

For bonds that are not free from the risk of default, the yield in Equation 13.1 includes a premium to compensate for risk. An alternative way of handling credit risk is described later.

Equation 13.1 may be altered in a variety of ways to more precisely match the terms of bonds actually trading. For example, in the United States, the formula must account for the payment of income spread over two payment dates per year. The formula can also be used to price bonds that are midway between coupon payment dates. The process is slightly more complicated than using fractional values for *t* because of industry standards defining the precise meaning of price and yield. In addition, it is common to subtract an amount equal to the prorated coupon income from the present value.

With this link between yield and price precisely defined, it is possible to create a mathematical gauge of price risk from the pricing formula in Equation 13.1. Named after Fredrick Macaulay, an insurance actuary, the formula combines a simple measure of risk called *average life* with the weights associated with the pricing formula in Equation 13.1 to more accurately measure the risk of a bond to an investor. Average life equals the time from now until a hypothetical average coupon or principal is received:

$$\text{Average Life} = \frac{\sum_{t=1}^{\text{Years to Maturity}} t \times \text{Cash Flow}_t}{\sum_{t=1}^{\text{Years to Maturity}} \text{Cash Flow}_t} \qquad (13.2)$$

This amount is displayed graphically in Figure 13.1, which shows the size and timing of the cash flows. The cash flows that appear in the numerator and denominator can be viewed as weightings that conveniently sum to 100 percent. Alternatively, the average life can be viewed as a balancing point, where cash flows occurring before the fulcrum point balance against cash flows occurring after the fulcrum point.

Average life appears to be a fairly reasonable measure of risk. Longer issues have a longer average life. Higher coupon bonds have

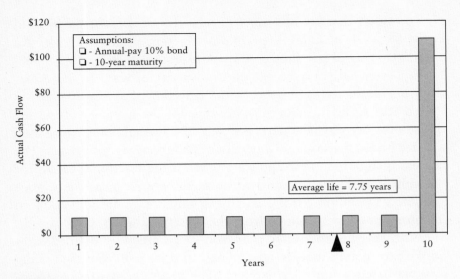

FIGURE 13.1   Average Life

more cash flow during the life of the bond, which is reflected in a shorter average life. (Two bonds with the same maturity have identical principal payments, but the bond with the higher coupon pays more income throughout the life of the bond, which shortens the average.) Unfortunately, it is not precise enough for a risk measure in a levered portfolio. Two bonds with identical average lives can have different sensitivity to interest rates. If a hedge fund established a long position in one bond and sold short an equal amount of bonds with an identical average life, the fund manager would not know whether it would profit or loss from a rise in interest rates. More important, if the fund wanted to be insulated from changes in rates, the manager would not know whether to buy more of the long issue or sell more of the short position until a gain or loss had occurred.

Macaulay noticed that he could combine parts of the pricing formula with the average life formula to get a much more accurate measure of price sensitivity. Macaulay's measure weighted the time to maturity by the present value of the cash flows instead of the nominal cash flows. The result is:

$$\text{Duration}_{\text{Macaulay}} = \frac{\displaystyle\sum_{t=1}^{\text{Maturity}} \frac{t \times \text{Cash Flow}}{(1+r)^t}}{\displaystyle\sum_{t=1}^{\text{Maturity}} \frac{\text{Cash Flow}}{(1+r)^t}} \qquad (13.3)$$

Like the average life, the present value of the cash flows, which appear in both the numerator and the denominator, can be viewed as weights of the time to maturity. The weights sum to 100 percent, just like the weights used in the average life calculation. The biggest difference between the average life weightings and the duration weightings is that the duration weightings put less weight on cash flows far in the future, because their low current value makes them less sensitive to changes in rates (all other things equal).

This present value weighting reduces the average weighted time to maturity. A duration estimate of bonds is almost always less than the average life estimate for the same issue.[2] Further, the weighting reduces the importance of the longest cash flows in the duration measure.

Figure 13.2 shows the fulcrum view of duration as a kind of average balancing the length of time to each coupon. The same 10-year 10 percent bond used for Figure 13.1 is used for this figure, too. The duration is shorter than the average life. Similarly, the fulcrum on the chart is closer to the time of shorter cash flows than the average life statistic.

Duration has an additional desirable characteristic very useful for bond hedging. When Macaulay's duration is divided by (1 + yield to maturity), the resulting statistic is called *modified duration*. It can be shown that this modified duration fairly precisely predicts the percentage change in price for a change in yield for small changes in yield.

Using modified duration, we can begin to construct rigorously weighted long and short positions. Suppose a hedge fund had a $100 million position in security A. The manager knows this bond has a duration of 5 (or 5 percent). Therefore, if yields moved 1 percent (100 basis points), the position could be expected to make or lose 5 percent

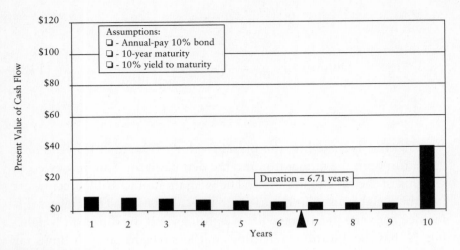

FIGURE 13.2   Duration

of $100 million, or $5 million. Suppose, too, that the fund manager wants to hedge that current position by selling short the second issue. If the manager sells short an equal $100 million, and the short issue has a duration of 4, the same yield change will create a gain or loss of only 4 percent of $100 million, or $4 million. By inspection, it is clear that the manager must sell $125 million short so that the size of the gain equals the size of the loss.

For several reasons, the math is not quite so tidy. First, the size of the position refers to the current market value of the position (including accrued interest), not the face amount of the bonds. Second, it is generally not true that the yield change on the short position exactly matches the yield change on the long position. Finally, the duration changes as yield changes, so the forecast is not as accurate for larger-yield changes.

A more general condition is given in Equation 13.4 to hedge a long position in the ith bond with a short position in the jth bond:

$$(\text{Price}_i + \text{Accrued}_i) \times \text{Par}_i \times \text{MDur}_i \times \Delta\text{Yield}_i$$
$$= -(\text{Price}_j + \text{Accrued}_j) \times \text{Par}_j \times \text{MDur}_j \times \Delta\text{Yield}_j \qquad (13.4)$$

Although there are quite a few terms in the equation, the idea is simple. Price plus accrued times par is the value of each position. The value multiplied by the modified duration gives the change in value for an arbitrary 1 percent (100 basis points) change in yield. The change in yield scales that gain or loss by the amount the yield is expected to change. Finally, the gain or loss for the long position is set equal (except for the negative sign) to the gain or loss for a short position.

The price, accrued interest, and duration of each bond are known or can be readily calculated. The change in yield is often assumed to be equal for both bonds, in which case they can be canceled out of the expression. The expression yields an exact weighting for one position given the starting position size for the other issue.

When the yields are not expected to move by equal amounts, it is important to clarify that it is not necessary to forecast the magnitude of particular yield changes. It is sufficient to forecast the change in yield of one issue relative to the second issue. For example, it is convenient to start with a change of 1 basis point. Given this change in the first issue, the second issue may be expected to move only half as much. In this situation, it may be prudent to overweight the issue with the steadier yield by an offsetting 2× overweighting compared to a duration weighting.

There are other differences between bonds besides duration. One extension of the duration-based view of risk management is called *convexity*. The formula for convexity (Equation 13.5) resembles the duration or modified duration formula. However, the purpose of the indicator is to measure how quickly the duration of individual bonds changes.

$$\text{Convexity} = \frac{\displaystyle\sum_{t=1}^{\text{Years to Maturity}} \frac{t(t+1)\text{Cash Flow}}{(1+\text{Yield})^t}}{(1+\text{Yield})^2 \text{Present Value}} \tag{13.5}$$

A bond with a high convexity will become more price volatile when rates decline and less volatile when rates rise. For this reason, convexity is generally seen as a good thing for long-only portfolio managers. For the hedge fund with short positions, convexity changes the duration of the position adversely.

It is a small next step to begin to treat positions as a portfolio of long and short positions. Just as weightings can be selected so that there is no net duration between the two positions, it is possible to combine three or more issues so that duration and convexity net to zero (including long and short positions).

The following example demonstrates the use of duration and convexity in hedging fixed-income securities. Consider two hypothetical notes, one bearing a 5½ percent annual coupon, maturing in 2 years and priced at 98 (per $100 face value), which yields 6.584 percent. The second has a 7⅛ percent annual coupon but matures in 5 years and has a price of 102, which yields 6.648 percent. The following calculation shows the proper hedge to carry to offset a long position of $100 million 5-year notes. For simplicity, both issues are assumed to move up and down by the same change in yield:[3]

$$(98 + 0.009) \times Par_i \times 1.86 \times 1 = -(102 + 0.012) \times 100 \times 4.16 \times 1$$

$$Par_i = -(102 + 0.012) \times 100 \times 4.16/(98 + 0.012)/1.86 =$$
$$\$233 \text{ million short}$$

Table 13.1 validates that the combined position is hedged for a parallel change in yield (where the yield on both issues moves by equal amounts).

As Table 13.1 demonstrates, the calculated weighting creates a position where the price sensitivity of the long position equals the price sensitivity of the short position. It is also clear that the position is not weighted to neutralize its convexity. It is possible to hedge both the duration risk and the convexity risk if there are additional positions in the portfolio. In addition, not every hedge fund will choose to hedge these exposures, but duration and convexity provide a methodology.

Bond portfolios are exposed to a variety of other risks, many of which can be quantified. One of the largest sources of risk to a hedge fund's bond portfolio is the yield curve. The yield curve represents all the yields on bonds of different maturities. Because hedge funds frequently carry both long and short positions, their positions may be more sensitive to the yield curve than to the general level of rates.

TABLE 13.1 Combined Hedge Position

Qty	Mat	Cpn	Price	Yield	Accd	Dur	Conv	Dur × Val	Conv × Val
–233	2-Yr	5.500	98	6.584	0.014	1.86	5.07	–42,468	–115,928
100	5-Yr	7.125	102	6.648	0.019	4.16	22.43	42,468	228,839
							Total	0	112,910

Notes: Qty = Quantity long or short in $ million; Mat = length of time until each bond matures; Cpn = annual coupon (as a percentage of $100 face); Price = quoted price of bond per $100 face; Yield = yield to maturity (percent); Accd = accrued interest per $100 face; Dur = modified duration; Conv = convexity; Dur × Val = Modified Duration × (Price + Accd) equal to change in value of the position for 1 percent change in yield; Conv × Val = Convexity × (Price + Accd), which is a gauge of how the duration weighting can change for each issue and the net position.

Most of the risks of the yield curve can be represented as changes in the slope of the yield curve and changes in the curvature of the curve. Over the past several decades, bonds of shorter maturities have had lower yields than bonds of longer maturities. That is not always the case, however, and the amount of difference between issues of various maturities can vary substantially.

The second yield curve risk reflects the degree to which yields bend upward or downward relative to a straight line. This type of flexing is constantly changing. In fact, even the location of the curvature may change over time.

Different strategies exist to measure yield curve risk. One of the simplest methods is to sort all the positions into a few "buckets" that subtotal the duration exposure for bonds in each maturity subinterval. For example, in Table 13.1, we could calculate subtotals for the Dur × Val calculation if the number of positions were larger and justified the additional effort. We could aggregate the risk for bonds in the money market maturity range, the 2-year range, the 5-year range, the 10-year range, and issues longer than 10 years. These buckets correspond with the maturities of benchmark Treasuries and the stated maturity of futures contracts, so it would be simple to eliminate undesirable risks.

A more ambitious method of measuring yield curve risk begins with a thorough review of the way yields can change. With this information, models for yield changes can be created. For example, regression can be used to measure how much short maturities move relative to longer issues. Risk measurement models then reprice the portfolio, following a short series to plausible scenarios for yield changes.

Currency and equity risk management differs considerably from fixed-income risk management. Yields on bonds in one country are highly correlated, and translating yield changes into price changes is routine. Yields on bonds in different countries are less well correlated. This makes international fixed-income risk management less precise and in many ways resembles the problems with currencies and equity positions.

Currency Risk Management

Currency trading desks are required to carry positions in a large number of currencies, but much of the volume of transactions occurs in a few currencies. These currencies (especially the euro, the Japanese yen, the Swiss franc, and the British pound) do not pose a major hedging problem for market makers, because traders can quickly and efficiently remove or hedge these exposures vis-à-vis the U.S. dollar or vis-à-vis each other. Although traders do not have a major problem with position management, risk managers must still be able to quantify the risk because traders do not always liquidate exposures.

Other currencies are much less liquid. Some currencies closely track other currencies and can be used as a proxy hedge. For example, all currencies that roughly track the U.S. dollar are accumulated separately from other currencies. Similarly, currencies that track the Japanese yen can be assumed to have the same risk as a position in the yen. By separating the positions into a manageable number of equivalent positions, the trader can get at least a rough gauge of the risk of the currency positions.

How well does this proxy hedging work? The answer depends on the nature of the positions. Some currencies do track other currencies fairly closely (at least most of the time). It is helpful if the exposure to any particular currency is small so that the currency position gets some benefit from diversification. Of course, this appeal to diversification is an admission that, although proxy hedging can be used to reduce risk, it does not eliminate it.

Proxy hedging also provides an imprecise measure of risk. Even when positions can be collapsed into a net position in several major currencies, proxy hedging provides no way to aggregate overall risk. In fact, dealers have lost substantial sums when proxy hedges have broken down, perhaps because the amount of risk changed without warning. For example, several currency dealers lost substantial sums related to the adoptions of the euro central currency in Europe.

Proxy hedging probably would not qualify for hedge accounting treatment of gains and losses (although some currencies track better than others). For more information on hedge accounting, see Chapter 11 (especially FAS 133).

Equity Risk Management

Beta, the lowercase Greek letter β, is a widely used measure of risk in the stock market and can provide the basis for a risk management methodology. Although it seems intuitive to use beta to weight long/short trades (and hence reduce risk), it appears to be somewhat complicated.

Beta is used to balance the trade-off between systematic (undiversifiable) risk and return for an investment portfolio. As Equation 13.6 shows, the expected return of a portfolio should equal the return on a risk-free asset plus some increment over that risk-free rate proportional to the risk of that portfolio:

$$\text{Return}_i = \text{Return}_{\text{Risk-free}} + \beta_i(\text{Return}_{\text{Market}} - \text{Return}_{\text{Risk-free}}) \quad (13.6)$$

The important distinction to make is that the required return of a particular stock is not proportional to the market return. Rather, it is only the difference between an individual asset return and the risk-free rate that is proportional to the amount the market return differs from the risk-free rate. The required return is not proportional to market return. This appears to make hedging with beta impossible.

TABLE 13.2 Comparison of Returns

Market Return (%)	Required Return$_i$ (%)	Ratio
−20	−33	1.65
−10	−18	1.80
0	−3	n.a.
10	12	1.20
20	27	1.35

Note: n.a. stands for not applicable.

In Table 13.2, a stock with a beta of 1.5 is compared with a range of possible returns for the market portfolio. A risk-free rate of 6 percent is used in the table.

It appears that there is no constant ratio linking the two returns that could be used as a hedge ratio. This could mean that no weighting is possible between the two assets that could remove the effect of the market from the combination. However, if possible different market returns are compared, the *difference* in the required returns is proportional to the beta of the asset. For example, the difference between the 20 percent return for the market and the 10 percent return is consistent with the beta of 1.5 (27% − 12% = 15%), as are all other lines in the table.

In fact, a consistent difference in the returns is revealed when comparing the total return of a levered position in both assets. Assume that the entire amount of the purchase price of the long position can be borrowed at the risk-free rate and that the proceeds of the short sale can be invested at the same rate. (Actually, it is only necessary to be able to borrow or lend the net difference in value between the long and short positions.)

From the levered perspective, all returns on long positions are reduced by the risk-free rate and all returns on short positions are increased by the risk-free rate. Table 13.2 becomes Table 13.3 (showing the returns on a long position in each case).

The returns are now proportional for the two assets because the fund earns only the excess return on its positions. It pays out (roughly) the risk-free rate to finance its long positions and it earns

TABLE 13.3   Comparison of Returns (levered perspective)

Market Return (%)	Required Return (%)	Ratio
–26	–39	1.50
–16	–24	1.50
–6	–9	1.50
4	6	1.50
14	21	1.50

(roughly) the risk-free rate as a rebate on the cash collateral support-ing the short positions (see Chapter 7). Those excess returns (or net returns from the hedge fund's perspective) are proportional, differing by the beta of the second asset relative to the first asset.

Hedge funds may be willing to go long one stock and short an-other (instead of investing in the market portfolio). The beta of the market equals 1.00 by construction. When betas are used to weight individual issues, the ratio of the betas of the two issues is the appro-priate weight for the positions.

To further clarify this methodology, it is the total market value of the longs and shorts that should be weighted by beta. Clearly, the price of each stock matters in that it determines the number of shares bought and sold, but the prices of the individual shares do not affect the aggregate value of the positions.

The method of trade weighting based on betas of the individual stocks carries with it all the implications of the assumptions used in deriving beta. In particular, it is only the systematic risk that is de-scribed by beta. Individual stocks may have wildly different amounts of total risk, much of which may be independent of the overall mar-ket return. This risk is considered diversifiable and is not considered in the weighting scheme.

This diversification requires a fairly large number of issues to make certain that diversifiable risk has been removed from the port-folio. But when used as a weighting scheme between two or even a few issues, very little of this diversification is present.

When only two issues are weighted, it may make sense to use the total risk on both issues. For a levered portfolio, the return can vary with the amount of leverage employed. To accommodate positions with different leverage (for example, futures contracts), risk of the individual positions can be represented as the standard deviation of price changes on the assets. In addition, the correlation between the two changes affects the volatility of the residual of the two positions (long versus short).

Using the volatility of the two assets (σ_{s1} and σ_{s2}) and the correlation coefficient (ρ), the optimal hedge ratio that minimizes the volatility of the hedged position is h:[4]

$$h = \rho \frac{\sigma_{S1}}{\sigma_{S2}} \tag{13.7}$$

This weighting scheme assumes that the two assets are multivariate normal. Each asset is normally distributed and the correlation coefficient describes the interaction between the two assets. Many assets owned by hedge funds, however, are rather skewed, do not have a stable standard deviation of returns, and may not have a stationary correlation coefficient. In addition, the objective to minimize variation may not be consistent with either hedge fund managers or its investors, who have limited downside and fairly unlimited upside. These investors may not be risk averse.

Nevertheless, this hedging scheme may make sense when a position is made up of pairs of long and short positions in fairly similar stocks. When the correlations are low and a fair number of positions are held by the fund, this weighting may be suboptimal relative to the entire position. The effect of each pair on the portfolio will differ, depending on the composition of the portfolio. As long as the correlation between stocks not paired together is nonzero, it makes sense to pick portfolios based on the volatility of the entire portfolio.

A large class of models is designed to build portfolios based on the expected profit and the risk of the entire portfolio. The technique is sometimes called *portfolio optimization* or *Markowitz programming* after the inventor, Harry Markowitz. The mathematical paradigm for optimization began with linear programming, a solution method widely used in a variety of applications in science and business. When risk is defined as variance in the models, a variation called *quadratic programming* is used for these models.

The problem establishes an *objective function* and a list of constraints. The objective function is sometimes called a *profit function*. In the portfolio context, the objective function is some measure of expected return or profit. The constraints limit the allowable risk in the portfolio. To get the best portfolio, the model must find positions that collectively create the best trade-off between risk (variance) and reward (expected return).

The beauty of this type of model is that risk management is embedded into the decision making about positions. Risk and reward may be as different as apples and oranges, yet a properly conceived model can force an efficient trade-off between the two.

The problem with this type of risk management is that it is inherently a front office application and risk management is also required in the back office. Making sure the portfolio is constructed wisely both from the view of expected profits and prudent risk is generally not the function of back office risk management. Instead, the back office focuses on risk measurement and perhaps enforcing maximum levels of allowable risk. This risk management can best be accomplished with a forward-looking model such as VaR described later.

Futures Risk Management

Futures can be an important part of a hedge fund portfolio. Generally, the risk characteristics of futures are derived from the underlying cash securities or commodities that are linked to the futures contract. The rules of the contracts can create complicated differences between the cash security or commodity and the future. In fact, an entire book has been written to describe the relationship between the cash Treasury markets and the Chicago Board of Trade futures on those Treasury issues.[5] Notwithstanding the differences, futures can be treated like cash instruments with the models mentioned previously.

Options Risk Management

Options can also be an important part of a hedge fund portfolio. Option hedging can be quite a bit more complicated than hedging of the underlying issues. The fair value of option prices depends on (1) the strike price; (2) the price of the underlying asset; (3) the time to expiration; (4) the volatility of the return on the underlying issue; and (5) the short-term rate associated with financing a long or short position in the underlying issue.

Generally, the strike price of an option does not change during the life of an option. One notable exception is on warrants or convertible bonds, where the strike price may change over time. Another exception involves some exotic options, such as Asian puts or calls and perhaps knockout puts or calls.

The most significant variable that can affect option hedging is the value of the underlying asset. For puts and calls that are significantly out of the money, the value of the option may not change much when the underlying asset moves up or down. As the price of the underlying asset moves to a level substantially above the strike for calls or below the strike for puts, the option becomes more valuable and more sensitive to changes in the underlying asset.

The sensitivity of a call or put relative to the underlying asset is called the *delta* (Greek letter Δ) of an option. The delta is important because it provides an approximate way to transform the risk of an option into the risk of the underlying asset, which can easily be incorporated into conventional risk management models.

Figure 13.3 is a graphical summary of the delta of a call plotted against the value of the underlying asset. The description of the option may affect the chart somewhat, but in general the delta begins at a value of zero at prices below the strike price and moves up to approximately 1 (the price of the option increase 1:1 relative to the underlying asset) as the price of the underlying increases.

The delta of a put (Figure 13.4) is nearly a mirror image of the delta of a call because the delta of a put and call with the same strike price sum to approximately 1. The put delta of an option is plotted against the value of the underlying asset. The delta begins at a value

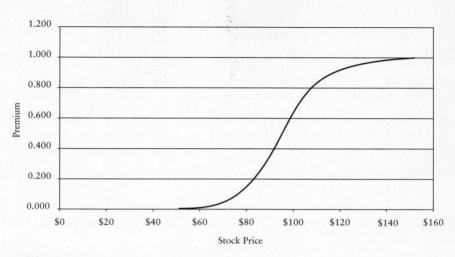

FIGURE 13.3 European Call Hedge Ratio (delta)

of approximately −1 at prices below the strike price and moves to a value of 0 as the value of the underlying asset increases.

Changes in the delta of an option create either a risk or an opportunity for an option trader. Holders of long positions in options

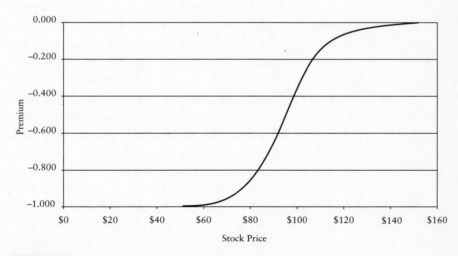

FIGURE 13.4 European Put Hedge Ratio (delta)

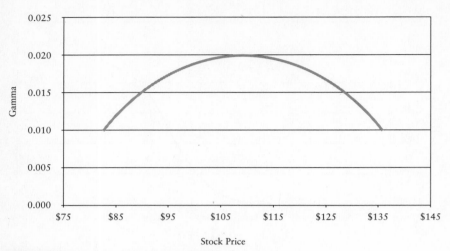

FIGURE 13.5   Gamma versus Underlying Price

benefit from changes in the delta. A market-neutral position becomes a long position in a rising market and a short position in a declining market. A measure of how fast changes are expected for the delta of an option is called *gamma* (Greek letter Γ). Figure 13.5 shows the gamma for a call option. The gamma of an option is largest near the strike price (give or take some adjustment for the time value of money and coupon or dividend income on the underlying asset).

For at-the-money options, the gamma is considerably larger as an option approaches the expiration date (see Figure 13.6). An additional risk factor for an options position is the volatility used to price the option. All option models use some form of probability distribution. For example, the Black and Scholes model assumes that the return of the underlying asset is normally distributed. Commonly used in mathematics and statistics, this distribution is no more than a way of assigning probabilities to all possible prices. Figure 13.7 shows the probabilities associated with two different levels of volatility. The area under each curve sums to 100 percent (that is, there is a 100 percent chance that something will happen and it is all represented somewhere in that area bounded by the curve). However, with the lower assumed volatility, many of the outcomes are near the starting level

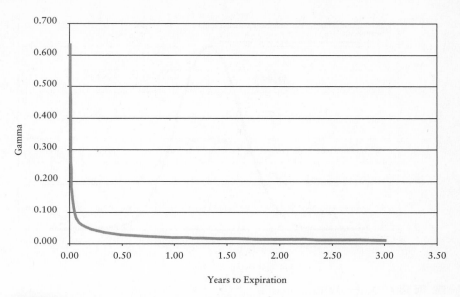

FIGURE 13.6   Gamma versus Time to Expiration

for the underlying asset. At higher volatilities, the chance of more extreme returns is much higher. Likewise, the probability that relatively little happens is reduced because all the outcomes must sum to 100 percent.

Higher volatilities lead to higher option prices because the higher volatilities are tantamount to increasing the chance of extreme outcomes (up and down). Because options cannot be worth less than zero, option holders benefit much more from extremely good price movements than from extremely adverse price movements.

Figure 13.8 shows the sensitivity of a call option to changes in volatility. The chart for a put would look very similar. This risk measure is sometimes called *kappa* (Greek letter K) but much more often called *vega* (not a Greek letter even though it sounds like it ought to be).

Options can be worth much more than their purchase price at expiration if the underlying asset moves favorably. At other times, the option may expire worthless, causing the trader to lose up to 100 per-

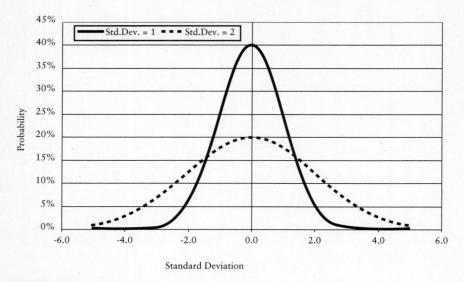

FIGURE 13.7   Normal Distribution

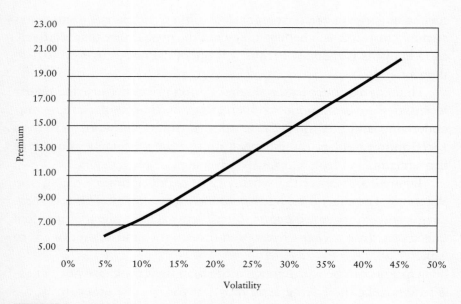

FIGURE 13.8   Call Premium versus Volatility

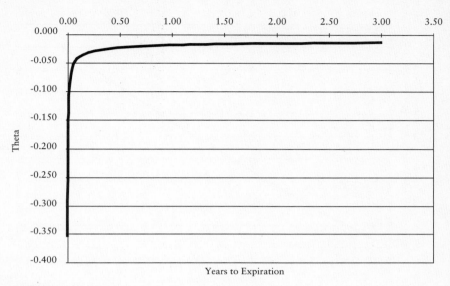

FIGURE 13.9   Time Decay (theta) versus Time to Expiration

cent of the value of the option. The Greek letter theta (Θ) measures how much an option loses in value if no other factors change (volatility, level of the underlying asset, financing rate, etc.). Figure 13.9 shows the theta or time decay of an at-the-money call.

The final option risk measure frequently discussed measures the sensitivity of the call or put to changes in the financing rate for the underlying issue. This risk factor is called rho (Greek letter ρ). Figure 13.10 shows the sensitivity of an at-the-money call to changes in the financing rate.

The chart of rho for a put looks somewhat different than the chart for a call. To hedge a call, the trader must sell short the underlying asset. The financing rate is used to measure how much income is earned on the proceeds of that short sale. Generally, a higher rate is better. Conversely, to hedge a put, the trader must buy the underlying asset. The financing rate is used to measure how much expense is paid to finance the long position. Generally, a lower rate is better (see Figure 13.11).

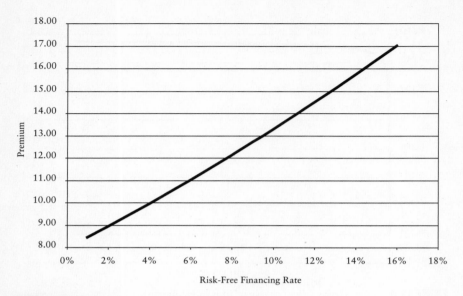

FIGURE 13.10   Call Premium versus Risk-Free Rate

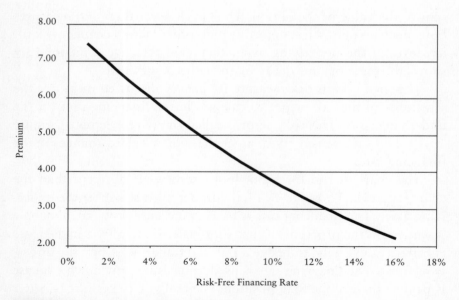

FIGURE 13.11   Put Premium versus Risk-Free Rate

While it is possible to measure any of these risk factors for an individual option position, the tools have value especially when they are accumulated for an entire option position. By monitoring totals of these option risk measures, the trader can assess the risk of the overall position.

Certain types of option positions have consistent and predictable risks. For example, a long calendar spread (short a nearby option and long a long-term option) is usually long vega[6] and long theta.[7] Other types of positions, such as a vertical spread (long one strike and short another for the same expiration date), can be long vega and short theta or short vega and long theta, depending on whether the underlying asset is closer to the strike of the long option or the short option.

Because volatility is one of the most important risks in an option position, it frequently gets special attention. In Chapter 5, a trading technique called GARCH models is described. As indicated, GARCH models use very short-term persistence in trends in volatility to make short-term forecasts of volatility.

Risk managers can use these GARCH forecasts. First, it is relatively easy to revalue the options portfolio at the levels of volatility predicted with the GARCH models. This failsafe prevents a trader from getting long or short options that the model predicts will be unprofitable if the forecast is accurate. Second, the goodness of fit of the GARCH model to the data provides an indication of the uncertainty of the volatility forecasts. Like any regression, the GARCH models calculate a confidence interval for the model parameters. A wide confidence interval is an indicator that the trend in volatility is uncertain and may argue for carrying minimal vega exposure.

RISK MODELS THAT RELY ON PROBABILITY

The models described in the previous section can provide considerable information about the nature of risks in a hedge fund position. They make it possible to forecast gains and losses stemming from a wide range of assumptions. As helpful as these scenarios are for risk management, they do not provide enough answers to hedge fund managers.

It is possible to create scenarios that look extremely profitable and other scenarios that are very risky. To be useful, the risk manager must have a way to know which scenarios are likely and which are unlikely. Alternatively, it may be sufficient to distill the possible scenarios into some inclusive indicator of risk.

Risk measures that incorporate probability are built from the same building blocks as the bond, stock, and currency hedging models described previously. In addition, these models overlay probability of outcomes onto the range of outcomes.

Value at Risk (VaR) and CreditMetrics are trademarked hedging strategies originally created by J. P. Morgan for internal risk management and for customers. Much has been written on these risk-modeling tools. This chapter does not attempt to incorporate all the revisions and extensions to the original ideas. Instead, the basic formulation is discussed from the point of view of hedge funds, which can be long or short a variety of assets.

Value at Risk (VaR) Risk Modeling

In Figure 13.7, the normal distribution was displayed with two different levels of volatility. For simplicity, one of the charts has been reproduced as Figure 13.12. The distribution that remains is called the standard normal distribution, which means that the distribution has a mean of 0.0 and a standard deviation equal to 1.0. This is the probability distribution that is discussed in this section.

The distribution shows the probability of every outcome. The chart continues from $-\infty$ to ∞, though the probability of getting more than 3 standard deviations to the right or left of 0.0 is very small.

It should be clear by inspection that there is exactly a 50 percent probability of being below the 0 mean and an equal 50 percent probability of being above the mean (because there is a very small chance of being exactly at the mean or at any one point). The probability of being at other points on the chart is also known. From the one-tail test in statistics, we recall that there is a 5 percent chance of being anywhere to the right of the line drawn at 1.65 standard deviations.

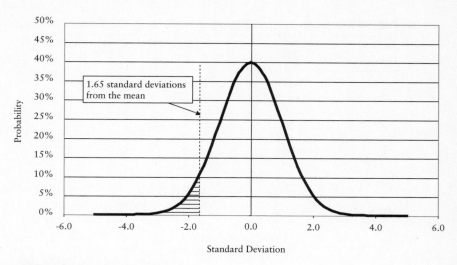

FIGURE 13.12 Normal Distribution

We will use that fact to build a probability-based report on risk. To simplify the initial calculations, we start with a single, unlevered asset. For illustration, we will work with a position worth approximately $1 million. In particular, we hold 10,000 shares of stock in XYZ Corporation that was priced as shown in Table 13.4.

We implicitly assumed that the return on XYZ was normal, which is approximately true for many assets. It really is not necessary to assume that XYZ was normally distributed, but it does simplify the discussion and is consistent with the original VaR formulation.

The share price is observed from actual price histories. The value of the position is just 10,000 times the share price. Because the number of shares did not change, the return could be calculated from either the price or the value of the position. The daily standard deviation was calculated using Excel's "stdeva" function, which returns the sample standard deviation. Although we do not need the annualized standard deviation in this example, the 43.40 percent number was calculated by multiplying the daily standard deviation by the square root of the number of days in a year. In this example, 2.74% × SQRT(251) equals 43.40%. To calculate VaR, multiply the

TABLE 13.4 Probability-Based Report on Stock XYZ

Date	Price ($)	Value ($)	Return (%)
1	98.778	987,778	n.a.
2	96.254	962,536	−2.59
3	96.724	967,239	0.49
4	99.193	991,932	2.52
5	101.571	1,015,705	2.37
6	105.091	1,050,912	3.41
7	100.502	1,005,017	−4.47
8	100.031	1,000,310	−0.47
9	102.222	1,022,217	2.17
10	100.000	1,000,000	−2.20

Daily standard deviation (%)	2.74
Annual standard deviation (%)	43.40
VaR(%)	4.52
VaR($)	45,197.66

daily standard deviation, 2.74 percent, times 1.65 standard deviations, which is 4.52 percent or a loss of $45,179.66 for the $1 million portfolio (assuming that the mean return is 0).

If the inputs are accurate, we can assert that 95 percent of the time, the position in XYZ will either make money or lose less than $45,179.66. If XYZ common had a standard deviation only half of the 2.74 percent calculated previously (1.37 percent), the VaR amount would also be half as large ($22,589.83). It is clear that this methodology translates the higher volatility of the position into a larger VaR and a smaller volatility into a lower VaR calculation.

Note that using the VaR framework does not really add any risk information. Instead, the method merely transforms the standard parameters for the normal distribution into a monetary amount.

It may surprise some readers that if a hedge fund borrowed half of the value of the above positions, the VaR would not change materially (see Table 13.5).

Although the volatility of the returns nearly doubled, the VaR for the position is calculated from the net investment in the position, which is half as much. As a result, the VaR measured in dollars did

TABLE 13.5 Probability-Based Report on a Hedge Fund

Date	Price ($)	Value ($)	Borrowed ($)	Net Investment ($)	Return (%)
1	98.778	987,778	493,889	493,889	n.a.
2	96.254	962,536	481,268	481,268	−5.11
3	96.724	967,239	483,619	483,619	0.98
4	99.193	991,932	495,966	495,966	5.11
5	101.571	1,015,705	507,853	507,853	4.79
6	105.091	1,050,912	525,456	525,456	6.93
7	100.502	1,005,017	502,509	502,509	−8.73
8	100.031	1,000,310	500,155	500,155	−0.94
9	102.222	1,022,217	511,109	511,109	4.38
10	100.000	1,000,000	500,000	500,000	−4.35

Daily standard deviation (%)	5.46
Annual standard deviation (%)	86.48
VaR(%)	9.01
VaR($)	45,034.99

not change. Yet the same market exposure is being borne by an investment half as large, reflecting the increased risk from leverage.

Conversely, if we held the equity in the fund equal and doubled the leverage, we would need to double the investment in each individual asset. Under these circumstances, the VaR calculated would double along with the position sizes.

It is not typical to account for leverage when calculating VaR on a levered portfolio. As the foregoing example indicates, it generally would not improve the calculation of risk. For positions where little or no investment is required (U.S. Treasury securities financed in the repo market, most over-the-counter derivatives, and, to a lesser extent, futures contracts), the indicated returns may approach infinite levels. Under these circumstances, it may be more intuitive to calculate returns and VaR using the nominal face amount.

Portfolio VaR

The previous VaR example tracked a single security. However, it is possible to track a portfolio exactly the same way. Assume that the position has not been changed for 10 days but is made up of a variety of securities (including long and short positions). In this case, the return calculated on the value of the position provides a valid means to estimate the standard deviation of the portfolio.

When a new security is entered into the portfolio or a security is removed from the portfolio, it is still possible to calculate the standard deviation of the updated portfolio by re-creating the past values as if the position equaled the current position. In this way, a VaR number can always be derived, even after portfolio adjustments.

Fortunately, there is an easier way to predict the volatility of a portfolio. The volatility of individual components can be added together to get the volatility of the whole. There is one complication, however. Diversification reduces the portfolio risk below the sum of its parts.

$$VaR_{1...n} = \sqrt{\sum_{i=1}^{n}\left(VaR_i\right)^2 + 2\sum_{i=1}^{n}\sum_{j=i+1}^{n}\rho_{i,j}VaR_i \times VaR_j} \qquad (13.8)$$

The formula for adding VaR numbers for assets in a portfolio is similar to the formula from statistics for adding variances. In Equation 13.8, the first summation adds up the VaR of each asset. The need to square the VaR before summing comes from the nature of VaR, which is a variation on the standard deviation, while it is important to add variances (which equal the square of the standard deviation). Because the VaR amounts are squared, the first term is always a positive number.

The second set of terms is called a *double summation*. The term incorporates information on the tendency of individual stocks to trade similar to other assets also in the portfolio. This expression accounts for the effect of diversification when individual assets are not perfectly correlated. Notice that, for a hedge fund, a large number of positions, up to half or more of the assets, can be short positions. The short positions have a sign opposite of the long positions. With a market-neutral hedge fund, a substantial number of the terms in this section summation are positive and many are negative. Even without the risk reduction of diversification, this set of risks can be much smaller than long-only portfolios.

The formula for adding the risk in a portfolio for adding VaR for assets that are not perfectly correlated involves many terms. The correlation between every stock versus every other stock in the portfolio all affects the risk of the composite portfolio. Spreading a portfolio over more stocks can reduce the risk of a portfolio, albeit by a decreasing amount for additional assets. Suppose the correlation between all stocks in a long-only portfolio all equal 50 percent. Further, suppose that the VaR on each asset equals $100. Figure 13.13 shows the benefits of diversification as the number of issues rises to 50. The chart demonstrates that most of the benefit from diversification can be achieved with 20 issues. Regardless of the level of correlation between the assets, there is an amount of systematic risk that cannot be eliminated with diversification. Notice, however, that for assets with low correlations, a residual portfolio risk is much lower than for highly correlated assets.

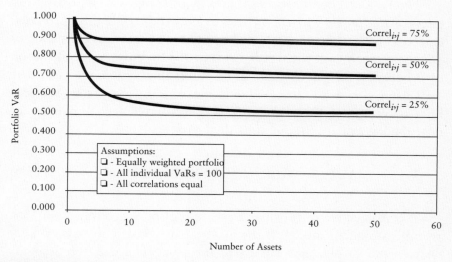

FIGURE 13.13 VaR Reduction from Diversification

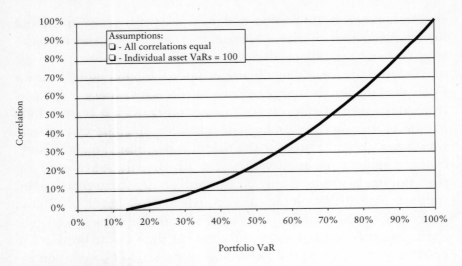

FIGURE 13.14   VaR of 50-Stock Portfolio

Figure 13.14 demonstrates the value of composing a portfolio of uncorrelated assets when compared to a portfolio of highly correlated assets. This chart was constructed by building portfolios consisting of 50 stocks, each with equal risk as measured by VaR. At a correlation of 0 between all assets, there is no remaining systematic risk. The VaR using this methodology would measure 0. Conversely, for very high correlations, the remaining undiversifiable risk remains very near the level of risk of the individual assets.

$$VaR_{i+j} = \sqrt{VaR_i^2 + VaR_j^2 + 2\rho_{i,j}VaR_iVaR_j}\qquad(13.9)$$

It is instructive to consider a position of pure arbitrage in a VaR risk measurement model. If the arbitrage is consistently priced very near to fair levels, then the correlation between the two assets is nearly 100 percent. In arbitrage, the pattern of one long position and one short position means that from the point of view of the hedge fund manager, the returns are perfectly negatively correlated. Under these circumstances, the VaR model would show a residual VaR for the combined position of 0. The formula in Equation 13.9 shows a $VaR_{i+j} = 0$ because $\rho_{i,j} = 1$ and $VaR_i = -VaR_j$.

Next consider a hedge between two assets that closely track each other but have a correlation somewhat less than 100%. Position sizes are selected so that VaR_i equals $-VaR_j$ and VaR_i^2 equals $-VaR_j\,VaR_j$, but the correlation reduces the second term. The VaR for the position is greater than 0 and is a measure of the basis risk on the position.

$$VaR_{i+j} = \sqrt{2VaR_i^2 + 2 \times 1 \times VaR_i VaR_j} = \sqrt{0} = 0 \qquad (13.10)$$

Because correlations are very high in much of the fixed-income market within a country and currency, there is little gained by adopting the more complicated and somewhat less precise VaR methodology. In fact, VaR could prove that duration and convexity hedging would be sufficient for risk control. When fixed-income positions are combined across currencies and national markets, the correlations decline. VaR can offer significant benefits over duration hedging country by country.

It should be obvious that proxy hedging implicitly assumes a correlation of 100 percent between the currency to be hedged and the currency selected to hedge the risk. VaR provides the means to quantify how much risk remains in the position after the proxy hedges are established.

There are plenty of criticisms of VaR. Returns are not normally distributed. Fairly extreme outcomes happen more often than predicted by the normal distribution. The problem is reduced somewhat by the typical 1-day horizon, where the probability of seeing these events is fairly small. To correct this problem, any distribution can be substituted for the normal distribution. For example, Monte Carlo simulation can measure a variation on VaR for any arbitrary distribution.

VaR may provide misleading risk measurements if the parameters used in the model are not stable. Volatilities are not stable. Neither are correlations between assets. It is not possible to appeal to diversification to moderate these inaccuracies. Volatilities shift and correlations change most when there are extreme movements in the market. They frequently create a situation where VaR does not properly describe portfolio risks.

Using VaR Methods for Skewed Hedge Fund Assets

All the examples of VaR measures rely on an assumption that the underlying returns are normally distributed. Returns of many of the assets held by hedge funds (including many types of derivatives) are not normally distributed. Although the normal distribution is part of the original VaR formulation, it is not necessary. In fact, VaR can and has been adapted to many probability distributions, including standard alternative distributions, proprietary models, and distributions created from recent history.

MANAGING CREDIT RISKS

A major risk for most bond portfolios involves the possibility of default. Very similar risks are present with derivatives transactions. Credit exposure can also exist in financing transactions and unsettled purchases and sales. The risk of default involves not just the actual event of default but also an assessment of the size of the recovery of value possible after a default. While it is possible to analyze each position for this credit exposure, it does not lend itself to simple models. Rather, analysts must study financial results, economic data, and other information to evaluate the credit risks.

Although default is an ever-present risk, the events are fairly uncommon and can be moderated by diversification, careful monitoring of financing exposure, and margining of derivative trades. The risk nevertheless affects bond portfolios all the time. As market participants perceive changes of risk of default or economic conditions that may limit the recovery of value in the event of default, the price of bonds reflects those attitudes.

Some managers use a credit "duration" on the portfolio. This analysis follows the same mathematical logic as duration used to construct Table 13.1, but the buckets are organized around similar types of bonds. The buckets might be divided by industry group, by the credit rating assigned by various rating agencies, or along other means. The purpose of the subtotaling is to measure the sensitivity of the entire portfolio to changes in yield caused by changes in credit quality, as opposed to changes in the overall level of rates.

A simple method to control credit risk is to limit the size of the portfolio's exposure to each industry and asset class. For example, funds often limit the amount of bonds issued by one issuer, an industry group, or other sources. This exposure traditionally has been measured in market value or face value. The credit duration methodology could be used to provide somewhat more robust diversification restrictions.

The more difficult challenge for credit risk modeling is to quantify the size of potential default. Little of a fund's credit exposure involves companies currently in default. There are two ways to measure uncertain credit exposure. One method develops the probability of default for individual bonds (or settlement risk, derivative trades, or trade credit). The second method reviews the probability of changes in value caused by perceived credit quality.

Default Credit Models

Consider first, a default model. This type of credit model looks at credit risk over the life of a bond. This method is similar to VaR in that it attempts to reassure the uncertainty of the credit events in terms of probabilities. The probabilities are generally derived from historical experience and do not represent well-known probability distributions, such as the normal distribution. Further, the time horizons are very long and require probabilities that are observed much less frequently than price changes are observed.

One method, popularized by J. P. Morgan's Creditmetrics, is driven by (1) the probability of not defaulting in each successive period and (2) the amount recovered from the assets if bankruptcy occurs. Table 13.6 shows an example typical of this methodology.

Table 13.6 begins with several assumptions. The time value of money equals 6 percent (continuously compounded). The probability of not defaulting in any year is 0.5 percent, contingent on the bond not having defaulted in a prior year. In the event of default, the debt holder can recover 75 percent of the face value of the issue by liquidating assets, reorganizing the company, or working out of default by other means. Finally, recognize that these are only assumptions and the user is free to change value. Although the values are the same for all 15 years in this example, the user may specify different interest rates, probabilities, and recovery in all periods.

Table 13.6 contains the column labeled Probability of No Default. Since there is an assumed probability of default equal to 0.5

TABLE 13.6 Credit Risk Over the Life of a Bond

Years	Probability of Default (%)	Probability of No Default (%)	Percent Recovered	Expected Value	PV @ 6%	PV of Expected Value
1	0.50	99.50	75	0.1250	0.9418	0.1177
2	1.00	99.00	75	0.2494	0.8869	0.2212
3	1.49	98.51	75	0.3731	0.8353	0.3117
4	1.99	98.01	75	0.4963	0.7866	0.3904
5	2.48	97.52	75	0.6188	0.7408	0.4584
6	2.96	97.04	75	0.7407	0.6977	0.5168
7	3.45	96.55	75	0.8620	0.6570	0.5664
8	3.93	96.07	75	0.9827	0.6188	0.6081
9	4.41	95.59	75	1.1028	0.5827	0.6426
10	4.89	95.11	75	1.2222	0.5488	0.6708
11	5.36	94.64	75	1.3411	0.5169	0.6932
12	5.84	94.16	75	1.4594	0.4868	0.7104
13	6.31	93.69	75	1.5771	0.4584	0.7230
14	6.78	93.22	75	1.6942	0.4317	0.7314
15	7.24	92.76	75	1.8108	0.4066	0.7362
Difference from default-free value						8.0981

Note: PV stands for present value.

percent in the first year, there is a probability of not defaulting equal to 99.5 percent (100 percent – 0.5 percent). In every year, there is a probability of not defaulting equal to 99.5 percent, assuming no default has yet occurred. There is, therefore, approximately a 99 percent change of no default after two years (99.5 percent × 99.5 percent). Likewise, there is around a 98.5 percent probability that the bond will service three years without default (99.5 percent^3). The remaining probabilities of not defaulting are completed in the same manner.

The probability of defaulting on or before a given year equals 100 percent minus the probability of not defaulting. For the first year, the probability is known from the assumptions. In each later year, the probability of default equals 100 percent minus the probability of no default by that year. In the second year, the probability of default is 100 percent less approximately 99 percent probability of no default.

If a default occurs, the loss is the amount not recovered. We assumed that 75 percent could be recovered regardless of whether the loss was to occur early or late in the life of the bond. Therefore, if a default occurred, the investor would suffer a loss of 100 percent – 75 percent, or 25 percent. The expected value of that loss is the 25 percent loss times the probability of default. For the example shown in Table 13.6, this expected value begins small and rises throughout the life of the bond, growing from $0.125 to $1.81 as later outcomes must endure the cumulative change of default.

Of course, because these events occur in the future, it is important to discount the values by the prevailing interest rate. Note that this methodology uses a constant 6 percent financing rate, which was assumed to be constant only for simplicity. It would not be appropriate to use the yield on this bond, however, because this methodology is separately accounting for the risk of default. To include a rate that also compensates for the risk of default would overcompensate for this risk.

Finally, the present values of each expected value are added together. The total, $8.10 in the present example, is subtracted from a price for the bond. This price should be based on a risk-free rate of interest appropriate for the maturity of the issue. For example, all the cash flows can be discounted by the zero coupon rates on the U.S. Treasury strip market (or comparable rates for non-dollar assets). In this way, the price of the bond is explicitly adjusted for the risk of default.

Before moving to another way to analyze credit risk, it should be pointed out that a variety of mathematical methods are used to translate assumptions about default over time into a pricing model and a risk model. For example, one approach that has been used has been to alter the binomial option model. Other models make somewhat different assumptions and follow different mathematical derivations but focus on the probability and economic significance of default.

The most popular credit default model modifies an option pricing model to track the entire assets of a firm, instead of the price of a single security. Under this methodology, the option owned by the shareholders to default and transfer the assets to bondholders and other creditors is modeled using methods similar to the derivation of the Black and Scholes model.

The most successful commercial version of this option-based default model is the KMV model. The authors of the model have derived the expected default frequency (EDF) from the option-based statement of the problem. The developers have attempted to configure the model to more accurately gauge this probability by shifting the point of default somewhat below the point when assets exceed liabilities. Even after this adjustment, the authors have observed that the rate of default is overstated by the option mathematics, so they have provided further adjustments to the probabilities. For a more detailed explanation of the KMV model and other credit default models, see Culp.[8]

Mark to Market Credit Exposure

The default credit methodology is a convenient way of translating a small number of assumptions into a price adjustment for a bond. This method is based on an analysis over the entire life of the bond. Usually, the horizon of bond investors is much shorter. Because bond credit spreads (or default probabilities and recovery rates) change from period to period, risky bonds can gain or lose value, affecting the performance of the investment.

Consider a 1-year horizon for a single-A rated bond. The bond bears an annual 6 percent and the 1-year interest rate for a comparable issue is 6¼ percent. The bond is likely to be rated single-A 1 year later (90.875 percent), but there is a chance that the bond will be rated as high as AAA (0.125 percent), a 2.27 percent chance of an upgrade to AA, a 5.375 percent chance of a downgrade to BBB, a 0.75 percent chance of being a BB bond, a 0.625 percent chance of being rated B, 0 percent chance of being CCC, and 0.125 percent chance of default.

Note these probabilities are roughly equal to historical rates of default. They represent averages over a business cycle but may be poor forecasts of changes in credit rating at times. The user is free to forecast these events, although the probabilities should sum to 100 percent.

The bond pays a 6 percent coupon in all situations except under default, when this model assumes that no interest will be received. Also, prices for the bond are estimated one year in the future under each credit rating. These levels may be based on current prices for bonds of different qualities (adjusted to the correct maturity), may be adjusted to reflect some theory of forward pricing, or may be based on additional analysis (see Table 13.7).

TABLE 13.7 Probability Distribution for Potential Upgrades and Downgrades

Current Rating	S&P Rating	1-Year Probability	Coupon ($)	Forward Value ($)	Total Value ($)	PV @ 6.25%	PV of Expected Value ($)
A	AAA	0.125	6.00	101.13	107.13	0.9394	0.13
A	AA	2.125	6.00	101.00	107.00	0.9394	2.14
A	A	90.875	6.00	100.75	106.75	0.9394	91.13
A	BBB	5.375	6.00	100.00	106.00	0.9394	5.35
A	BB	0.750	6.00	97.63	103.63	0.9394	0.73
A	B	0.625	6.00	95.75	101.75	0.9394	0.60
A	CCC	0.00	6.00	72.25	78.25	0.9394	0.00
A	Default	0.125	0.00	50.63	50.63	0.9394	0.06
							100.13

Note: PV stands for present value.

Discount the total of the bond value and coupon under each scenario in Table 13.7 to get the fair value of the bond. The discount rate to use should be based on the relevant holding period (1 year in this example), not the yield to maturity of the bond. Fair value for the bond under uncertainty is the expected value of the present value of these outcomes.

UNIQUE RISKS FOR HEDGE FUNDS

Hedge funds face many risks not captured by models measuring the risk of the positions. The history of hedge fund disasters proves that these risks are significant and pose a real threat to the success of any hedge fund.

Settlement Risk

Settlement risk is mostly a nuisance risk for most hedge funds. The category involves a wide range of things that can cost a fund some performance but generally should not threaten the fund's existence.

The bond market requires quick and efficient delivery of large blocks of securities. Nearly all positions are financed as repurchase agreements (repos) or reverse repos, so a similarly sized financing trade accompanies any purchase or short sale. On settlement date, the fund must pay for purchases with intraday overdrafts, then resolve the overdraft by settling the financing trade. When things go wrong, one side remains unsettled (called a fail to deliver), leading to an overnight overdraft. The cost of a fail to deliver can be expensive, especially if the fail spans many days.

Sometimes an issue is hard to borrow. When short positions are large relative to the floating supply, it may be hard to borrow an issue at any price. More often, it just costs more to borrow the issue, because most institutional holders are willing to lend the securities they own. When an issue is "tight" or hard to borrow, a type of fail called a round robin can develop, which does not tend to go away without some extra effort to break up the situation. A round robin occurs in financing where A borrows an issue from B, who expects to receive the issue from C. C thinks it has the issue to lend because it bought it from A. Each party waits for the others to deliver and they cannot clear up the fail because no one holds any securities to deliver.

Dealers have several advantages over retail customers to allow them to efficiently make and take delivery of large volumes of securities. The cutoff time for dealers delivering to customers is later than the cutoff for customers delivering to dealers. Unless a hedge fund negotiates dealer time with its trading and financing counterparties, the fund may find itself in the situation where dealers can deliver securities to them after the fund is beyond the deadline for redelivery.

Equity short sellers face a risk when borrowing securities. This problem is worse for small companies with a small float of stock. It can be hard to borrow issues of larger companies involved in merger or divestiture.

Much of the stock loan is controlled by a small number of custodian banks and master trustees. This concentration makes it easy to locate shares to borrow for short sales. However, it also means that small-time short sellers and new players may have a hard time locating and keeping shares of hard-to-borrow securities. Young hedge funds frequently discover that they must return a borrowed security if a larger customer wants to borrow the same issue.

Short Squeeze

The consequence of these problems borrowing stocks and bonds can lead to a short squeeze. A short squeeze occurs when borrowing a security gets prohibitively expensive or impossible and the short seller must buy in the position, usually at a high price.

Sometimes the short squeeze can be engineered. If players discover a large short position in an issue, they may borrow shares or bonds just to make them unavailable to the short seller. Traders may buy more of the issue and refuse to lend the position back to the short sellers.

A short squeeze can force the price of an issue higher. The higher price makes the issue more attractive as a short candidate, even if high financing costs are expected.

An investor who holds a long position can lose no more than 100 percent of the value because the price cannot go below zero. A short seller has no limit on the size of a loss. In principal, a short can go up 100 percent, 200 percent, or more, causing a loss greater than the value of the position. In practice, gains and losses are rarely that extreme, but losses on short sales are nevertheless skewed to more extreme outcomes.

A short seller risks changes in the liquidity of the underlying issue. In an actively traded stock or bond, a trader may feel that a short or long position is prudent because the position could be liquidated in a fairly short period of time. When liquidity dries up, the short seller is much more vulnerable to the squeeze simply because the long seller has the security and needs only to convince someone to buy the issue. In contrast, to unwind a short position, the buyer must either convince a holder to liquidate or convince another trader to sell short the issue. It is more difficult to motivate a potential seller to sell than to motivate a potential buyer to buy.

Short Financing Risk

Although a short seller faces the risk of a buy-in (when the lender closes out a financing trade by buying the security to replace the securities loaned), in at least one respect, the short seller has less risk than the levered buyer. As described in Chapter 7, loans of both stocks and bonds are usually collateralized with cash. This cash collateral earns a return somewhat below short-term financing rates. Conversely, the lender of the security has access to the cash collateral because the collateral is structured as a (slightly) below-market loan.

When issues get tighter, the submarket rate goes lower and the lender earns a higher spread on the security loan, because the cash can be reinvested at prevailing short rates to earn a wider spread. Nevertheless, the financing rate generally cannot go below zero, because that is the rate consistent with a fail to deliver. When general interest rates are low, the risk of special financing rates is fairly small.

In some countries, it is not acceptable to fail to deliver. In these markets, borrowing rates can go negative. There is no natural limit to the amount it can cost to borrow a short position.

Of course, the holder of a long position faces little or no risk in borrowing money against a particular issue. The short seller has few options because he or she must borrow a particular issue. The levered long holder is merely borrowing money. There are many more parties who are in a position and are willing to lend cash than parties who are in a position and willing to lend securities.

Credit of Counterparties

Hedge funds face significant counterparty credit risk. There are many sources of counterparty risk. When a fund buys or sells securities with a broker-dealer, the fund has a credit exposure. The more the price of the security has moved from the trading price, the larger the credit exposure to the counterparty.

For most transactions, the time from trade to settlement is short. Stock and bond regulators are pressuring broker-dealers, futures markets, and stock exchanges to reduce the delay between trade and settlement.

Mortgage trades remain one of the largest sources of credit exposure. Mortgage trading involves long forward purchases and sales. Credit policies differ as to how margin is maintained (if at all) on forward mortgage trades.

Over-the-counter derivatives can create large credit exposures. Options and swaps can change significantly in value from the time of trade until the trade is closed out, exercised, matured, or expired. Many of these trades allow for maintenance margin to be assessed by either counterparty. It is important to monitor this exposure.

Financing transactions can create significant counterparty risk. At the time securities are borrowed or lent, margin is usually established equal approximately to the value of the issue. Financing trades are not structured to tie the value of positions in the fund to the value of their financing positions. As positions make or lose money, the investors reap all gains and bear all losses. A fund must repay the entire loan balance regardless of the value of the position. However, when the NAV of the fund declines sharply or turns negative, the financing counterparties face the risk of loss on trades.

Both long financing and short financing can involve credit risk. If a fund borrows securities from a dealer and posts cash collateral, the fund becomes an unsecured creditor of the dealer if the price of the security declines, while the dealer becomes an unsecured creditor of the hedge fund if the price of the security rises. Similarly, if a fund borrows cash from a dealer and posts securities as collateral, the fund becomes an unsecured creditor of the dealer if the price of the security increases, while the dealer becomes an unsecured creditor of the hedge fund if the price of the security decreases.

Most hedge funds are not registered as broker-dealers. Most hedge funds finance their long and short positions with broker-dealer financing desks or at banks, because security regulations require a business to register as a broker-dealer to finance trades with retail clients. (There is little credit exposure to financing trades with retail customers that are not levered.) However, most of a hedge fund's financing trades are conducted with a levered counterparty that is a potential credit risk.

It is fairly easy to monitor counterparty risk, although firms frequently do not have easy access to the necessary data. With the information, it is easy to calculate the difference between the value of the security and the collateral for each unsettled trade, financing transaction, or derivative position. Further, it is not especially difficult to simulate different market scenarios to see when credit exposure gets critical.

It is sometimes more difficult to make the credit exposure go away. Not all trades with the dealer are consistently margined. Mortgage trades may be unmargined until a large threshold level is exceeded. A dealer does not always net margin exposure that a customer may have with the dealer. Reg T may limit borrowing levels. Dealers may be uncooperative about trading out of positions with customers that have substantial intrinsic value.

Ability to Borrow Cash

A levered fund must finance long and short positions to implement its investment strategies. The fund must comply with borrowing limits imposed by financing counterparties, including margin, haircuts (excess collateral provided to the financing counterparty), and total loan size limits. When positions lose money, the financing limits are based on the new, lower borrowing power of the fund.

If a fund borrowed the maximum possible amount allowed by the financing counterparty limits, it would be extremely vulnerable to a financing squeeze. Any time the fund had any material loss in NAV, it would need to reduce positions. Most funds maintain their leverage levels below the maximum amount of leverage in part to avoid this exposure and in part because the funds would be too risky if maximum leverage were employed.

When a fund has a significant loss, it is often forced to reduce positions. If a fund does not reduce positions in the face of losses, it is increasing its leverage. Consider an example of a fund that has $100 million in assets (it does not matter if they are long or short positions, but it may be easier to consider a long-only example) and $50 million in partnership capital. If the assets decline to $75 million, then capital would decline by $25 million. Leverage would increase from 2:1 ($100:50) to 3:1 ($75:25).

When a fund must reduce positions in the face of losses, it is placed in a vulnerable position. Hedge funds often take large undiversified positions in illiquid securities. Several times in the past, hedge fund losses have been aggravated by the limited liquidity of the market for the securities in the fund. With knowledge of the vulnerability of the hedge fund, trading counterparties may bid and offer at prices that increase the losses in the fund.

Sometimes, changes in credit standard are sufficient to force the distressed liquidation of positions. For example, following the demise of the Granite Fund, a mortgage derivative hedge fund, other funds that remotely resembled the Granite Fund were forced to reduce leverage. The poor performance this liquidation caused was enough to close several funds, even though they never posed a credit risk to thier lenders.

Liquidity Risk

It is clear from the problems faced by several large hedge funds in the past decade (see Chapter 16) that the lack of liquidity has played a role in their demise. Market regulators have concerns that these risks place stress on the entire financial system. As a result, banks that lend to hedge funds are allowed under the Basel II accord to request a numerical calculation of liquidity and operational risks.

Various measures of liquidity exposure capture some of the liquidity risk in a hedge fund portfolio. For example, measures of diversification (the number of issues held, the average weight of an individual issue as a percent of the portfolio, the largest position(s) as a percent of the total) give some idea of the sensitivity of the fund to liquidity of individual issues. Other measures, such as the position size divided by the daily trading volume, provide a rough gauge of how quickly and easily positions could be liquidated under ordinary market conditions.

Such measures provide little insight on the vulnerability of individual funds to extreme market situations where selling or buying is one-sided, liquidity diminishes, and the bid/offer spread widens. Lacking adequate information for precise measurements, hedge funds may substitute "stress testing," which analyzes the portfolio over widely varied assumptions of trading volume, costs, and interaction between different asset classes. Perhaps data from previous market crises (for example, the 1987 stock market crash and the stress to world markets caused by currency turmoil a decade later) can eventually provide better information about liquidity of hedge fund position.

DUE DILIGENCE

Hedge funds can limit their risks significantly by conducting due diligence research on trading counterparties and futures commission merchants (FCMs). Due diligence is difficult because most broker-dealers are not incorporated as separate entities. Instead, they exist as wholly owned subsidiaries of holding companies. Many times, the counterparty is an offshore entity. The capital from the parent may be in the form of noncash purchase of subordinated securities. Meanwhile, the capital of the holding company supports positions in a vast array of businesses, most with positions that are not disclosed to trading partners.

Nevertheless, hedge funds should attempt to monitor the creditworthiness of their trading partners. The fund should take advantage of as much information about these counterparties as possible. It may be possible to discuss exposures with other dealers and other hedge funds. In the past, credit departments of several organizations have taken the lead on extending credit. Other dealers and hedge funds follow the lead of these respected leaders. Traders that do business with marginally sound counterparties may have profitable trading businesses because the counterparty may have fewer choices. These short-term profits must be balanced against the greater chance of loss due to credit exposure.

Members of the exchange execute trades on the exchange for the benefit of clients. However, the futures exchanges have a clearing corporation that assumes the opposite site of all trades. Hedge funds rely on the futures clearing corporations of each exchange to honor all trades. Clearing corporations have failed, although very rarely. Most futures traders believe that the chance of a failure of a clearing corporation is very small. Nevertheless, the manager of a hedge fund should review this exposure from time to time and determine the risk the fund has to nonperformance by the clearing corporation.

Customers with large futures positions may be required to post substantial margin at futures member firms. These margins almost always exceed the value of the positions at the FCM. Clients that have several accounts may have a considerable required margin for offsetting positions. As a result, these clients have substantial balances that are, at least theoretically, a credit exposure.

Margin at futures commission merchants is segregated. Exchanges impose substantial requirements on their members. Most futures clients believe these controls are adequate protection. Some customers choose to limit their exposure by doing business with FCMs that are subsidiaries of the most creditworthy parents (AAA-rated bank holding companies). Others maintain accounts with multiple FCMs to spread out their exposure. This can be self-defeating at times, because it increases the chance that the hedge fund will have margin requirements imposed on their gross positions larger than their net positions.

The Alternative Investment Management Association (AIMA) has prepared a sample questionnaire for potential investors in hedge funds. The AIMA suggests that investors ask hedge funds to fill out the form and provide it to potential investors. The form is seven pages and includes basic information, such as the types of instruments held, what the positions are designed to accomplish, and a biography of the key employees. The form asks the manager to identify the major sources of return, to document how ideas are developed, and to identify ways the fund manager monitors and controls risk.

Zurich Capital Markets, Inc. has created a substantially more complete due diligence survey and has offered the survey to the industry as a potential standard for due diligence. The survey consists of four documents constructed in Microsoft Word and an additional document constructed in Microsoft Excel. Like the AIMA survey, the goal of the Zurich forms is to allow investors to learn key information about funds. Because the forms are extensive and fairly comprehensive, Zurich hopes that fund managers will complete the forms and offer them as standardized disclosure for due diligence. Although considerable effort is required to fill out and update the content of the forms, fund managers should be saved effort if most disclosure can be accomplished with the standard form.

Individuals often feel they need to ask questions not covered by the AIMA form or the Zurich package. Neither organization warrants their product to be complete. It is up to the individual or institution and advisors (lawyers, accountants, and investment advisors) to determine what additional review is required consistent with the nature of the fund, its style, and other relevant factors.

BEST PRACTICES

The Basel Committee on Banking Supervision pointed out[9] that most of the risk of loss to counterparties after the near collapse of Long Term Capital Management involved financing transactions and outstanding derivatives. Derivative transactions pose a credit exposure when the terms of these trades make the positions valuable. The counterparty faces a risk equal to that value less any previously collected collateral if a default interrupts the cash flows demanded by the trade.

The Basel Committee on Banking Supervision has recommended that hedge funds should have a substantial risk management capability.[10] This generally means that a hedge fund should have a quantitative risk measurement system (probably designed and implemented independent of the trading desk). The firm should establish risk guidelines.

The President's Working Group on Financial Markets has noted in *Hedge Funds, Leverage and the Lessons of Long Term Capital*[11] that there is an increasing trend in using collateral to mitigate credit exposures. The committee recognized the limits of collateral but nevertheless recommended greater use of it. In particular, policies should be reciprocal, so large broker-dealers and hedge funds should also post collateral with smaller counterparties.

The President's Working Group further recommends that hedge funds and broker-dealers each establish credit limits that reflect the financial strength of each counterparty, the policy concerning collateral or other margin, and whether exposures are netted. Credit exposure should be reevaluated daily.

In addition, the President's Working Group noted that leverage as measured by financial statements did not adequately measure risk. The committee suggested a measure based on the size of expected gains and losses relative to the capital base. Rather than impose arbitrary rules, the committee preferred to force disclosure of that risk, and trading and financing counterparties could determine their limits and price their services accordingly. Nevertheless at the time of this writing, there is no best practice policy consistently enforcing disclosure of potential risk levels.

The Basel Committee recommended the hedge funds and their trading partners sign master agreements.[12] The International Swap Dealers Association (ISDA) and the Public Securities Association (PSA) have constructed agreements that spell out collateral requirements, delineate the rights of parties to close out positions, and document each party's rights under bankruptcy. Fund managers should be certain these agreements are in place with all trading counterparties (including relevant subsidiaries) and apply to the types of securities traded by the fund.

A committee of industry participants recently released a series of best practice recommendations for the industry.[13] This document endorses many of the recommendations from previous quasi-governmental committees. In addition, this group called for hedge funds to establish clear investment objectives and risk targets. The fund should allocate traditional authority and budget risk consistent with these objectives and targets. Management should also create an internal risk auditor to document the degree of compliance to senior management. It is noteworthy to mention that senior management, not the trading desk, should direct each of these steps (with the exception of the day-to-day trading).

The industry committee also called for hedge funds to monitor (but not necessarily disclose to investors) various measures of liquidity risk, including an attempt to determine the extent that credit risk, market risk, and liquidity risk interact. In particular, the committee proposed a measure called *asset liquidity* based on the extent that the value of the asset changes in response to changes in the liquidity of the market for the asset.[14] The committee proposed additional metrics, including the number of days to liquidate or hedge a position and an estimate of the amount the fund would lose due to liquidity if the positions were liquidated or hedged within a specified time interval.

In addition, the committee challenged hedge funds to implement liquidity policies including monitoring systems to assure adequate liquidity even under stress.

The committee has proposed that hedge fund managers should stress test hedge fund portfolios. The fund should analyze (but not necessarily disclose to investors) the effects of changes in yields, the shape of the yield curve, and changes in volatility and should look for "nonlinearities" (the effects of option gamma and bond convexity) between asset prices and fund returns. Should this recommendation become accepted as standard care required by the manager, the fund would be required to conduct such analysis or risk lawsuits from investors.

NOTES

1. For general risk management, see Christopher L. Culp, *The Risk Management Process,* Wiley, New York, 2001. For a more complete review of the techniques, see Carol Alexander, *Mastering Risk,* Volume 2: *Application,* Financial Times, Prentice Hall, 2001.
2. A fairly common exception is the average life of a zero-coupon bond, which equals the Macaulay duration. Also, if interest rates equal zero, the two measures are also equal because the present value terms all equal 1.
3. Each bond was assumed to have one day of accrued interest in this example.
4. For a derivation of the optimal hedge ratio, see John C. Hull, *Options, Futures and Other Derivatives*, 4th ed., Prentice Hall, Englewood Cliffs, NJ, 2000, page 39.
5. Galen D. Berghardt and Terrence M. Belden, *The Treasury Bond Basis: An In-Depth Analysis for Hedges, Speculators and Arbitrageurs,* McGraw-Hill, New York, 1993.
6. An option position is long vega when the entire position makes money when volatility rises and loses money when volatility declines. An option position is short vega when the entire position loses money when volatility rises and makes money when volatility declines.
7. An option position is long theta when time decay on the entire position is positive, meaning that the position makes money over time if the underlying asset does move. An option position is short theta when time decay on the entire position is negative, meaning that the position loses money over time if the underlying asset does not move.
8. Culp, Christopher L., *The Risk Management Process,* Wiley, New York, 2001, pp. 372–417.

9. *Banks' Interaction with Highly Leveraged Institutions,* Basel Committee on Banking Supervision, January 1999, page 2; available at http://www.bis.org/publ/index.htm.
10. Ibid., page 4.
11. *Hedge Funds, Leverage and the Lessons of Long Term Capital Management,* April 1999, page 9; available at http://www.ustreas.gov/press/releases/docs/hedgefund.pdf.
12. *Banks' Interaction,* page 3.
13. *Sound Practices for Hedge Fund Managers,* February 2000; available at http://planethedgefund.com/articles/Sound_Practices.doc.
14. Ibid., paragraph 9.

CHAPTER 14

Marketing Hedge Funds

The chapter about marketing appears near the end of this book because it is necessary to understand much background information about the hedge fund industry before marketing concepts are applied, but it is wrong to conclude that marketing should be one of the last things considered when forming a hedge fund. On the contrary, the marketing perspective developed here is that an aspiring manager should approach the creation of a new fund much like a food company would develop a new product, beginning by identifying needs and following an orderly path through the classic marketing issues.

It also should not be assumed that the chapter on marketing is unimportant. On the contrary, the success of a hedge fund management company and the success of an individual fund depend very much on the success of efforts to market the product. This chapter explores classic marketing concepts as they apply to hedge funds.

CORE CONCEPTS OF MARKETING

Many of the ideas and theories developed to sell consumer goods have been applied to services, including investment products. Indeed, many of the techniques described here are used by hedge fund sponsors.

The purpose of this review of marketing is to challenge hedge fund sponsors to apply the marketing model to their organizations. "Marketing is a social and managerial process by which individuals and groups obtain what they need and want through creating, offering, and exchanging products of value with others."[1]

Traditional marketing begins by identifying *needs, wants,* and *demands.* It may seem wrong to include needs on this list. When applied to consumer goods, this generally implies goods that are essential to life itself. Investors that have money to invest (especially in hedge funds, which are generally available only to the affluent) have already provided for those basic needs. In fact, investing often fulfills the basic need for retirement (individuals and pension plans), fund basic services (university endowments), or fund critical social needs (foundations). In practice, it may not matter whether the desire for hedge funds stems from a need, a want, or a demand. The resulting desire for hedge funds creates an opportunity for organizations seeking to satisfy that desire.

It is tempting to think about these issues solely from the point of view of a potential investor in a hedge fund. However, to understand the market environment, it may be necessary to think of these needs, wants, and demands as they create desires that can be satisfied not only by other alternative investments but also by traditional investments.

One of the most basic needs for investors is to account for the time value of money. A decision to invest today involves a choice not to consume today. In order for the investment to make sense, the deferred cash flow must be "sweetened" by a reasonable return. The most fundamental need for investors is to receive a rate of return to compensate for this delayed consumption.

Many possible portfolios can be assembled from a variety of assets. Hedge fund investors may seek out hedge fund investments to increase return, to reduce risk, or in some other way alter the payoffs available.

Hedge fund investors may satisfy additional wants while providing an investment return. The exclusive nature of hedge funds may confer on the investor social status or an impression of sophistication as an investor.

Index mutual funds have consistently performed better than funds following an active strategy. One explanation for why investors continue to invest in the actively managed mutual funds is that a sizable number of investors get pleasure out of *seeking* to outperform the benchmarks even if it does not happen most of the time. This same logic has been used to explain the appeal of state lotteries, where the probability of success is much more remote than for hedge funds to provide a superior return.

Unlike most goods and services, a buy decision refers to a decision to invest in a particular fund. A fund is bought when an investor makes an investment in that fund. The purchase is completed only when fees are collected for providing this service. However, in some sense, the investor buys the product over and over again each time the investor decides to leave the investment intact.

Although it is convenient to take an all-inclusive view of investor needs, wants, and demands and the full range of investment products that can fulfill consumer desires, much more attention will be focused on those investors who are able and willing to "buy" the product. Hedge fund sponsors are concerned about those possible investors willing and able to invest.

To a marketing organization, a *product* is anything (physical product or service) that can fill a need. Frequently, the need is abstract from the actual product. A homeowner buys a drill to fill the need for a hole. Similarly, an investor may be buying diversification, peace of mind, or even a dream of attractive investment success.

Frequently the consumer must choose between many products that can solve the need. To choose, the investor weighs *value, cost,* and *satisfaction*. The customer perception may not correspond with historical performance or the level of incentive fees. In fact, the investor must conclude that the high level of expertise in a hedge fund justifies the higher fees relative to mutual funds. Incentive fees may enhance customer satisfaction and a sense of value because the fee is not charged when returns are low. In fact, clients are usually most happy when incentive fees are high, because net performance is also high.

Other factors may reduce satisfaction. Some factors, such as taxes, may be beyond the control of the hedge fund manager. Returns on substitute investment products also affect satisfaction. Investors may be much more happy with low positive returns if other assets have had negative returns.

Hedge funds seek to improve perceived value. The most direct way to improve the perception is to increase the return (through excellent performance). Hedge funds may find that additional customer knowledge leads to higher perceived value and greater satisfaction. Similarly, an excellent customer relationship can augment perceived value.

For many consumer goods, a company can create an impression of value by lowering the price. This is not commonly used with hedge funds. Like many physical luxury goods, high pricing creates an impression of excellence that may actually heighten the product's appeal.

Hedge funds have several indirect ways of measuring customer satisfaction. Do investors refer other potential investors to the fund managers? To what extent does the fund experience turnover in its capital base? Finally, the fund can get feedback from client contact.

The *purchase* or *exchange* in most markets is different from an investment transaction. As mentioned earlier, the good actually purchased and consumed is the investment of those funds, so the transfer of money is not, by itself, the transaction. The purchase may come bundled with other arrangements, perhaps undisclosed to the investor. The manager may execute trades under a soft dollar arrangement whereby customers' commissions pay for computer systems or other goods used by the manager to perform the investment services. Commissions may also be directed to sales agents who market the hedge fund.

Hedge fund clients may get additional investment advice beyond the actual purchase and sale of securities. In face-to-face meetings, in letters to investors, and in marketing literature, the fund manager may discuss investment strategies, relative value, tax issues, and portfolio considerations.

Unlike most consumer goods, hedge fund management services must be repurchased each break period. The client makes an explicit decision to make an investment. Then, at each period that the investor may withdraw the funds, a decision to not withdraw money is equivalent to a purchase decision. It is like a newspaper subscription that can be canceled at regular points but also automatically renews if no action is taken.

A hedge fund builds many types of relationships that can affect the success of the fund. The relationship between the investors and the fund is affected by past performance and investor contact. The fund also has relationships with trading counterparties. These relationships can be a valuable source of returns. The fund has important relationships with lending counterparties. Without these lenders, many hedge fund strategies would be impossible to implement. The fund has relationships with regulators, accountants, lawyers, third-party marketers, and even other investment providers. The network of all these relationships makes it possible to satisfy the needs and wants of the investors.

The *market* can be defined narrowly or broadly. "A market consists of all the potential customers sharing a particular need or want who might be willing and able to engage in exchange to satisfy that need or want."[2] A market to a hedge fund manager may be just those investors who could invest in a particular hedge fund strategy and the managers that offer that strategy. A somewhat broader view would include all hedge fund strategies (perhaps also including managed futures, private equity, and venture capital funds). The broadest definition would include a wide range of assets or significantly different risk and return. This definition may be useful to a large investment organization interested in providing a financial supermarket of alternatives to its customers.

It is typical to define the market as the universe of hedge funds. This market has grown rapidly in the past decade. Both the total assets under management and the number of hedge funds continue to grow. As of December 1999, nearly one-third of all hedge funds had between $5 million and $25 million. Another approximately one-third of the funds had between $25 million and $100 million.[3] Perhaps because of the rapid increase in the number of funds (or the closing of several large funds), the size of the average hedge fund has been decreasing. (See Tables 14.1 and 14.2.)

Marketers are those individuals or organizations actively seeking an exchange with another party, which usually involves the seller of

TABLE 14.1   Breakdown of Hedge Fund Investors

Individual
Pension fund
Endowment
Domestic
Offshore

TABLE 14.2   Breakdown of Hedge Fund Strategies

Equity hedge
Equity market neutral
Fixed-income arbitrage
Convertible arbitrage
Emerging markets
Others

a product but could involve the consumer in some cases. In the case of a hedge fund, the marketer is the fund sponsor, not the fund itself. The prospect usually is the end investor. In some cases, it may be useful to view a fund of funds investor as an intermediary between the investor and the hedge fund, which serves as the prospect. A hedge fund may seek to establish a relationship with a possible joint marketing partner or a private banker that may use the fund in portfolios. Each of these prospects is not the fund investor but may make the investment decision.

COMPANY CONCEPTS

The goal of marketing is to organize all the company's efforts around filling consumer needs. However, there are many other business models.

Companies may be oriented by a *product concept*. This organization seeks to build a product with the presumption that the customer will buy it because of product advantages. When a senior trader leaves a broker-dealer or another hedge fund to create a new fund based on prior trading experience, a product-oriented fund manager is created. When a life insurance company creates a new product combining the tax savings of life insurance with the investment characteristics of a hedge fund, the company is operating as a product-oriented company.

A company may be built on a *sales concept*. Under this point of view, customers will not buy enough of a product without a significant selling effort. This type of organization may use unique skills and contacts to encourage consumption. In the hedge fund business, this orientation is common in the fund of funds sector. It is also typical of a hedge fund created by a retail broker-dealer as a sales product.

The third type of business organization is a *marketing concept*. Here, the business is devoted to discovering and satisfying customer needs, wants, and demands. Knowledge of these desires precedes the product creation and forms the basis for selecting the type of product(s) to create. In fact, marketing issues pervade the business plan from the beginning. This type of organization is not commonly found in the hedge fund community, because hedge fund principals are more likely to have investment expertise than marketing expertise.

GROWTH STRATEGIES

Classic marketing analysis separates growth strategies into *intensive growth strategies, integrative growth strategies,* and *diversification strategies*. One way to grow intensively is to increase *market penetration*. For hedge funds, this might mean prospecting for business among competitors' investors. This type of marketing represents a major part of the marketing effort for institutional investors (that make multiple hedge fund investments). Funds also market to their own clients to increase their allocation to hedge fund strategies. Hedge fund investors frequently make small initial investments in a hedge fund and increase the stake over time. Marketers can also seek to increase the number of investors in hedge funds. Most funds devote a large marketing effort toward individuals who have not invested in hedge funds before.

A second form of intensive growth strategy is called *market development strategy*. This strategy looks to find new hedge fund investors. However, instead of increasing efforts to find investors using established techniques, new channels are created. For hedge funds, this may involve developing new joint marketing agreements or creating engineered products to be sold to investors unlikely to invest directly in hedge funds. The most common example of market development strategy is when a fund enters a new geographical area (a domestic fund creating an offshore ability, for example).

The third way a fund manager can create intensive growth is called *product development strategy*. This strategy might involve creating additional funds following different investment strategies. It might involve product improvement. For a hedge fund, that might involve changes to the investment decision making to improve risk or return characteristics. It also may involve changes in terms to investors (transparency, lockup rules, etc.). Finally, many funds choose to implement multiple strategies to provide investors with the benefit of diversification.

A second strategy for growth is called *integrative growth*. This strategy usually means vertical integration (Ford making its own steel). For hedge funds, vertical integration might involve creating a broker-dealer to execute trades. Because the fund does not participate in those profits and the fund sponsor does, such arrangements are regarded with suspicion. Perhaps the best (limited) example of integrative growth is when a fund eliminates outsourced services and provides the services for the fund.

The third strategy for growth is called *diversification growth*. Diversification growth involves selling new, related products to existing customers (for example, a mutual fund starting a hedge fund), selling different products to existing clients (a hedge fund starting a fund of funds), and selling unrelated products to new customers. Well-established hedge fund managers may employ this strategy, especially when the core strategies are running into capacity limitations. By offering quite different products to a new group of customers, the firm greatly strengthens its revenue base.

MARKETING MIX

The marketing mix has been described by Jeremy McCarthy as the Four P's: *product*, *pricing*, *promotion*, and *place*.[4] The product is determined by all the key decisions made when the fund was created. Each product is distinguished by the characteristics of the return, the degree of transparency, lockup provisions, whether the fund follows a single, pure style or multiple strategies, and whether the fund has any special features. For example, some funds invest in real estate and private equity (including initial public offers) using special accounting rules called *side pocket allocations*.

The second P is pricing. Funds do not generally compete much on price, but there has been a modest decline in management fees over time. Funds do differ as to whether incentive fees acknowledge a hurdle rate below which no fees are assets. The manager may make decisions concerning ticket charges that can meaningfully affect the total cost to the investor. Funds can use some portion of commissions to hire some administrative services or software. Funds may also allocate some of the futures commission to a third-party marketer. Finally, the manager may elect to waive some of the disclosed fees when the assets under management are small when the costs are distributed over too small a base of assets.

The third P is promotion. Promotion is broadly defined in the marketing literature, but it includes direct marketing efforts to the extent allowed. There is a relatively small number of potential institutional investors and getting contact information is fairly straightforward. Getting information about individuals, especially offshore individuals, may require the aid of third-party marketers where cross-selling of hedge fund assets is not possible.

Promotion also includes public relations, Internet marketing, and advertising. Although most U.S. hedge funds are not allowed to advertise, the promotion budget includes the costs of developing hand-outs and mailings. It may be possible to advertise related products. By speaking regularly at conferences, the managers can disseminate material in a favorable light.

Offshore funds may be able to advertise in some markets and not others. Several loopholes make it possible to advertise hedge fund products in many jurisdictions. For example, a fund may be able to advertise in a British periodical commonly read by French investors.

Offshore funds have the flexibility to select a domicile, perhaps set up a master-feeder structure instead of a mirror fund, and even change the way they do business.

All funds can differ as to how they are sold. Some hedge funds are sales products for a team of high net worth stockbrokers. The hedge fund management company sells others directly. Perhaps more commonly, the fund directs the assets to a fund of funds that reallocates the money to different strategies. Many hedge funds outside the United States trade on European stock exchanges. Finally, it is possible to indirectly sell the fund by using derivatives to make the pattern of return available to investors unwilling to invest in a fund.

MARKET RESEARCH

Relatively few data are available for hedge fund marketers. Fund managers need both aggregate data (to make strategic decisions) and investor details (used to market to potential investors).

Data are classified as *primary data* and *secondary data*. Primary data have been collected for a specific purpose. These data might include a list of current customers and associated financial details and can also include a list of potential customers.

Secondary data have been gathered for a previous need or for an ongoing need. For a hedge fund, this primarily means contact information on existing and potential investors. It probably makes sense to centralize the data with contact management software. This allows the fund to have continuity in its marketing efforts amid staff turnover. It allows the hedge fund management company to cross-sell different funds to its customer base.

Secondary data may be plentiful in another kind of financial institution that has extensive contact banking, brokerage, or conventional money management product lines. The private placement rules that prohibit advertising may also prohibit the financial institution from soliciting these customers. It is important to clear marketing efforts with the fund's legal advisor. However, when the existing relationships have an advisory nature, the fund has much more leeway to cross-market. Treading a tight line, the fund manager can also inform existing customers about a new hedge fund opportunity for clients and encourage existing customers to seek out information on the product.

For most businesses, the government is a major source for secondary marketing data. For hedge funds, the secondary data are not extensive. Most funds are exempt from Securities and Exchange Commission (SEC) registration. In any case, data reported to the SEC, the Commodity Futures Trading Commission (CFTC), and the National Futures Association (NFA) would be more interesting to investors than to marketers within the fund organization. A minor exception might be income and wealth statistics derived from Internal Revenue Service (IRS) information and other disclosures on the growth of pension assets that may help in formulating marketing goals.

Pension consultants have valuable data collected from their clients and published periodically. This source of data can be expensive—hundreds or even thousands of dollars—compared to the standards of mass-circulated books and periodicals. These data are extensive, however, including information about the size of plans, the range of their investments, risk tolerance, geographical distribution, and both historical and forecasted growth.

The financial press publishes lists of the largest pension funds, endowments, and foundations. These lists can be useful checklists for marketing. The lists generally do not include contact information other than that available from other sources. In using this information the fund marketers again must be careful to comply with marketing rules prohibiting unsolicited marketing to potential clients.

Business publishers have a large amount of data on potential clients. Feature articles in *Business Week,* the *Wall Street Journal, Fortune,* and *Forbes* can be a valuable source of secondary marketing data. Reports from Standard & Poor's, Moody's, and Duff and Phelps primarily intended for investors can also provide information valuable to marketers.

A fund manager can acquire secondary marketing data in a variety of ways. The simplest way is to hire third-party marketers that already possess these data, including an extensive list of potential clients. Third-party marketers are valuable to the new hedge fund primarily because of these secondary data. The fund manager should not expect the independent marketer to share much of this information with the fund. Instead, they reduce the need for this information.

One of the best sources of secondary data for a hedge fund committed to marketing its own products is its own effort. Such information should be preserved and organized as if the data will be used for later marketing decisions. It often is useful.

The mutual fund industry can be a source of secondary market information. The hedge fund industry tends to be quicker to adopt new investment vehicles, which creates the impression that whatever happens in the mutual fund industry is old news. However, with the sheer size of the money under management and the variety of products, the mutual fund industry can reveal information about changes in investor preferences.

Traditional marketing techniques to acquire secondary data have not worked in the hedge fund industry. Many hedge fund investors are very concerned about privacy. The investors that would participate in a focus group may not represent the attitudes of the fund's potential investors. Not surprising, many hedge fund prospects refuse to complete a survey about hedge funds.

Most hedge funds are small organizations. As mentioned in Chapter 1, the average fund has approximately $100 million in assets and most funds have fewer than 50 employees. A fund manager may have no employee exclusively devoted to marketing the fund. It is not reasonable to expect the manager to pay for expensive contract research.

ANALYZING THE CONSUMER

Traditional marketing literature includes extensive theories of personality or psychology to systematize theories of consumer purchase decisions. Perhaps these theories are more relevant for studying the buyers of toothpaste or laundry detergent than for studying buyers of hedge funds.

For example, Maslow's Theory of Motivation identifies five levels of needs.[5] Consumers have little need for products at a particular level until the needs in the previous level are satisfied. The five levels are: (1) physiological needs (food, water, shelter); (2) safety needs (security, protection); (3) social needs (sense of belonging/love); (4) esteem needs (self-esteem, recognition, status); and (5) self-actualization (self-development and realization). Private placement rules pretty much ensure that all potential clients can satisfy the first two levels of needs. Hedge funds are not in a position to supply social needs. While some clients satisfy needs for self-esteem, it is not clear how that affects a firm's marketing effort, because clients could get the same self-esteem from other hedge funds.

Herzberg's Theory of Motivation may be somewhat useful for hedge funds marketing to existing clients. Herzberg's theory predicts that motivation is determined by satisfiers (things that causes satisfaction) as well as dissatisfiers (things that cause dissatisfaction).[6] The absence of dissatisfactors does not seem to predict purchase motivation. However, dissatisfiers explain why a fund finds clients withdrawing money. Some of those dissatisfiers may be out of the control of the manager. For example, once an investment strategy is selected, losses will occur from time to time. However, the nature of the investment base may influence the choice of an investment strategy. In other words, it may be able to market a fund that has narrower swings in performance even if the average return is lower.

A particular fund may discover that its clients are not strongly dissatisfied by losses. Hedge fund investors are often sophisticated investors that may be more disturbed by variance from a stated strategy than short-term losses from that strategy. Clients may be dissatisfied with long delays in producing tax reporting information or poor communication. By eliminating these unnecessary sources of dissatisfaction, a fund can hold on to investor money longer.

Because individual investors must satisfy the private placement requirements that limit hedge fund investment to high income or high net worth individuals, there is fairly little difference in the demographics of the individual investors. They are in a high tax bracket. They tend to be older.

Nevertheless, there has been an attempt to distinguish between the moderately wealthy (for our purposes, those who marginally qualify to invest in hedge funds) and the very wealthy. There appear to be clear differences in the psychographics of these two groups. There are many more moderately wealthy individuals than very wealthy individuals. The moderately wealthy individual may have only recently achieved that status, so is less likely to have already received numerous solicitations from other hedge funds. Naturally, the potential investment from this type of individual is smaller than from a very wealthy individual, which may affect the economy of marketing to this group. This group may appeal most to fund of funds marketers because these investors can benefit from the diversification in a fund of funds.

The very wealthy individual may already have hedge fund investments. The very wealthy individual who does not have hedge fund investments probably made a decision not to invest in funds because this group has been thoroughly solicited already. These investors are capable of making large investments. In addition, they have the resources to invest directly, rather than through funds of funds.

THEORIES OF ORGANIZATIONAL BUYING

Some of the theories about selling to organizations are useful in marketing to fund of funds, pensions, and endowments. Selling to industrial buyers differs from selling to consumers. There are relatively few buyers, but they are capable of making large transactions, especially relative to small hedge funds. In marketing to organizations, there is often a close relationship between the buyer and the seller. That may be obvious when describing a large auto manufacturer and its suppliers. In the case of hedge funds, the buyer is the investor and the seller is the hedge fund manager. Like the institutional buyer, these investors tend to be geographically concentrated in large cities in the large industrial states. As a group, they may be less price sensitive than individual investors, concerned more with net performance, correlations, and risk characteristics.

These institutional investors are not particularly sensitive to the level of economic activity because they are investing an existing pool of funds. They are sophisticated buyers relative to the typical individual. They tend to make investment decisions by committee. Finally, like the institutional buyer, they are repeat purchasers, often requiring the fund manager to create semicustomized versions of their product.

MARKET SEGMENTATION

The hedge fund market is a niche of the entire investment market. In Chapter 1, we note that there are some 6,000 funds, although some sources estimate a much smaller total. If there are 6,000 funds worldwide that average $100 million in assets, the entire size of the hedge fund industry is only $600 billion ($100 million × 6,000). This industry is dwarfed by the banking and insurance industries.

The fund of funds industry is a smaller niche within the hedge fund market. Hedge funds can be segmented by the industry categories described in Chapter 3. Most hedge fund investors seek out funds that can contribute something very specific to their portfolios. An investor may review all categories of hedge funds and narrow the search to one or a couple of sectors, then consider particular funds.

Fund of funds investors usually pick several funds in a small number of fund categories.

Within a country there is little geographical segmentation. An American individual is as likely to invest in a fund located in New York as in California. An Indian investor is as likely to invest in a fund in Calcutta as in New Delhi. However, an American individual will not invest in a fund outside the United States.

At first it would appear that the category of offshore fund represents a single geographical segment. It matters little to an offshore investor if an American institution or a British company runs the fund that is domiciled in Bermuda. Nevertheless, there are differences between different Caribbean domiciles that affect the perception of the fund based on its choice of host domicile. Europeans have a preference for funds domiciled in Ireland, the Channel Islands, or several continental sites, just as Asian investors have a preference for funds domiciled near them. Those differences may reflect the convenience of nearby time zones, language barriers, or just a better understanding of the desires of nearby investors, but this is what defines a segment.

The hedge fund industry clearly segments hedge funds according to age or life cycle. Most investors that make a decision by committee (especially pensions and endowments) are not willing to invest in a fund that has been in existence less than 5 years. There are some exceptions because young funds tend to perform better than more established funds.[7] Some fund of funds managers are a prominent exception, actively seeking out new promising managers and attempting to get preferential access to the fund's capacity for new investment.

Traditional marketing frequently tries to segment across income or social class. The market for investments by individuals is not very segmented by income perhaps because it can only market to the wealthy with substantial income. As mentioned in Chapter 10, nonprofit organizations avoid highly levered funds to avoid unrelated business taxable income (UBTI). Segmentation will develop as managers attach additional weight to the effect of taxes on return, creating a segment of tax-neutral investors (pension funds) and taxable investors.

DIFFERENTIATING THE PRODUCT

Hedge funds have several ways to differentiate their product from the competition. The mix of assets (stocks, currencies, convertible bonds, private equity, etc.), the fee structure, the degree of leverage, the amount of risk assumed, the amount of transparency, the reputation of the manager, and the image of the fund all distinguish the fund from potential competitors. The fund manager has control of all these variables but generally makes policy decisions without sufficient consideration to the marketing implications of those decisions.

NEW PRODUCT DEVELOPMENT

Engineers and marketing departments control the introduction of most new products. Investment professionals assume the role of new product engineers for the hedge fund. Hedge funds often create new products in response to demand from existing or potential clients.

The marketing literature classifies new products according to six categories:

1. New-to-the-world products. Any asset can represent a completely new product if it has not been used as the basis for a hedge fund.
2. New product lines that compete with existing lines. Banks, investment managers, and insurance companies that create hedge funds know that a successful fund will cannibalize existing products.
3. Additions to existing product lines. Hedge funds set up multiple funds to make it easy for their investors to diversify some of the fund-specific risk of investing in their products while keeping the investor from investing with competing products.
4. Improved products. Usually, a hedge fund does not create a new fund when it revises its investment techniques. Following a period of poor returns, a manager may create a new fund to try to hide that history from potential investors.

5. Repositioned products. Fund of fund managers tend to invest in the trendiest strategies. They may be guilty of not seeking funds with the best prospects, but their fund may be easier to market.

6. Cost reductions. Usually, cost reductions are negotiated individually, with largest investors getting better pricing.

NEW PRODUCT PROCESS

Creating a new fund is not so different from creating a new consumer product. The first step is to generate a new idea or ideas. According to the philosophy of marketing management, the process should begin with customer needs not satisfied in the marketplace. In practice, it is more common to generate ideas from trading and investment specialists and explore whether these ideas would have sufficient demand (satisfy needs). Hedge fund managers can also get new ideas from competitors, from sales staff, and from leaders in the management company.

A company uses several stages to adopt a new product. The first stage builds awareness of the product. For hedge funds, this stage may mean drafting press releases, setting up meetings with hedge fund journalists, and (probably most important) making sales calls to existing clients. The next stage is evaluating the interest from these parties. The third stage involves an evaluation of the fund. The manager may begin with a paper portfolio, emulating actual purchases and sales in a real-time simulation. The manager may seed a new fund and begin to build a track record. The next stage is a trial. Certainly at this point the fund would be operational and should have some money from outside investors. The final stage is adoption, when the management company commits to offer the product, invests in trading and accounting systems required to run the fund at a reasonable size, and begins to market the new fund.

Many factors affect how quickly investors adopt the new product. For consumer goods companies, the relative advantage of the new product influences how fast customers adopt the product. The hedge fund business is a numbers game, so this advantage pertains to risk, return, and factors such as tax advantages. Communicability also affects how quickly customers respond to a new fund. Customers must be able to understand the fund and also understand how it differs from existing products. Other factors, such as compatibility, complexity, and divisibility, affect consumer goods more than hedge funds.

Hedge Funds and Product Life Cycles

Like many consumer goods, hedge funds have clear life cycles. These life cycles exist in part because the popularity of fund styles changes. The relative value of underlying assets changes and along with this change comes change in the demand for the product. Finally, there are both economies of scale for small funds and diseconomies for large funds.

The product life cycle can be broken into four stages: introduction, growth, maturity, and decline. Four introduction strategies are used to promote consumer goods, depending on characteristics of the product life cycle. Each strategy has an analogous example in the financial product arena. A *rapid skimming strategy* is typical of financial engineering at broker-dealers. This is a high-price, high-profit strategy. It requires intense promotion to build a base of business before competitors imitate the product. This strategy makes the most sense if the market is not generally aware of the product. The second strategy is called *rapid penetration*. Futures exchanges follow this strategy when they introduce a new futures contract. The product is priced aggressively and promoted intensely. It makes sense when customers are not aware of the product, customers are price sensitive, the industry has decreasing marginal cost to scale, and there are no problems increasing the scale of business. The third strategy is called *slow penetration*. An index mutual fund is priced aggressively but is not promoted much. This strategy makes sense when customers are aware of the product, are price sensitive, and when the size of the market is large. The final strategy is the *slow skimming strategy* in which the product is introduced at a high price with a high profit margin. It is not promoted extensively (in this case because regulations prohibit heavy promotion). The strategy works when the market is small, when potential customers are well informed, and when competition is not anticipated.

During the growth stage in the life cycle of a hedge fund, the fund experiences rapid growth. Competitors emerge, perhaps imitating the new product. The manager must invest in additional staff and computer systems to keep up with the demand for the fund. Nevertheless, profits soar because costs grow much slower than revenues.

For most products, the maturity stage is the longest period. For hedge funds, it may be less true, in part because seven years (the expected life of a fund) is so short. It may be that the life cycle of hedge funds more resembles an inverted V. Funds that fill a narrow niche of the hedge fund market are most vulnerable to having a short maturity stage. Large funds may have more persistence simply because of their size. In the maturity stage, the fund experiences slower growth. The manager has added to staff and support rapidly, so probably has excess capacity. Marketing in the mature stage should focus on increasing the size of the fund by marketing to existing customers (perhaps cross-marketing other funds), with an effort to attract sticky money (money that is not likely to be withdrawn quickly).

Decline is the final stage for a business. The nature of decline can vary significantly. For funds that experienced a performance disaster, decline can be a very short period. A high-water mark may encourage a fund manager to close a fund even when adequate demand exists for the product. Funds in shrinking niche markets can exist indefinitely if the scale of the business adjusts to the absence of growth.

GOING GLOBAL

The hedge fund industry is much more global than most products. Nevertheless, many hedge funds are created as domestic funds (within the United States, United Kingdom, or Germany, for example) because they cost more to register offshore and are more complex to administer. Many managers of these domestic funds want to expand internationally to increase demand for the product.

Many of the issues involving a move offshore can be organized around the Four P's (product, pricing, promotion, and place). A company must decide whether to maintain the product worldwide or to modify the product for individual markets. Hedge fund managers can convert a fund into an offshore fund or create a new fund (or even a series of new funds). Fortunately, the master-feeder structure (see Chapter 6) allows considerable flexibility to get maximum advantage from registration and tax rules.

Manufacturing companies face complicated pricing decisions when they take products global. Hedge funds have a much simpler time pricing their product because they can offer undisclosed price discounts to investors. A buyer of pharmaceuticals can pay a substantially lower price for a product outside the United States than within. Tax law in the United States prohibits the U.S. citizen from representing himself or herself as a German to get a discount on hedge fund fees. In any case, the fund manager would likely grant breaks in the posted fee schedule because of the size of investment but not the point of origin of the investment.

The fund manager should be aware that regulations differ from country to country. It is important to rely on competent legal and accounting advisors to assure compliance. The fund manager should also be mindful that tax laws differ substantially across borders. These tax differences can rise to the level of a marketing issue if the investments from particular tax jurisdictions are substantial enough to justify adapting the investment implementation to the advantage of certain citizens.

The fund manager must promote its products globally. The fund wants to build an international "brand," both to make its investments sticky and to generate interest from potential investors. The performance of the fund tends to be the strongest promotion tool. Fund managers will have difficulty taking a fund global if performance is mediocre. However, advertising restrictions are most severe in the United States and are all but unregulated in some countries. In much of the world (outside the United States), hedge funds can be promoted much like mutual funds.

The fourth P is place. A hedge fund can be distributed through a variety of channels, even within a country. Globally, the manager must use an even greater variety of channels. For example, a fund may allow an independent marketer to sell the fund domestically. Most independent marketers are small operations that could not hope to distribute the product outside the home market. A hedge fund manager may allow one large brokerage firm to promote the fund in Europe but may allow a Japanese bank to distribute the fund in the Far East.

Regulations and tradition affect the choice of channels. For example, many hedge funds are nominally listed on European stock exchanges, even though few sales occur on the exchange.

THE UNIQUE CHARACTER OF THE HEDGE FUND PRODUCT

Throughout this chapter, we apply traditional marketing ideas to hedge funds. The ideas are relevant because many of the marketing issues apply to the hedge fund product. It would be irresponsible, however, to fail to explore how hedge funds differ from most marketing products.

A hedge fund investment is a service product, albeit a nonstandard service product. It is created and consumed simultaneously. It cannot be stored. Its buyers face the uncertainty of investment results, making it difficult (at least over the short run) to distinguish a poor product from poor results. Also, because hedge fund results are so measurable, it is difficult to market quality as a characteristic of the manager's product.

Although hedge funds have existed for more than 50 years, the hedge fund business is still young. Instead of offering an investment product, the hedge fund industry will offer a marketing product that just happens to be an investment product. The nature of the product, how it is priced, how it is promoted, and how it is distributed will certainly evolve. Responsive marketing organizations will take advantage of these changes.

NOTES

1. Philip Kotler, *Marketing Management,* 9th ed., Prentice Hall, Englewood Cliffs, NJ, 1997, page 9. This classic marketing textbook provides the model around which I have organized this chapter.
2. Ibid., page 13.
3. According to Van Hedge Advisors as quoted by Alexander Ineichen, "In Search of Alpha," *Global Equity Research UBS Warburg,* October 2000, page 8.
4. E. Jerome McCarthy, *Basic Marketing: A Managerial Approach,* 12th ed., Irwin, Homewood, IL, 1996; cited in Kotler's *Marketing Management,* pages 92–94.
5. Abraham Maslow, *Motivation and Personality,* Harper & Row, New York, 1954, pages 80–106; cited in Kotler's *Marketing Management,* page 184.
6. Frederick Herzberg, *Work and the Nature of Man,* William Collins, Cleveland, OH, 1966; cited in Kotler's *Marketing Management,* page 185.
7. "The Young Ones," in *Absolute Return Fund Investment,* April 2001; available at http://www.hedgeworld.com/research/reports.

CHAPTER 15

Derivatives and Hedge Funds

Hedge funds create several embedded options for the investor, the fund manager, and the fund creditors. This chapter describes some of the most important optionlike patterns and the impact these options have on hedge fund participants. The chapter also explores some recent developments by reinsurance companies and underwriters to reengineer hedge fund returns.

INCENTIVE FEE AS CALL OPTION

The typical hedge fund collects a management fee of around 1 percent of assets.[1] The management fee is collected regardless of the return on the assets in the portfolio. If performance is attractive, the fund may grow in size and the fixed management fee may grow proportionately with the assets under management. Nevertheless, the fee remains fixed with respect to a given amount of money under management.

In contrast, an incentive fee varies directly according to the performance of the fund. Typically, the fund manager collects 20 percent of the net profits (before incentive fees are applied but after management fees are subtracted).

Table 15.1 lists various levels of return, along with incentive fees, stated as a percent of the assets under management. The incentive fees are calculated as 20 percent times the return. For a fund with no hurdle rate, the incentive fee is:

$$\text{Max}(0, \text{Return} \times 20\ \%)$$

TABLE 15.1 Incentive Fees (20%)

Return (%)	No Hurdle Incentive Fee (%)	5% Hurdle Incentive Fee (%)
−10.0	0.00	0.00
−7.5	0.00	0.00
−5.0	0.00	0.00
−2.5	0.00	0.00
0.0	0.00	0.00
2.5	0.50	0.00
5.0	1.00	0.00
7.5	1.50	0.50
10.0	2.00	1.00
12.5	2.50	1.50
15.0	3.00	2.00
17.5	3.50	2.50
20.0	4.00	3.00

Note: Incentive fee (with 5 percent hurdle rate) = Max(0, (Return − 5%) × 20%).

If the fund is subject to a 5 percent hurdle rate, no incentive fee is collected until the fund return exceeds 5 percent:

$$\text{Max}(0, (\text{Return} - 5\%) \times 20\%)$$

The payoff to the manager closely resembles a call option as shown in Figure 15.1. Like a call option, the manager participates proportionately in the profits of the fund but is not liable for losses. The payoff to a fund manager with a hurdle rate simply represents an out of the money call. Similarly, a high-water mark also places the call out of the money. The expiration on the call is equal to the time left in the performance period.[2]

The performance period is the time used to calculate the incentive fee. It may be monthly, quarterly, or annually and may be subject to special provisions (lookbacks, high-water marks, and hurdle rates, for example) that complicate the payout.

It is possible to value this incentive fee. Perhaps more important, it is easy to see that the manager has an incentive to increase the risk

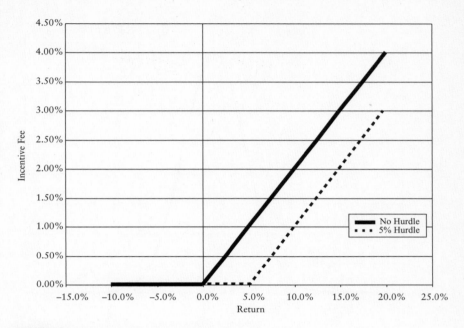

FIGURE 15.1   Incentive Fee (as percentage of assets)

(that is, the volatility of returns). The manager gains without bound if extremely good performance occurs. Under low or moderate volatility, the probability of extremely high returns may be very small. At high levels of volatility, the probability of these extreme moves improves. While there is also a symmetrical increase in the probability of extremely bad results, these results are borne completely by the investors, not the manager. As a result, the manager has an incentive to enter into more risky trades than does the investor.

Figure 15.2 shows the effect of changing the volatility on the probabilities of extreme outcomes. The figure reproduces the distribution also printed in Figure 13.7. The area under each curve represents the probability of all outcomes. In each case, this area represents 100 percent because we include all outcomes. The higher volatility attributes a higher probability to extremely good and bad outcomes and less probability to moderate returns. From the previous chart of

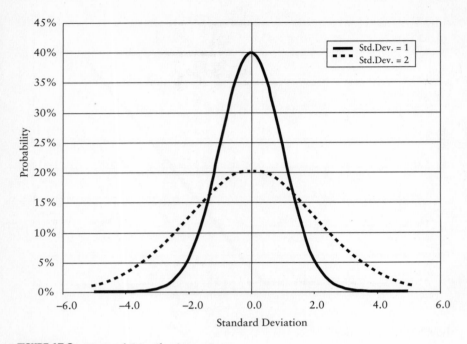

FIGURE 15.2   Normal Distribution

incentive fees, we can observe that this would increase the probability of large incentive fee payments and also increase the probability of no incentive fee (because of loss). Nevertheless, the lower bound on incentive fees creates an incentive for the manager to take more risk.

To control for this risk, many hedge fund investors insist that the hedge fund manager must make a substantial investment in the fund. On those investments, the manager has the same incentive as the investor and hence acts somewhat as a check on the incentive to take excessive risk. This investment does not eliminate the optionlike structure of the incentive fees.

Investors generally prefer less volatility of return to more volatility.[3] If the manager adopts an extremely volatile strategy, the funds will become less attractive to investors. The incentive to control risk and grow the assets under management appears to be a strong motivation to refrain from excessive risk taking.

EMBEDDED PUTS ON HEDGE FUND RETURNS

The limited partner (or limited liability corporation [LLC] shareholder) has a built-in put option on the assets of the firm. In the absence of leverage, this put does not appear valuable because it is difficult to lose more than 100 percent of the assets without leverage. In contrast, with leverage of 10:1, a 10 percent decline in the value of the assets is sufficient to wipe out the capital (net asset value) of a fund.

In Figure 15.3, we assume a 2:1 leverage. Because the investors cannot lose more than their original investment, the payoff resembles a put option. The chart, however, shows the return of the assets and the put together. The combination therefore resembles a call option.

The investor has an incentive to allow the manager to take more risk. Figure 15.4 shows the theoretical value of a put option at vari-

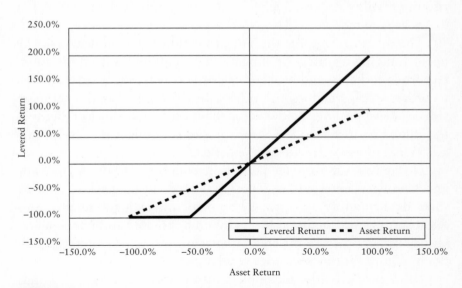

FIGURE 15.3　Hedge Fund Returns as Put-Protected Assets

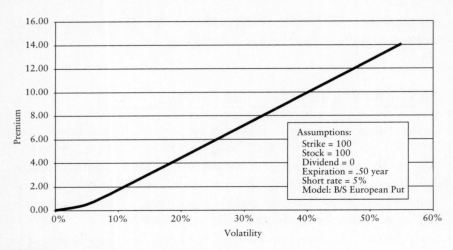

FIGURE 15.4 Put Premiums versus Volatility
(BS stands for Black and Scholes.)

ous volatilities. Like the incentive fee/call, the put gains value with a rise in volatility because higher volatilities apply to large gains, but losses are limited.

The investor acquires the put protection from the lenders. The hedge fund has a variety of obligations: to employees, to trade counterparties, to banks and broker-dealers who lend money or securities, to office supply vendors and others. In the event that the net asset value (NAV) declines below zero, these creditors may lose because the limited partners and LLC investors are not obligated to contribute additional money to make up the deficit.[4]

Hedge funds must make periodic accounting disclosures to trade and lending counterparties. Typically, funds must disclose balance sheet data monthly and provide audited statements annually. This disclosure is a precondition for maintaining trading and financing relationships imposed by the credit managers of trading counterparties, not a requirement by securities regulations.

Disclosure provides incomplete information to creditors. Funds routinely reduce leverage for month end. Creditors do not know the size of positions on other dates. Statements are aggregated so that the fund does not disclose specific positions. Derivatives are generally not listed on the statements and only aggregate information about the derivatives is disclosed in footnotes.

USING DERIVATIVE INSTRUMENTS TO DELIVER HEDGE FUND RETURNS

There are several ways to structure derivative securities based on hedge fund returns. A total return swap is a synthetic long (or short) position in the fund bundled with financing for that investment. In other words, this swap replicates the net cash flows associated with borrowing money and investing the money in a hedge fund. One party receives a periodic payment as if it owned the fund (including distributions, if any, and capital gain) and pays periodic interest payments as if it borrowed the funds. In reality, the principal balance is nominal because both the initial cash flows and the final cash flows net to zero (the amount of money "borrowed" equals the amount of money "invested" and the amount of money "repaid" equals the amount of money "redeemed" because the periodic swap payments account for the hedge fund performance).

It is also possible to create a synthetic hedge fund as a structured note. Because hedge funds generally do not make dividend or income distributions, these structured notes may resemble a zero-coupon bond with no stated maturity. Instead, the value increases by the return on the fund. Alternatively, the note may have a final principal payment. In this case, the structured note replicates a protective put on the hedge fund investment. To pay for the put, this type of note may pay a lower interest rate than the hedge fund return.

Organizations have traded calls and puts on hedge fund returns. UBS sold calls to the partners of Long Term Capital Management (LTCM) and invested an amount equaling the notional amount in the fund as a hedge. Because they also reinvested the call premium in the fund, UBS actually invested more than the notional amount in the fund. When the hedge fund suddenly lost nearly 100 percent of the NAV of the fund, UBS lost $680 million.[5]

Insurance companies have issued puts on hedge fund returns. In the examples that have been disclosed, a fund of funds issues a structured note based on the returns of the fund of funds. The notes vary in structure but resemble the structured notes described previously. Investors gain because they get a strong guarantee of principal. Puts can allow some investors to make hedge fund investments that would otherwise be prohibited by law or policy. The fund of funds benefits because it is fairly certain to retain the money under management for an extended period. The insurance company benefits because the premium charged exceeds the expected losses.

Tax savings motivated most of the early derivative hedge fund transactions. In the case of LTCM, the partners replaced direct investment in the fund with calls on the fund. The partners paid ordinary tax rates (up to 39.6 percent federal plus state tax) on most of the return. They hoped to defer the income and convert it to long-term capital gain, which is taxed at a maximum of 20 percent.[6]

The Tax Relief Extension Act of 1999 (TREA) made it much more difficult to create derivatives exclusively to create tax savings. TREA created Internal Revenue Code Section 1260, which required the derivative buyer to treat the position for tax purposes as if the underlying asset were owned directly. The law did not restrict derivatives based on hedge fund returns but removed any tax incentive to substitute the derivative for a direct investment.

Most of the hedge fund derivatives now being created are being used to limit the downside of a hedge fund investment. There has been interest in creating this downside protection for a long time. Earlier attempts bundled zero-coupon bonds with long options. For example, at an 8 percent interest rate, it was possible to buy 10-year zero-coupon bonds for 46 percent of the money invested in the fund.[7] Under this structure, the fund can lose all of the remaining 54 percent of the funds because the zero-coupon bonds eventually mature for 100 percent of the hedge fund investment. By limiting the risk trading to the excess 54 percent, it was possible to create somewhat diluted hedge fund returns with high probability of returning at least the original investment.

At a 5 percent interest rate, the discount on the 10-year zero-coupon bonds is smaller.[8] At the lower rate, 28 percent less money is available for investment in hedge fund strategies. The zero-coupon bonds provide a modest 5 percent return on 61 percent of the funds invested. At lower interest rates, the zero-coupon structure makes it difficult to provide competitive returns. Substituting puts and diversification improves the expected level of return.

Because the fund manager has an incentive fee that closely resembles a call option, it is reasonable to expect some managers to want to sell over-the-counter calls on their performance. The value of the incentive fee varies directly with fund performance and is subject at least in part to factors beyond the control of the manager. By selling some of that exposure in advance, the manager can make the outcome more certain. The manager has the best information about the size of future profits and may believe that the price paid for options is excessive. Also, if the incentive fee tempts a fund manager to take excessive risk, then selling some of that incentive reduces the bias for risk taking.

Investors would no more accept a fund manager selling options on the fund performance than shareholders would accept a chief executive officer of a company buying puts on the company. The transaction would have the appearance that the manager had no confidence in the investment. In addition, the sale would subvert the motivation for the manager to do well for all the investors. It is painful enough for investors to disgorge 20 percent of their profits to the manager. Under the foregoing scenario, the manager would thereby profit, even when the fund lost money. Finally, the incentive fee creates an incentive at least roughly similar to investors because the manager and the investors both participate when the fund does well. Without the incentive, factors other than performance may motivate managers' behavior.

BEST PRACTICES—THE TRADER'S OPTION

Managers should be aware that traders under their employment have an incentive that closely resembles the incentive fee call option. Trades typically receive a salary plus a bonus. The bonus may be tied directly to the individual trader's performance, the fund performance, or may be at the discretion of the fund manager. In all cases, the size of the bonus usually is closely related to the trader's performance.

Like the incentive fee that the fund manager is granted by the fund inventor, the trader has an incentive to invest in risky trades, because bonuses are also never smaller than zero.

Managers can do several things to limit excess risk taking by employees. First, the firm can monitor the risk of positions and limit the risk individuals can create for the fund. Second, the fund usually pays bonuses annually. For much of the year, when a trader has an accumulated profit, the trader has a symmetric payoff to gains and losses (further gains increase the bonus, but losses from a midyear profit lead to lower or no bonus). Third, some funds have somewhat complicated provisions that can force an employee to disgorge bonuses in recent prior periods when losses follow gains in different trading years. Fourth, it might be possible to tie the bonus to both the trading profit and the risk of the positions.

NOTES

1. This fee is usually collected pro rata monthly or quarterly.
2. However, if an investor does not withdraw from the fund, the option is renewed during the next performance period.
3. There are some exceptions, perhaps resembling the motivation of the lottery ticket buyer.
4. A general partner theoretically has unlimited liability but generally has little capital beyond its investment in the fund. The general partner is almost always a limited liability entity that also cannot be made to make additional contributions to the fund in the event of bankruptcy. See Chapter 6 for a more complete description of this structure.
5. See Laderman, Jeffrey M., "UBS Failed Risk Management 101," *Business Week,* November 9, 1998.
6. This advantage to the partners was not offset by a corresponding disadvantage in taxes for the broker-dealer because UBS treated both sides of the transaction as ordinary income.
7. $1/(1 + 4\%)^{20} = 45.6\%$ of face.
8. $1/(1 + 2.5\%)^{20} = 61.0\%$ of face.

CHAPTER 16

Lessons Learned from the Hedge Fund Industry

T he news media cover disasters in the financial markets because readers seem to enjoy reading about them. Whole books have been written about some of these disasters. The fall of a financial institution (bank loan problems, Drexel Burnham, E. F. Hutton, zombie savings and loans, bridge loans at broker-dealers, etc.) or the actions of rogue traders (Dorothy Conway at Marsh & McClennan, Nick Leeson at Barings Bank, Arnold the computer at Drysdale Securities, etc.) motivate market participants and governmental regulators to call for action so that whatever just happened could never happen again.

It is outside the scope of this narrative to chronicle these events, but we have learned lessons from some of them. With the warning that the followings sections do not necessarily represent the most newsworthy disasters for the past decade, we briefly describe several hedge fund disasters that provide insight to managers currently running hedge funds.

THE GRANITE FUND

The Granite Fund was created to invest in exotic mortgage instruments and provide a market-neutral pattern of return. Mortgage derivatives start as ordinary home loans secured by single-family houses, apartments, and commercial real estate. The loans are bundled together by Fannie Mae, Freddie Mac, and the Federal Home Loan Mortgage Corporation. These agencies sell securities called *pass-throughs* that, in effect, let investors own parts of portfolios of these mortgages. In addition to consolidating these monthly cash flows from many smaller loans, the agencies add a guarantee to the cash flows.

Nevertheless, these pass-through securities have some disadvantages compared to noncallable government bonds. Because homeowners can repay the loans when rates decline, these pass-throughs resemble callable bonds. To make the pass-throughs more desirable to potential investors, portfolios of these pass-throughs are assembled and the cash flows are redivided. The resulting securities are called collateralized mortgage obligations (CMOs) or real estate mortgage investment conduits (REMICs). Some of the cash flows resemble short-term government bonds. Others resemble long-term bonds or zero-coupon bonds. More importantly, some cash flows are fairly certain in magnitude and timing. Others bear most of the prepayment risk for the loan portfolio.

The uncertainty inherent in the pool of pass-throughs gets distilled to a small collection of bonds called *residuals* and *Z bonds*. These securities are very sensitive to changes in interest rates and can lose much of their value when rates decline.

The securities most sensitive to changing rates can be valued and hedged with powerful computer models. The models are rather sensitive to input assumptions. The inputs are not known with certainty at any point. More important, the inputs change from day to day, requiring the positions to be constantly reevaluated.

The Granite Fund owned many sensitive CMO securities in 1994. Perhaps its hedging analysis was somewhat inadequate. Perhaps it should have hedged with interest rate options. Perhaps the fund was levered too much. It seems clear that Granite Fund could have managed its positions better. However, these mistakes were not enough to cause the investors to lose all or nearly all of their investment.

Granite's lenders became concerned about their loans to the

hedge fund. The fund had lost money and lenders (generally the large broker-dealers that are active in the mortgage market) worried that the collateral they held would be inadequate to protect them from loss. One by one, the lenders demanded either additional collateral or reduction in the loan balances. The lenders were collectively willingly lending 10 times the fund's capital but suddenly reduced it to 8 times the fund's capital at a time when the capital was eroding. Positions needed to be sold. However, the more Granite sold, the more prices declined and the more the lenders were concerned that they were unprotected.

One by one, the lenders called the loans, demanding immediate repayment. When Granite could not comply, the dealers sold the collateral at whatever price they could get, to recover as much of the loan balance as possible. There were accusations and lawsuits accusing the dealers of liquidating at artificially distressed prices.[1]

In a spiral resembling a run on a bank, the process fed upon itself until Granite had lost all of the capital in the fund.[2] Other mortgage funds were at risk. For example, Ellington Capital conducted an impromptu auction on Columbus Day, a holiday when the mortgage dealers are usually closed, to liquidate positions quickly enough to avoid following Granite down the spiral of liquidations. After the auction, the fund's prime broker reportedly refused to clear the trades and the fund had to arrange for buyers and lenders to exchange securities for cash without using the prime broker to settle the trades.

The lesson learned from the losses at the Granite Fund is that leverage creates a unique risk independent of the assets being managed. Lever a stock, for example, and the risk is not just that the returns swing twice as wide. A fund run by Illinois Institutional Investors (also called III or Triple I) had many positions similar to Granite Fund and Ellington Capital. However, the III fund used the interest rate swap market as a hedge, instead of U.S. Treasuries and Treasury futures. It made up much of the loss on the mortgages because swap spreads also widened. By creating a more effective hedge, it was not vulnerable to a raid by its financing counterparties.

FENCHURCH CAPITAL MANAGEMENT

Fenchurch Capital Management ran mirrored fixed-income arbitrage funds. The funds totaled $35 million in 1990 and rose to a peak of $850 million in mid-1995. Performance was good (midteens per year or higher) and the volatility of returns was very low.

The combination was extremely attractive to investors, producing one of the highest Sharpe ratios in the industry. The fund closed to new investment several times to digest the growth in assets under management and adjust to the growing asset base. Probably, closing the fund made it even more desirable.

The funds were invested in a combination of basis (futures) trades, options arbitrage, and yield spreads between a variety of high-quality fixed-income assets (spreads between Treasuries of adjacent or nonadjacent maturities, Treasuries versus eurodollar futures, mortgage pass-throughs versus Treasuries). The funds were invested in arbitrage trades or nondirectional relative value trades.

Because of the nature of the trades employed, Fenchurch had developed a style of trading it felt improved its results. The manager established modest-sized positions in many trades that were somewhat mispriced. Some of these trade relationships corrected quickly and were unwound. Others became more mispriced. The managers increased their exposure to these trades. The manager set a goal to have the maximum exposure when the trade was most mispriced.

The fund's owners decided to replicate the business in the European markets and established a trading desk in London to manage a new pool of investments devoted to this variation. The performance was not as attractive and growth in assets under management was disappointing. The company decided to merge the two operations (the management companies) and the funds. The offshore fund run in the United States was merged with the offshore fund run in London and the fund for U.S. investors was rebalanced to mirror the merged international arbitrage fund.

One motive to merge the operations is that the Fenchurch performance could be used to market the combined investments. The manager also believed that the European markets were less efficient and provided greater profit potential for the Fenchurch clientele. By one estimate, the relationships followed in the European portfolio were 10 times as volatile as the U.S. relationships, even though considerable effort was made to construct arbitrage-like relationships.

The fringe benefit to this greater volatility is that the fund could run 10 times as much capital with the same asset base. In other words, the funds could reduce leverage and gross positions and accommodate the growth in assets under management without running into capacity constraints.

Fenchurch found that the relationships it traded were considerably more volatile than the trades it had previously emphasized. Unfortunately, it did not significantly reduce the leverage on the portfolio. The combination caused considerably more volatility in net asset value.

Faced with losses and redemptions from investors, the funds needed to dramatically reduce position size. With cash, futures, and options positions *each* up to 60 times the capital of the funds, that meant that tens of billions of dollars of positions had to be closed out. The disruption caused by the liquidation aggravated the losses to investors.

Investors learned to be cautious about changes in strategy designed to avoid capacity constraints. Capacity constraints are real but not necessarily insurmountable. At every successful fund, the managers made changes to operations to accommodate the growth. These changes do not inevitably lead to disaster but usually increase the probability that future returns will be lower than past returns.

Managers should note the risk Fenchurch took in merging the two operations. If the new trading strategy had been implemented on only the smaller European pool, the manager would have still had a successful U.S. product when the experiment failed. The smaller experiment may have been more likely to succeed because the position sizes were not large enough to attract attention. With their huge size in less liquid markets, the funds became price makers, instead of price takers, which dramatically increased the cost of downsizing the portfolios.

LONG TERM CAPITAL MANAGEMENT

Long Term Capital Management (LTCM) may represent the best-chronicled investment disaster ever. Readers seeking more detail should have no trouble finding newspaper articles, hearings by regulators and legislators, and books. These accounts reveal many of the details of the disaster and lessons to be learned. Nevertheless, no primer on hedge fund management would be complete without a review of the story.

LTCM was founded by senior traders from Salomon Brothers. Regulators had chastised the firm for manipulating the U.S. government securities markets. John Meriwether, the former vice chairman and head of Salomon's proprietary trading group, found it was easy to attract key traders to join him in creating a hedge fund that would employ many of the strategies developed at Salomon Brothers.

Merrill Lynch raised billions of dollars for the fund under very attractive terms to LTCM. The management company hired a large research team to support trading and develop new strategies. On the strength of the paid-in capital and the reputation of the key employees, the fund established massive credit lines with trading counterparties.

The fund enjoyed extremely good performance, which further boosted capital and strengthened the reputation of the firm. In part to cope with capacity constraints, the firm returned capital to many investors. The partners also sought to replace the capital with increased investment of their own money. Some of that investment took the form of options on the fund.

Perhaps never has the risk of the positions been more studied than the LTCM positions were studied prior to their massive losses in 1998. The study showed very little risk, despite leverage that unofficially was reported to have exceeded 250 times the fund capital. Perhaps the greatest source of risk reduction was diversification between the many strategies employed. In some ways, the large leverage was a means to reduce risk, rather than increase it.

The fund experienced extreme losses that were believed to be virtually impossible to occur in practically all the positions the firm carried. There is a belief that when markets are in disarray, correlations revert to 100 percent. Whether that is true in the general case, it was the case for LTCM.

In hindsight it may be true that such correlation was inevitable for LTCM. Despite being extremely secretive, the positions carried by LTCM were copied by other hedge funds and by traders at broker-dealers. This may have occurred innocently enough because these other traders looked at the same markets with the same analytical tools. Because LTCM needed to finance its positions and needed counterparties for its derivative trades, other traders knew many of the positions it carried. Therefore, once the fund needed to reduce positions (for whatever reason), it is no surprise that Wall Street could not or would not accommodate its need for liquidity.

The investment community learned or relearned that leverage brings risks that may be inevitable, despite a research department dedicated to mitigating those risks. For a single trade, leverage (for either long or short positions) creates risk not present with unlevered positions. This risk did not prove to be a major factor in the demise of LTCM.

The aggregate risks of a levered portfolio are more than the sum of the individual risks. Leverage magnifies the effect of gains and losses on positions. The fund carried positions that were designed to reduce all risks except those consciously created. For fixed-income positions, it means that at any point in time the aggregate book was not sensitive to the overall level of rates. It might have been sensitive to the shape or steepness of the yield curve, the level of rates in one country in particular, spreads between high-grade and low-grade instruments, spreads between liquid and illiquid issues, or currency exchange rates. These risks may be less than risks of the underlying assets. But with sufficient leverage, these residual risks can be massive.

Diversification acts to dampen this risk. Historical data can help reveal whether these risks tend to occur together or randomly. If previous data create a sense that diversification can control these risks, then leverage can be increased. However, with the greater exposure, the fund begins to rely on diversification.

When position sizes become large enough to affect prices, a hedge fund is vulnerable to predatory trading by other funds and broker-dealers. As with the Granite Fund and Fenchurch, forced liquidation created opportunities for other traders to profit from LTCM's problems. When these funds found themselves in a vulnerable position, losses greatly exceeded reasonable estimates of the worst-case scenario.

TIGER AND BOWMAN FUNDS

Julian Robertson ran a highly successful family of funds over an 18-year period based on the intuitive idea of buying stocks that are underpriced and selling short issues that are overpriced. The formula was successful and allowed the Tiger funds to grow to be the world's largest hedge funds. Money invested at the outset would have grown to a peak value of more than 150 times the initial investment. Yet from August 1998 until April of 2000, investors lost nearly half their investment at a time when the Standard & Poor's Index was up nearly as much.

Many trades, indeed many strategies, were to blame for these losses that eventually led Robertson to close the funds and return the remaining balance to his 700 investors. No single sector affected the fund more than the high-tech electronics and software boom.

Ironically (but in hindsight, not surprisingly), the same sectors led to problems at a hedge fund concentrated in those sectors. The Bowman Technology fund was down more than 20 percent year to date in early May of 2001 when it announced it would return $1 billion to investors and close the fund.

Investors can take many lessons from the foregoing examples. It is clear that narrowly focused strategies can be vulnerable to persistent periods of bad performance beyond the control of the manager. This performance can be significant enough and last long enough to force funds out of business.

Hedge fund creditors may learn how to more accurately appraise how vulnerable particular funds are to a bad run. Probably, a multi-strategy fund would be less likely to suffer drawdowns sufficiently large to affect the prospect of repayment. Intuitively, a nondirectional strategy should also be less likely to suffer severe drawdowns, but that intuition is challenged by the losses with Granite, Fenchurch, and LTCM.[3]

It is not true that such examples prove hedge funds are excessively risky. The volatility of hedge fund returns has been declining. Many funds are less risky than the Standard & Poor's 500. An even larger percentage of funds is less risky than the Nasdaq index (again with the benefit of hindsight).

It also is not true that such examples prove that these individual managers took excessive risk or imprudent risks. Obviously, in hindsight, they made poor choices because they lost sufficient money to warrant closing their funds. However, one purpose of a hedge fund is to create a pattern of return different from what is otherwise available with traditional assets and perhaps to be different from other hedge funds. It is up to the marketplace to decide if such funds deserve a place in portfolios. While hedge funds with more modest risk exposure have enjoyed faster growth in assets under management, there will always be investors looking to invest in funds that may be able to provide astonishingly high returns.

MANHATTAN FUND

Michael Berger established a long-short value hedge fund and raised some $400 million from 300 investors over several years. Whether or not Berger ever expected to make money for these investors, he did not. Instead, he falsified results to claim that he had been profitable.

The fraud went undetected by auditors, investors, regulators, and credit committees at trading shops that extended credit to the fund. The additional time gave the Manhattan Fund a chance to recover, but it did not recover. Instead, as the scheme grew in size, it greatly increased the size of the loss.

In this and similar cases, investors and creditors have looked to auditors, prime brokers, and financial advisors for compensation for losses. To date, these lawsuits have not been successful for the investors seeking restitution. These legal developments demonstrate that legal advisors, accountants, brokers, and marketers are potentially exposed to the risk of lawsuits.

Due diligence can reduce the risk of loss to fraudulent funds. Avoiding losses may be one of the most underemphasized methods of improving performance. Due diligence will not be able to detect every instance of fraud. For the investor, avoiding some losses may be sufficient incentive. Perhaps as important, due diligence may uncover other irregularities that would affect investors or lenders. Finding such irregularities may still be useful in deciding how much trust and confidence to place in a fund manager.

There is a second benefit from conducting due diligence that may be more useful to prime brokers, investment advisors, and auditors. Over time, a certain number of funds will experience severe losses whether or not fraud is present. By conducting thorough due diligence in advance of investment and on an ongoing basis thereafter, these advisors will be in a much better position to defend against lawsuits from investors seeking restitution. In other words, it may make sense to do some due diligence merely as a legal defense even if there is no duty to conduct such research. The issues are different in every case and the outcome cannot be predicted with certainty, but in general, the courts do not expect advisors to indemnify investors against losses.

Investors with limited resources to devote to due diligence may be better off investing in a fund of funds, where considerable effort can be devoted toward researching each fund. The fund of funds also benefits from diversification when fraudulent losses occur.

REMINDERS

The descriptions in this chapter include lessons for both the investor and the hedge fund entrepreneur. The investor is reminded of the value of conducting a thorough due diligence review of possible hedge fund investments. The investor may greatly underestimate the risks of an investment if he or she does not understand the nature of the investment and does not have some basis for holding the manager accountable.

The hedge fund entrepreneur is reminded that the liquidity of the securities the fund trades may dry up and force a survival challenge beyond the control of the fund managers. Managers should establish a maximum fund size and stay small enough to remain viable as an investment. Changing investment strategies or expanding into new markets greatly increases the risk of underperforming.

NOTES

1. Under this theory, Dealer A liquidated positions with Dealer B at below-market prices and Dealer B reciprocated by liquidating positions with Dealer A also at below-market prices.
2. However, the fund has recovered some damages in subsequent lawsuits.
3. This sample is neither representative nor large enough to say that nondirectional funds are riskier than other strategies.

glossary

Accredited investor Allowable purchaser of private placement under Section 3(c)1 for the Investment Company Act of 1940. An individual with $1 million net worth or income exceeding $200,000 per year for 2 years or certain business entities with at least $5 million in assets. For more information, review Section 4(2) of the Securities Act, SEC Regulation D, and Internal Revenue Code Rule 501.

Accrual basis Basis for recognizing income and expenses that does not rely on actual transfer of cash for the accounting event to be realized.

Aggregate tax allocation A simplified method for allocating taxable revenues, expenses, gains, and losses to investors that aggregates these items each period before allocating. The resulting allocations can differ somewhat from layered tax allocation.

AIMR Association for Investment Management and Research. Source for most widely accepted minimum standards for presenting investment performance.

At risk The investment that an investor could lose. For a limited partnership and a corporate owner, this usually equals the paid-in investment. Either owner can contract to commit additional funds if necessary, which raises the amount at risk. A general partner has unlimited liability, so has no specific amount at risk.

Backup withholding A provision in U.S. tax law that requires U.S. investment entities to withhold 30 percent of investment returns for foreign investors. This withholding can be reclaimed only by filing a tax return in the United States and proving no U.S. tax liability exists.

Blue-sky laws State regulations designed to protect investors from unethical investment schemes.

Break period Each period when investors may enter or exit the fund or ownership percentages may change for other reasons. The break period becomes the interval used to allocate all results to investors.

BUMAB Beginning unrealized memorandum account balance. Used for aggregate tax allocation.

Cash basis Basis for recognizing income that times the realization of income and expenses with the actual transfer of cash. Cash basis is used for most individuals and is generally not allowed for businesses. The exception is the S corporation, which is on a cash basis because it must be on the same basis as the individuals.

CFTC Act of 1936　Created the Commodity Futures Trading Commission, established the need for an industry self-regulating body, and established rules governing disclosure and conduct.

Clearance account　A special type of bank account used to buy and sell securities. Unlike a typical bank account or brokerage account, the clearing bank allows substantial intraday overdrafts to facilitate buying and selling of securities.

Clearing corporation　A third party that assumes and guarantees the off-setting positions of all futures and futures options transactions. The clearing corporation requires futures brokers to collect margin to ensure performance by customers carrying positions. The clearing corporation assumes the risk of shortfall if margin is insufficient when a customer fails to honor a purchase or sale.

Commodity Futures Trading Commission (CFTC)　Agency authorized to regulate fair disclosure and trading in futures or futures options. The CFTC does not regulate registered securities. *See also* Securities and Exchange Commission (SEC).

Commodity pool　A type of investment defined and regulated by the NFA for the CFTC. Trades in futures contracts or commodity options.

Commodity pool operator (CPO)　A category of investment manager defined and regulated by the NFA. This manager runs pooled commodity accounts. A manager may need to register as a CPO and a CTA.

Commodity trading advisor (CTA)　A category of investment manger defined and regulated by the NFA. This manager runs separate (unpooled) commodity accounts. A manager may need to register as a CPO and a CTA.

Convertible arbitrage fund　Category of hedge fund using convertible bonds, convertible preferred stock, and the underlying common to create market-neutral portfolios.

Credit　(1) In accounting, the part of a pair of entries posted on the right side of the ledger. (2) In futures, the amount of money deposited to the account because of a combination of trades. (3) In futures, a positive balance in excess of required margin.

CreditMetrics™　Brand name of method of quantifying risk developed by J. P. Morgan.

Debit　(1) In accounting, the part of a pair of entries posted on the left side of the ledger. (2) In futures, the amount of money withdrawn from the account because of a combination of trades. (3) In futures, a negative balance relative to required margin.

Dedicated short bias fund   Type of hedge fund predominantly short stocks with minimal long exposure to stock prices.

Delaware Chancery   The state court system of Delaware.

Derivative   An investment whose price or return is determined by another asset or price.

Domicile   Legal location of a business (even if all business is conducted elsewhere).

Downside variance   A version of statistical variance that ignores positive deviations from the mean. This measure of risk ignores positive differences from the mean (profits) and accumulates only negative differences (losses).

Drawdown   The percentage of loss from a high point in cumulative return to the lowest point observed until a new cumulative high is achieved.

Due diligence   Research aimed at satisfying that an investment is not fraudulent or inappropriate. The research is primarily concerned with whether the risks are reasonable and much less concerned with the prospects for profit.

Duration   One of several risk measures linking bond price changes to yield changes. *See also* Macaulay duration; Modified duration; Price-weighted duration.

Emerging markets fund   Type of hedge fund investing predominantly in stock and/or bonds of emerging market nations.

Employee benefit plan   Provides retirement income to employees resulting from a deferral of income by employees for periods extending to the termination of covered employment or beyond (from ERISA).

Equity market-neutral fund   Type of hedge fund having long and short diversified portfolios of stock.

Equity pairs trading fund   Type of hedge fund specializing in arbitraging between nearly identical securities issued by the same company.

ERISA   Employee Retirement Income Security Act of 1974. U.S. legislation defining rules for pension fund investing.

Event-driven fund   Type of hedge fund that seeks returns through restructuring, takeovers, mergers (risk arbitrage), liquidation, bankruptcy, or other corporate structure events.

Exchange for physical (EFP)   A type of futures trade executed off a futures exchange floor where a futures contract and the underlying cash commodity are simultaneously bought and sold. All other transactions in futures must occur via open outcry within the exchange (either in a physical pit or in electronic trading).

Family office   The accounts of several affiliated investors run by a private investment counselor(s).

FAS 133   Statement from the Financial Accounting Standards Board requiring that derivative securities be marked to market and establishing whether a related cash asset must also be marked to market.

Finder's fees   Allocation of management and incentive fees to third-party hedge fund marketers.

Flow-through entity   A business unit that pays no tax; instead, all taxable items are allocated to owners and reported on the investors' tax returns. Partnerships, limited partnerships, limited liability corporations, and subchapter S corporations are flow-through business entities.

Forward   A physical or financial transaction that settles in the future. The transaction may require parties to post margin, is not standardized, and involves no clearing corporation.

Front running   To place an order to buy or sell a security in front of a known order for additional securities.

Future   An exchange-traded variation on a forward transaction. Unlike forwards, futures are standardized, introduce a clearing corporation as the counterparty on each trade, and impose daily margin requirements.

Futures commission merchant (FCM)   Category of futures broker created by the NFA that executes futures trades and maintains margin for customers.

General/limited partnership   See Limited partnership (LP).

General partner   A special class of partner in a limited partnership who bears unlimited liability for partnership activities.

Hedge fund   An unregulated investment pool.

High-water mark   The highest net asset value or highest cumulative return experienced by a client over a period of time.

Hot issue allocation   Special allocation of shares of initial public offerings designed to prevent National Association of Securities Dealers members and related parties from indirectly benefiting from these assets.

Hurdle rate   A threshold rate of return. Incentive fees are earned for returns above the hurdle rate.

Hypothecate   To pledge an asset. Frequently partnership agreements prohibit partners from using their partner interests as collateral or security.

Identified straddle   An election made at the time a long and a short position are established that allows the investor to mark both positions to market for tax purposes.

Incentive fee   Fee paid to manager based on the performance of the fund. Typically a manager charges 20 percent of fund profits before fees.

Initial margin   Margin required by a clearing corporation for a future or futures options. Initial margin may be cash or high-quality short-term securities (U.S. T-bills for domestic exchanges). *See also* Variation margin.

Introducing broker (IB)   A category of futures broker defined and regulated by the National Futures Association. This broker passes all trades through to a full-service futures commission merchant, which maintains the position, collects margin, and reports results to the client.

Investment Company Act of 1940   Governs registration of securities offerings.

K-1   Tax form provided to investors in flow-through entities that reports income and expenses allocated to the investor for inclusion on the tax form of the investor.

Layered tax allocation   Form of tax allocation in which each lot of each asset is treated as if the investor individually bought or sold a portion of the asset directly (outside the partnership). Each time the partnership ownership percentages change, a new layer with cost and ownership allocation is created.

Ledger   Accounting data organized around debits and credits to emphasize the double-entry nature of the inputs.

Ledger data   Information that can be fit into the general ledger format (for example, the number of shares purchased is not a ledger item, but the cost of the shares is). *See also* Nonledger data; Subledger data.

Leverage   Borrowing money or securities in an investment account.

LIFO layering   Layered tax allocation using last-in, first out matching of realized gains and losses to investor gains and losses.

Limited liability corporation (LLC)   A business structure that combines the flow-through tax treatment of a partnership with the limited liability of a corporate structure.

Limited partner   A type of partner in a limited partnership that is not liable for the activities of the partnership beyond its committed investment.

Limited partnership (LP)   Partnership that has both one or more general partners and one or more limited partners.

Lockup   A provision in some hedge fund subscription agreements requiring that investments may not be withdrawn for a specified amount of time.

Lookback   A provision where a hedge fund will refund incentive fees if the fund loses the gain in a specified period.

Macaulay duration   Present value weighted time to maturity.

Management fee   A fee assessed that is not related to the level of performance. Generally a management fee is defined as a percentage of assets under management. This percentage is quoted on an annual basis.

Margin   Performance bond on futures account or minimum equity requirements for option and levered stock and bond accounts.

Master-feeder structure   Type of hedge fund structure that creates a U.S. fund that invests all of its money in an offshore fund that accepts only non-U.S. investors. This structure provides the features of the mirrored funds with simpler administration. Also called *spoke and hub*.

Mirrored funds   A manager runs proportionally identical funds within the U.S. and offshore and seeks to provide identical returns in each fund.

Mixed straddle election   A declaration to the Internal Revenue Service that all trading will be treated as straddles. All positions will be marked to market at the end of each tax year.

Modified duration   Percentage change in price for 1 percent (100 basis point) change in yield. Modified duration is Macaulay duration divided by (1 + yield).

Mutual fund   Investment company regulated by the Securities and Exchange Commission. Although mutual funds are structured as a special-purpose corporation, they receive flow-through tax treatment as long as substantially all income (as dividend) and gains/losses (as a noncash distribution) are distributed to investors.

Net asset value   Net equity in an investment company (mutual fund, real estate investment trust, venture fund, or hedge fund) divided by the number of shares or units outstanding.

Nonledger data   Types of data that cannot be conveniently preserved within the double-entry books. Examples of important nonledger data include partnership ownership percentages, share quantities, trade counterparties, and credit exposure. *See also* Ledger data; Subledger data.

Notice   (1) (noun) The amount of time an investor must allow before a request to withdraw will be honored. A fund has a 7-day notice if the investor must request a withdrawal 7 days in advance. (2) (verb/noun) To advise the fund that the investor will redeem some or all shares or units in a partnership.

Offshore administration   Operation of substantially all the back-office functions of a fund outside the United States. This offshore administration avoids the need for backup withholding for investments by non-U.S. entities in funds run by U.S. managers.

Offshore fund   A hedge fund organized and legally operated outside the United States.

Onshore fund   A hedge fund organized and legally operated within the United States.

Open outcry   A requirement that futures and options on futures must occur in a trading pit (or electronic equivalent) and all members must have an opportunity to participate in the trade. *See also* Prearranged trade.

Prearranged trade   A futures or futures option trade executed between buyer and seller without giving other exchange members a chance to bid, offer, or participate. *See also* Open outcry.

Price-weighted duration   Nominal change in price for a 1 percent (100 basis point) change in yield. Price-weighted duration is equal to modified duration times price (as a percent of $1 face value).

Prime broker   A clearing account with credit enhancement. The customer reports trades to the prime broker who guarantees and effects settlement of the trade.

Private placement   A sale of securities exempt from registration under the Securities Act of 1933 and the Investment Company Act of 1940.

Private placement memorandum (PPM)   A legal document describing the terms of an unregistered security.

Qualified eligible participant (QEP)   A person with $2 million in securities or $200,000 in margin or certain institutions with $5 million. If all investors are QEPs, a commodity pool can invoke CFTC rule 4.7, which reduces disclosure burdens.

Qualified purchaser   Allowable investor in a private placement under Section 3(c)7 of the Investment Company Act of 1940. Individuals must have investments of at least $5 million.

Realized gain/loss   A gain/loss that results from a closeout of an opening purchase or sale.

Rebate   Interest paid on cash used to collateralize stock loan trades. Rebate (for stocks) is the same as repo interest (for bonds).

Recognized gain/loss   Any realized or unrealized gain or loss that is acknowledged in the accounting and/or tax records.

Reg T   Rules established by the U.S. Federal Reserve Bank that limit the minimum margin on securities held at broker-dealers. Reg T limits margin on exchange-traded equities to 50 percent. Broker-dealers are exempt from Reg T, allowing them to create derivative securities that effectively eliminate Reg T for other investors.

Repo   Repurchase agreement. A short-term financing agreement in which bonds are exchanged for cash as a secured loan and then "repurchased" at the end of the loan. Although originally deemed to be matched sale and purchase transactions in bankruptcy, revision to the Uniform Commercial Code established that repos are to be treated as secured loan agreements.

Reverse   *See* Reverse repo.

Reverse repo   A variation on a repo transaction where securities are borrowed and collateralized with cash. *See also* Repo.

Risk arbitrage fund   Type of fund seeking returns by investing in companies involved with merger and acquisition.

Risk disclosure document   Document provided to private placement investors in substitution for a prospectus. In practice, the risk disclosure document (sometimes just called the disclosure document) protects the sponsor of the private placement/hedge fund from liability.

RiskMetrics™   Brand name for value at risk developed by J. P. Morgan to quantify portfolio risk.

Scalability   The ability to increase the assets under management for a hedge fund strategy without reducing the returns.

Section 1256   Tax provision in Section 1256 of the Commodities Exchange Act of 1974 that establishes a split of 60 percent long term and 40 percent short term for all gains and losses on commodity trades regardless of holding period.

Securities Act of 1933   Governs registration of securities.

Securities and Exchange Commission (SEC)   Agency authorized to regulate fair disclosure and trading in registered securities. The SEC does not regulate futures or futures options. *See also* Commodity Futures Trading Commission.

Separate accounts   Rather than pooling investments into a single account run by a commodity pool operator, a commodity trading advisor executes trades in individual accounts for each client.

Sharpe ratio   A measure of the trade-off of risk versus reward named after William Sharpe. Excess return (return minus the risk-free rate) divided by the volatility of return.

Side pocket allocation   A special allocation used for illiquid assets. Generally, the allocations do not change as partners enter and leave the fund and are not routinely marked to market. Manager generally collects no incentive fee until the assets are liquidated.

Soft dollar arrangements   Agreements by brokers to pay for products or services used by an investment manager out of commissions paid by the investment manager's clients.

Sortino ratio   A variation on the Sharpe ratio named after Frank Sortino that substitutes downside variance for volatility.

Spoke and hub   Copyrighted name for master-feed structure.

Statutory representation   Businesses that specialize in acting as the formal site to receive notices for a business.

Sticky   Adjective describing capital unlikely to be removed from the fund for a significant period or following poor performance.

Subchapter S corporation   A precursor to the LLC. A sub-S corporation may have only one class of stock, no more than 35 different shareholders, and the shareholders must be U.S. residents. Financial results flow through to shareholders.

Subledger data   These data could be included in the general ledger of debits and credits but, for convenience, may be maintained outside the accounting software and data. For example, individual shares and costs may be carried in detail on spreadsheets and the accounting records may contain only totals created from this detail. *See also* Ledger data; Nonledger data.

Subscription agreement   Legal document filed as part of an investment in a hedge fund creating a contract between the investor and the fund.

10 Commandments   Set of 10 rules that established a safe harbor, ensuring an investment entity would be deemed offshore. Legislation defining offshore rules eliminated this safe harbor.

Transparency   Disclosure of specific holdings to investors. Managers may refuse to disclose this information because they believe they are vulnerable to predatory practices if the positions are disclosed.

Turn   The last business day of the year (for financing leveraged positions).

Unrealized gain/loss   A mark to market gain or loss not associated with a closing purchase or sale. Hedge funds use this unrealized information as a basis for partnership allocations. Unrealized gains/losses are generally not recognized unless the fund makes a mixed straddle election.

Unrelated business taxable income (UBTI)   Income taxable to a tax-exempt organization because the business is not related to the tax-exempt portion of the organization's activities.

Value At Risk (VAR)™   A measure of investment risk that establishes an amount where one-day losses will be smaller 95 percent of the time and larger 5 percent of the time.

Variation margin   Adjustment to futures account reflecting changes in price of established positions. Additional margin must be satisfied with cash deposits only. Excess variation margin can be withdrawn.

Volatility   A measure of risk. Generally defined as the standard deviation of return (annualized).

Window dressing   Making changes to positions at an accounting statement period to make statements more desirable. This practice often involves reducing leverage. For funds that disclose positions, it might involve buying stocks that have performed well and selling stocks that have performed poorly before statements are prepared.

bibliography

Articles, Online and In Print

Alternative Investment Management Association Staff. 1997. "Due Diligence Questionnaire: Applicable to Hedge Fund Managers." Sample questionnaires for due diligence. Recently updated version for AIMA members only. http://www.aima.org/aimasite/indexfrm.htm.

Alternative Investment Management Association Staff. 1997. "Due Diligence Questionnaire: Applicable to Managed Futures.pdf." Sample questionnaires for due diligence. Recently updated version for AIMA members only. http://www.aima.org/aimasite/indexfrm.htm.

Amin, Gaurav S., and Harry M. Kat. 2001. "Hedge Fund Performance 1990-2000; Do the Money Machines Really Add Value?" *Working Paper,* http://planethedgefund.com/articles.php3. Fees are only justified when viewed in portfolio context.

Arvedlund, Erin E. 2002 (January 7). "Hedging Their Bets." *Barron's Online.* Trends in mutual funds, especially quasi-hedge funds.

Association of Investment Management and Research Staff. 1997. "AIMR Soft Dollar Standards." AIMR also has a new set of standards available in the comment stage. http://www.aimr.org/standards/ethics/soft_dollar/index.html.

Association of Investment Management and Research Staff. 2001. "AIMR Performance Presentation Standards." http://www.AIMR.org/standards/pps/ppsstand.html. De facto standards for performance presentation.

Bank for International Settlements. 2000. "Banks' Interactions with Highly Leveraged Institutions: Implementation of the Basel Committee's Sound Practices Paper." http://www.bis.org/publ/bcbs68.pdf. Best practices for banks.

Bank for International Settlements. 2000 (September). "Best Practices for Credit Risk Disclosure." http://www.bis.org/publ/bcbs74.htm. Best practices recommendations.

Bankman, Joseph. 2000. "The Economic Substance Doctrine." NYU Law Colloquium on Tax Policy and Public Finance. http://www.law.nyu.edu/tppf/economicsubstance.html. Problems with hedge fund shelters.

339

Barreto, Susan. 2001 (November 20). "Commonfund Study Finds Investors Taking on New Asset Allocations." http://www.hedgeworld.com/news/read_excite.cgi?storyfile=/sections/peop/peop546.html. Endowments and foundations increasing alternative assets and cash.

Barreto, Susan L. 2001 (December 11). "Art Institute of Chicago: A Lesson in Transparency?" http://www.hedgeworld.com/news/read_excite.cgi?storyfile=/sections/dail/dail5515.html. Problems with endowment invested in hedge fund.

Basel Committee on Banking Supervision. 1999. "Banks' Interactions with Highly Leveraged Institutions." http://www.bis.org/publ/index.htm. Best practices for banks.

Basel Committee on Banking Supervision. 1999. "Credit Risk Modeling: Current Practices and Applications." http://www.bis.org/publ/index.htm. Summary of current credit risk measurement.

Basel Committee on Banking Supervision. 2000. "Principals for the Management of Credit Risk." http://www.bis.org/publ/bcbs75.htm. Best practices for credit risk management.

Basel Committee on Banking Supervision. 2000. "Supervisory Guidance for Managing Settlement Risk in Foreign Exchange Transactions." http://www.bis.org/publ/index.htm, Best practices for credit risk management.

Best, Sarah. 1999 (second quarter). "Hedge Funds Demand Fair Treatment." *International Securities Lending,* pp. 22–30. Roundtable discussion of prime brokerage.

Best, Sarah. 1999 (fourth quarter). "Passing Judgment on Prime Brokers." *International Securities Lending,* pp. 54–56. Prime brokerage from manager's point of view.

Beyer, Charlotte. 1999 (February 22). "The Rich Are Different." *Investment News,* http://www.e-hedge.com/articles/articles_08InvNews.htm. Rich are more sophisticated than marketers believe.

Burton, Katherine. 2000 (July). "Hedge Funds Come Full Circle." *Bloomberg Magazine,* pp. 65–68. Trend in hedge funds is lower risk, equity.

Calvin, James N., and Thad Chrupcala. 1997. "Buyer's Guide to Partnership Allocation Systems." *HFR Investment Technology,* pp. 23–30. Not brand-specific.

Carpenter, Jennifer. 1999. "Does Option Compensation Increase Managerial Risk Appetite?" *NYU Stern Working Papers,* http://www.stern.nyu.edu/fin/workpapers/papers99/wpa99076.htm. Effect of incentive fee on behavior; theoretical.

Chicago Mercantile Exchange Staff. "Futures and Options Trading for Hedge Funds." http://www.cme.com/market/institutional/strategy_papers/hedge.html. Short description of regulatory requirements for hedge funds.

Clash, James M., Robert Lenzner, and Michael Maiello with Josephine Lee. 2001(August 6). "$500 Billion Hedge Fund Folly." *Forbes,* Vol. 168, Issue 3, pp. 70–75. Negative story on hedge funds.

Clow, Richard. 2001 (June 7). "Max Re IPO to Throw Light on Obscure Hedge Fund Vehicle." *Financial Times.* Financial engineering to reduce taxes.

Committee on Global Financial System. 2001 (March). "Collateral in Wholesale Financial Markets." http://www.bis.org/publ/cgfs17.htm. Shortage of collateral limits using secured transactions to reduce risk.

Cote, Denise. 2001 (April 17). "Cromer Finance LTD and Prival et al. v. Michael Berger et al.: Opinion." U.S. District Court, Southern District of New York. Opinion from trial. http://www.legalcasedocs.com/120/241/696.html.

Coy, Peter. 2001 (February 26). "The Wrong Way to Regulate Hedge Funds." *Business Week,* page 90. Argues that Basel II will destabilize hedge fund investing.

Cross Border Capital. 2001 (April). "The Young Ones." *Absolute Return Fund Research,* http://www.hedgeworld.com/research/reports/. Quantifies common view that young funds outperform.

Cullen, Iain. 1999 (October). "Marketing Hedge Funds." *Alternative Investment Management Association Staff Special Report.* http://www.aima.org/aimasite/ indexfrm.htm. Laws re: France, Germany, Switzerland, and U.K.

Culp, Christopher, and Ron Mensink. 1999 (Fall). "Measuring Risk for Asset Allocation, Performance Evaluation, and Risk Control." *Journal of Performance Measurement,* pp. 55–73. Review of risk measurement as grounded in finance theory.

Derivatives Strategy Staff. 1998. "How UBS Lost $680 Million." *Derivative Strategies,* http://www.derivativesstrategy.com/magazine/archive/1998/1098shrt. asp. Account of calls on LTCM.

Derivatives Strategy Staff. 2000. "Another Way to Trade Hedge Funds On-Line." *Derivative Strategies,* http://www.derivativesstrategy.com/magazine/archive/ 2000/0400shrt.asp. FundsPlus exchange for trading hedge funds.

Dugan, Ianthe Jeanne. 2001 (December 12). "The Art Institute of Chicago Files Suit Over Alleged Fraud." *Wall Street Journal.* Allegations of fraud at Integral Hedging.

Feinberg, Phyllis. 2000 (May). "Clearing Up the Transparancy Issues." *Pensions & Investments,* Vol. 28, Issue 9, pp. 119–120. Survey of investors and managers on transparency.

Fortune, Peter. 2000 (September/October). "Margin Requirements, Margin Loans, and Margin Rates: Practice and Principle." *New England Economic Review.* Primer on margin rules.

Frankel, Michael G., and Avran S. Metzger. 1998 (December 2). "The History of Section 704(b)." *Tax Management Real Estate Journal*. Technical; does not cover aggregate allocation.

Fuerbringer, Jonathon. 2000 (October 20). "When Companies Talk, Who Gets to Listen?" *New York Times*. Vinik exiting hedge fund business.

Fung, William, and David Hsieh. 1999 (June). "A Primer on Hedge Funds." *Journal of Empirical Finance,* pp. 309–331. http://schwert.ssb.rochester.edu/f411/hedge.pdf. Basic information, data, commodity trading advisors, bibliography.

Gallagher, Kathleen. 2001 (March 21). "SEC Freezes Funds." *Journal Sentinel*. http://www.jsonline.com/bym/news/mar01/heart22032101.asp. Heartland Funds to be liquidated.

Gallo, Peter. 2001 (March 19). "Foxhound Fund Liquidates; Investors Migrate to Other Bulldog Funds." *The Alternative Edge*. http://www.hedgeworld.com/news/alt_edge/. Following major drawdown, fund closes but retains most of the investors.

Gallo, Peter. 2001 (April 2). "Prime Broker Landscape." *The Alternative Edge*. http://www.hedgeworld.com/news/alt_edge/. Market share of prime brokers.

Gallo, Peter. 2001 (April 23). "The Berger Legacy: How a Massive Fraud Changed the Hedge Fund Industry." *The Alternative Edge*. http://www.hedgeworld.com/news/alt_edge/. Account of fraud, trial, and opinion.

Gallo, Peter. 2001 (May 29). "Bowman Returning $1 Billion." *The Alternative Edge*. http://www.hedgeworld.com/news/alt_edge/. Problems with Bowman large cap tech fund.

Gallo, Peter. 2001 (June 11). "Max Re Readies for IPO." *The Alternative Edge*. http://www.hedgeworld.com/news/alt_edge/. Description of company and its partners.

Gallo, Peter. 2001 (June 25). "Bear Stearns Battles $1.9 Billion Lawsuit." *The Alternative Edge*. http://www.hedgeworld.com/news/alt_edge/. Second Berger suit versus Bear Stearns.

Gallo, Peter. 2001 (August 6). "CDC to Sell $3.3 Billion Hedge Fund Business." *The Alternative Edge*. http://www.hedgeworld.com/news/alt_edge/. Selling funds operation as ongoing business.

Gallo, Peter. 2001 (December 13). "SEC Accuses Hedge Fund Manager Sagam of Fraud." *The Alternative Edge*. http://www.hedgeworld.com/news/alt_edge/. Currency Ponzi scheme involving Yehuda Shiv.

Gallo, Peter. 2001 (December 13). "Yagalla Pleads Guilty to $50 Million Fraud." *The Alternative Edge*. http://www.hedgeworld.com/news/alt_edge/. Fraud at Ashbury Capital.

Geczy, Christopher C., David K. Musto, and Adam V. Reed. 2001 (June 30). "Stocks Are Special Too: An Analysis of the Equity Lending Market." *Working Paper*. Thorough description of the stock loan market.

Gerber, Geoffrey. "Using a Nonparametric Approach to Market-Neutral Investing." Reprinted in Jess Lederman, and Robert A. Klein, editors. *Market Neutral State-of-the-Art Strategies for Every Market Environment*. McGraw-Hill, New York, 1996. Compares linear multifactor valuation with nonparametric models for pairs trading.

Goetzmann, Ingersoll & Ross. 1998 (January 27). "High Water Marks." *Working Paper*. http://papers.ssrn.com/sol3/delivery.cfm?cfid=182062&cftoken=84418214&abstractid=57933. Valuing high-water mark provision; why they exist.

Gould, Carole. 2000 (October 8). "More Funds Using Outside Managers." *New York Times*, p. 3. Brief description of Fund of Funds.

Hedge Fund Industry Committee. 2000 (February). "Sound Practices for Hedge Fund Managers." http://planethedgefund.com/articles.php3. Recommendations for risk management; glossary.

HedgeFund.Net. 2000 (February 15). "Due Diligence Guide for Investing in Hedge Funds." http://www.hedgefund.net/dd_index.php3. Due diligence best practices.

Hoenig, Jonathan. 2001 (April 12). "Hedge Funds for the Masses." Smartmoney.com. Hedge funds should be available to Mom and Pop.

Hsieh, David, and Bill Fung. 2001. "Asset-based Hedge-Fund Styles and Portfolio Diversification." *Working Paper*. http://www.london.edu/hedgefunds/Working_Papers/HF-005/hf-005.html. Analysis of hedge fund performance.

Ineichen, Alexander. 2000 (October). "In Search of Alpha." *Global Equity Research UBS Warburg*. http://www.research.ubswarburg.com/. Thorough review of hedge fund industry.

International Association of Financial Engineers. "Hedge Fund Disclosure for Institutional Investors." www.iafe.org/conferen/2000_notes/InvestorOct12 consensus.pdf. Best practices on disclosure.

International Organization of Securities Commissions (IOSCO) Committee on Payment and Settlement Systems. 1999 (July). "Securities Lending Transactions: Market Development and Implications." http://www.iosco.org/iosco.html. International review of lending market and regulations.

Investor Risk Committee of the International Association of Financial Engineers. 2001 (July 21). "Findings on Disclosure for Institutional Investors in Hedge Funds." http://www.hedgeworld.com/research/. Introduces a new classification system and lists best practices.

Jereski, Laura. 1995 (June 23). "Feeding Frenzy." *Wall Street Journal,* p. A1. Forced liquidation of Granite Fund.

Jorion, Phillipe. 2000 (January). "Risk Management Lessons from LTCM." *Working Paper.* http://www.hedgeworld.com/research/reports/top_dl.cgi. Criticizes VaR type risk modeling.

Karas, Robert. 1999 (October). "Looking Behind the Non-Correlation Argument." http://www.aima.org/aimasite/research/lgtoct99.htm. Correlation of hedge funds and commodity trading advisors reviewed.

Kess, Kenneth M. 1999 (Spring). "Starting and Operating a Hedge Fund: Tax and Business Issues." *Journal of Tax and Investments,* Vol. 16. Structural issues including the "10 Commandments."

Kim, Steve, Mika Toikka, Pankaj Patel, Kevin Chang, and Ed Tom. 2001 (September 8). "How Hedge Funds Have Performed." *CSFB Equity Research.* Performance review 1994–2001.

Laderman, Jeffrey. 1998 (November 9). "UBS Failed Risk Management 101." *Business Week.* Call option trade with LTCM.

Lamm, R. McFall, Jr. 1999 (Winter). "Portfolio of Alternative Assets: Why Not 100% Hedge Funds?" *Journal of Investing.* Prudence of hedge fund investing; value of diversification.

Leib, Barclay T. 2000. "The Future of Innovation." *Derivative Strategies.* http://www.derivativesstrategy.com/magazine/archive/2000/0700fea3.asp. Hedge fund derivatives.

Leib, Barclay T. 2000. "Who Blew Up Phoenix?" *Derivative Strategies.* http://www.derivativesstrategy.com/magazine/archive/2000/0500fea2.asp. Meltdown of fixed-income arbitrage fund.

Lucchetti, Aaron. 2001 (April 3). "Janus Capital Keeps Investors." *Wall Street Journal.* Janus keeps most investors despite significant losses.

Lucchetti, Aaron, and Carrick Mollenkamp. 2001 (July 5). "Marsico Funds Falter After Fetching Premium." *Wall Street Journal.* Marsico sold funds to BoA in February 2000; results now spotty.

Lux, Hal. 2001 (April). "The Great Hedge Fund Reinsurance Tax Game." *Institutional Investor.* http://www.iimagazine.com/channel/insurance/20010412000967.htm. Offshore reinsurance as tax device.

MacRae, Desmond. 1995 (third quarter). "What's Happening with Prime Brokers." *International Securities Lending.* General discussion of prime brokerage.

McCrary, Stuart. 1999 (Fall). "Put and Call Structures in Hedge Funds." *Derivatives Quarterly,* pp. 27–38. Discussion of optionlike payoffs in hedge funds.

McHugh, Robert W., Jennifer Ward, and Jon G. Arfstrom. 1996. "A Tale of Two Allocation Methods." *HFR Journal of Hedge Fund Research*, Vol 1, No. 1, pp. 1–3. Lot layering versus aggregate partnership allocation.

Meyers, Howard S., and Robert G. Heim. 2001 (September). "An Overview of U.S. Hedge Fund Regulation." *Alternative Investment Management Association Staff Newsletter*, pp. 44–47. http://www.aima.org/aimasite/indexfrm.htm. Short but thorough description of regulations.

Mina, Jorge, and Jerry Yi Xiao. 2001. "Return to Riskmetrics: The Evolution of a Standard." Published by RiskMetrics Group. http://www.riskmetrics.com/r2rovv.html. Update to 1996 Technical Document.

Moody, John. 1995 (October 23). "A Farewell to Hedges." *Time*. Steinhardt exiting hedge fund business.

Nadel, Steven B. 1998. "An Accountant's Guide to the Major Legal Issues Affecting Hedge Funds." *CPA Journal*. http://www.luca.com/cpajournal/1998/1098/Departments/D721098.html. Short but thorough review of legal issues affecting hedge funds.

National Futures Organization. 2001. "Disclosure Documents: A Guide for CPOs and CTAs." http://www.nfa.futures.org/compliance/dd2001.html. Review of disclosure requirements for commodity pool operators.

Neely, Christopher J., and Paul A. Weller. 2001 (September). "Predicting Exchange Rate Volatility: Genetic Programming vs. GARCH vs. Riskmetrics." *Federal Reserve Bank of St. Louis Working Paper*. http://www.stls.frb.org/docs/research/wp/2001-009.pdf. Forecasting volatility using various methods.

Nelsestuen, Linda. 1999 (fourth quarter). "Derivative Tax Shelters." *The Ohio CPA Journal*, pp. 22–23. http://www.ohioscpa.com/Journal/journal_articles/Oct99/Oct99_Derivative_Tax_Shelters.pdf. Tax changes in 1999 limiting tax savings from hedge funds.

New York Department of Banking. 1999 (March 4). "Review of Hedge Fund Activities." http://www.banking.state.ny.us/hfreport.htm. Due diligence best practices.

Oliver R. Witte. 2001 (February 26). "An Index Is an Index, Is an Index—Well Not Really." *The Alternative Edge*, p. 4. http://www.hedgeworld.com/news/alt_edge/. Review of hedge fund data vendors.

Oppel, Richard A., Jr. 1999 (February 2). "A Depleted Omega Loses a Key Advisor." *New York Times*. Short account of Omega Fund.

Ottomanelli, Angela J. 2001. "Foundations, Endowments Making Changes." Firefund.com. Report on recent Commonfund Study.

Pacelle, Mitchell. 1999 (February 12). "Hedge Funds Face Tougher Times." *Wall Street Journal*. Description of prime broker pressures on mortgage hedge fund.

Perry, Michael. 2001. "Building a Better Barrier to Entry?" *Brooklyn Law School Center for the Study of International Business Law Working Paper*. http://planethedgefund.com/articles.php3. Description of U.S. and U.K. regulations.

President's Working Group on Financial Markets. 1999 (April). "Hedge Funds, Leverage, and the Lessons of Long Term Capital Management." http://www.ustreas.gov/press/releases/docs/hedgfund.pdf. Hearings following the collapse of LTCM.

Pricewaterhouse Coopers Staff. 1998 (October). *Structural, Tax, Accounting and Reporting Issues Affecting Investment Partnerships,* 3rd ed. Nice technical overview of business.

Quinn, Thomas F., Karen Garre, and Wendi Hangebrauck. 2001 (Spring). "Foreign Partnerships: Rules, Issues, and Planning Opportunities Regarding U.S. Filing Requirements." *International Tax Journal,* Vol. 27, No. 2, pp. 1–46. Changes from Tax Relief Act of 1997.

Record, Charles. 1997. "Automating the Partnership Accounting Process." *HFR Investment Technology*, pp. 18–22. Using commercial software for partnership allocation.

Risk Management Association. 1999 (September). "Guidelines for the Equity Lending Trader." http://www.rmahq.com/Sec_Lending/guideqltrd.html. Best practices on securities lending.

Ritzi, Andreas. 2000. "The Safe Way to Play Hedge Funds." *EuroHedge*. http://www.eurohedge.co.uk/reports/2000_08/safeway.htm. Limited downside derivatives.

RSM Robson Rhodes. 2001 (August). "UK Direct Tax Considerations for Offshore Funds." http://www.hedgeworld.com/research/reports/. Review of U.K. tax issues.

Schneeweis, Thomas, and George Martin. 2000 (September). "The Benefits of Hedge Funds: Asset Allocation for the Institutional Investor." *Center for International Securities and Derivatives Markets Working Paper*.

Schneeweis, Thomas, Richard Spurgin, and Vassilos N. Karvas. 2000 (Summer). "Alternative Investments in the Institutional Portfolio," AIMA Commissioned Paper. www.aima.org/aimasite/research/aiip@202000.pdf.

Scholl, Jaye. 2000 (April 3). "Humbled Tiger." *Barron's Online*. Demise of Tiger Fund.

Scholl, Jaye. 2001 (July 31). "Back to the Future." *Barron's,* Vol. 80, No. 31, p. 32. Downward pressure on fees.

Securities and Exchange Commission. 1998 (October). "Compliance Guide to the Registration and Regulation of Brokers and Dealers." http://www.sec.gov/investor/pubs.shtml. Reference guide to SEC regulations.

Securities and Exchange Commission. 2000 (January 19). "Litigation Release No. 16412." http://www.sec.gov/litigation/litreleases/lr16412.htm. Description of Manhattan Investment Fund scheme.

Shapiro, Alan, and John Wells. 2000 (June 9). "New Foreign Partnership Information Reporting Requirements." *Tax Management International Journal*.

Sidel, Robin. 2001 (June 14). "Takeover Traders Are Pained by GE-Honeywell Deal Fallout." *Wall Street Journal*. Consequences of a broken takeover deal.

Silk, Roger D. 2000. "How Privately Placed Tax Advantaged Products Can Benefit Investors." http://www.hedgeworld.com/research/reports/viewer.cgi?doc_id=401. Using insurance products with hedge funds.

Small Business Administration. 1993 (October). "Selecting the Legal Structure for Your Business." http://www.sba.gov/library/pubs.html#mp-25. Background on basic business forms.

Sortino, Frank A., and Lee N. Price. 1994 (Fall). "Performance Measurement in a Downside Risk Framework." *Journal of Investing*. www.sortino.com/htm/performance.htm. Using semivariance and variations for risk measurement.

Sortino, Frank A., and Lee N. Price. 1996 (Winter). "On the Use and Misuse of Downside Risk." *Journal of Portfolio Management*. http://www.sortino.com/htm/ontheu.htm. Using semivariance and variations for risk measurement.

Staff. 2000 (April). "New Foreign Partnership Reporting Requirements." *The Tax Advisor*. Changes from Tax Relief Act of 1997.

Sunit Gopalan. 2001 (April 23). "Momentum Raises $250 MM in Hedge-linked Structured Notes." *The Alternative Edge*, p. 4. http://www.hedgeworld.com/news/alt_edge/. Structured notes about hedge fund returns.

Taggart, William, Jr., and Gina M. Biondo. 1996. *Hedge Funds: A Comprehensive Tax Planning Guide*. Pricewaterhouse Coopers LLP. Great tax reference for hedge funds.

U.S. Congress. "Commodities Exchange Act." http://www.nfa.futures.org/compliance/publications.html. Created the Commodities Futures Trading Commission.

U.S. Congress. "Internal Revenue Code (Section 1.704(b))." Partnership tax allocation.

U.S. Congress. "Investment Advisors Act." Created regulations affecting money managers.

U.S. Congress. "Investment Company Act of 1940." http://www.law.uc.edu/CCL/sldtoc.html. Created regulations controlling investment pools and partnerships.

U.S. Congress. "National Securities Market Improvement Act of 1996 (Sec 3(c)7 of 1940 Act)." Exceeding the 100-investor rule.

U.S. Congress. "Securities Act of 1933." http://www.law.uc.edu/CCL/sldtoc.html. Created the registration requirement for public offerings.

U.S. Congress. "Securities Exchange Act of 1934." http://www.law.uc.edu/CCL/sldtoc.html. Created the Securities and Exchange Commission.

U.S. Congress. "Taxpayer Relief Act of 1997." Eliminated "10 Commandments" and eased creation of offshore funds.

U.S. Federal Reserve Bank. "Regulations T and X." http://www.bankinfo.com/72719981.pdf. Updated list of marginable securities.

U.S. House of Representatives. "The Hedge Fund Disclosure Act Hearings." http://commdocs.house.gov/committees/bank/hba63382.000/hba63382_0f.htm. Hearings pending disclosure of positions.

Weber, Eric C. 2001. "Changing Tides Report 2001 (First Quarter)." Freeman-co.com. Statistical review.

Weiss, Gerald. 2001 (February). "Dynamic Rebalancing." *Journal of Financial Planning*, Vol. 14, No. 2, pp. 100–108. Dynamic allocation and retirement withdrawals.

Witte, Oliver. 2001 (February 14). "Rebel with a Cause." http://hedgeworld.com/news/read_news.cgi?section=strt&story=strt670.html. Tax efficiency in hedge funds.

Zuckerman, Sam. 1998 (October 17). "D. E. Shaw Explains BofA Loss." *San Francisco Chronicle*. Losses at D. E. Shaw and Band of America due to statistical arbitrage.

Zurich Capital Markets Staff. Zurich Due Diligence Documents. Sample questionnaires for due diligence proposed as industry standards and available in public domain.

Books

Barham, Susan. 2001. *Starting a Hedge Fund: A U.S. Perspective*. Hong Kong: ISA Publications. Short, but benefits from the perspective of many practitioners.

Barham, Susan, and Ian Hallsworth, editors. 1999. *Starting a Hedge Fund: A European Perspective*. Hong Kong: ISA Publications. Short, but benefits from the perspective of many practitioners.

Bekier, Matthias. 2000. *Marketing of Hedge Funds*. Bern: Peter Lang. Ph.D. dissertation discussing hedge fund marketing from the academic marketing framework.

Bowen, John J., Jr. *Creating Equity*. 1997. New York: Securities Data Publishing Books. Although this book is directed at financial planners, it provides valuable insights on the entrepreneuerial issues in setting up a hedge fund.

Burghardt, Galen D., and Terrence M. Belden. 1993. *The Treasury Bond Basis: An In-Depth Analysis for Hedgers, Speculators and Arbitrageurs*. New York: McGraw-Hill. A great summary of one of the most basic fixed-income arbitrage trades.

Crerend, William J. 1998. *Fundamentals of Hedge Fund Investing: A Professional Investor's Guide*. New York: McGraw-Hill. This is a good summary of hedge funds aimed at a potential investor.

Culp, Christopher. 2001. *The Risk Management Process: Business Strategy and Tactics*. New York: John Wiley & Sons. Great source book for risk management.

Dunbar, Nicholas. 2000. *Inventing Money: The Story of Long Term Capital Management and the Legends Behind It*. New York: John Wiley & Sons. Somewhat technical account of the rise and fall of Long Term Capital Management.

Edwards, Robert D., John Magee, and W. H. C. Bassetti (eds.). 2001. *Technical Analysis of Stock Trends*, 8th ed., New York: AMACOM. The original bible on technical analysis and still a valuable reference book.

Kaufman, Peter J. 1998. *Trading Systems and Methods*. New York: John Wiley & Sons. This book has been one of the most popular books on the subject of technical analysis for decades because it is comprehensive and clear, and has been updated regularly to keep it current.

Lederman, Jess, and Robert A. Klein (eds.). 1995. *Hedge Funds: Investment and Portfolio Strategies for the Institutional Investor*. New York: McGraw-Hill. Considerably technical background on hedge funds intended for institutional investors.

Lowenstein, Roger. 2000. *When Genius Failed: The Rise and Fall of Long Term Capital Management*. New York: Random House. The more popular of two books describing the story of Long Term Capital, it includes more biography and less description of the trades and strategies.

Murphy, John J. 1999. *Technical Analysis in the Financial Marketplace: A Comprehensive Guide to Trading Methods and Applications*, Englewood Cliffs, NJ: Prentice Hall. A good reference book for someone wanting to build a hedge fund with technical analysis tools. Very comprehensive.

Nicholas, Joseph G. 1999. *Investing in Hedge Funds: Strategies for the New Marketplace*. New York: Bloomberg Professional Library. Very good hedge fund primer written for the potential investor.

Nicholas, Joseph G. 2000. *Market Neutral Investing: Long/Short Hedge Fund Strategies*. New York: Bloomberg Professional Library. Describes hedge fund trades for the potential investor.

Parker, Virginia Reynolds (ed.). 2000. *Managing Hedge Fund Risk: From the Seat of the Practitioner—Views from Investors, Counterparties, Hedge Funds and Consultants*. London: Risk Books. A valuable collection of articles on risk management from a wide range of perspectives.

Peters, Carl, and Ben Warwick (eds.). 1997. *The Handbook of Managed Futures: Performance, Evaluation and Analysis*. Chicago: Irwin Professional Publishing. Unlike most texts, this text has more content geared to traders rather than to investors.

Reverre, Stephane. 2001. *The Complete Arbitrage Deskbook*. New York: McGraw-Hill. Describes many of the equity trading strategies used by equity hedge funds.

RiskMetrics Staff. 1997. *CreditMetrics Technical Document*. New York: J. P. Morgan. Description of the RiskMetrics approach to credit risk.

Riskmetrics Staff. 1996. *RiskMetrics Technical Document*, Volumes 1 to 5. New York: Morgan Guaranty Trust Company. http://www.riskmetrics.com/rmcovv.html. Documentation for VaR. Also called *RiskMetric Classic*.

index

The letter "n" indicates a note number found on the page cited.